The Theology of Marriage

The Theology of Marriage

*The Historical Development of
Christian Attitudes Toward Sex
and Sanctity in Marriage*

by JOSEPH E. KERNS, S.J.

SHEED AND WARD – NEW YORK

Library of Congress Catalog Card Number 63-17145

IMPRIMI POTEST:
> JOHN M. DALEY, S.J.
> PROVINCIAL OF THE MARYLAND PROVINCE
> OCTOBER 25, 1963

NIHIL OBSTAT:
> JOSEPH T. NUGENT
> CENSOR LIBRORUM
> JANUARY 6, 1964

IMPRIMATUR:
> ✠ ROBERT F. JOYCE
> BISHOP OF BURLINGTON
> JANUARY 7, 1964

The Nihil Obstat and Imprimatur are official declarations that a book or pamphlet is free from doctrinal or moral error. No implication is contained therein that those who have granted the Nihil Obstat and Imprimatur agree with the contents, opinions or statements expressed.

Manufactured in the United States of America

*To my colleagues and students
at Wheeling College*

"Yahweh God said, 'It is not good that the man be alone. I must make him a helpmate of his own kind.'"

PREFACE

THIS EXPLORATION of married life cannot be expected to present a complete spiritual program for husbands and wives. Most husbands and wives are also parents, and parenthood will not be considered here.

Our attention will be centered on just one aspect of their life together: the effort they make to improve each other. Isolating a subject is often a help to studying it more closely, and this one seems to deserve this special attention.

At different speeds in different countries, but all over the world today, a profound change is taking place in family life.[1] There is a drift from the farm to the city, from a patriarchal to a democratic style of decision making, from a complicated social network that included cousins and in-laws and aunts to an isolated set of parents and children. Newlyweds find themselves freer but more alone. With limited resources and experience, they are expected to found an institution so complex and expensive and awesome in its consequences as a family.

Their relationship to each other in this joint endeavor is not what it would have been in former times. The city apartment is not, like the farmhouse, the base of an economic enterprise. They do fewer jobs together. During most of the day and most of the week each must face the problems of a world that the other cannot share.

This naturally affects their life together. There is a new

emphasis on companionship, a craving for satisfaction of deep emotional needs. Marriage is seen, not as the start of a family, but as a means to personal fulfillment.

Whether or not this change is for the better, it is a fact. And in view of this fact it seems important to study the religious implications of being bound in this way to another human being. Does marriage demand any really basic change in a man's dealings with God? What connection is there between his own spiritual growth and that of this companion?

Experience, the social and behavioral sciences, the present state of the world in which married couples live—data from these and other sources would have to be synthesized before there could be anything like an answer. These pages are an effort to contribute to that synthesis by seeing what light the Christian revelation throws on the subject. The reader, however, should be reminded not to interpret any particular view as representing the full teaching of the Church.

This may not always be easy to determine. What the Apostles were given was not a course of lectures but a companionship with a person, climaxed on Pentecost by a dazzling realization of who this person was. As they looked back, a new meaning appeared in those days of listening to Him, watching Him in action, eating and drinking with Him. Beholding Him in this new and wonderful way, they also beheld themselves and the meaning of life. They had to tell the world about it.[2]

But what you know about a person cannot really be put into words. You speak, and what you say may not be false; but it is so painfully incomplete. Words keep calling for other words to help them. You can tell others if things they say about the person are true, but meanwhile you blush at your own description. You keep groping for one that will say what you know.

This has been the Church's experience. In the light of almost two thousand years of communion with her Spouse, reflection on Him, and ever greater experience in describing what she sees, she has continued Peter's discourse to the crowd at Pentecost. A

Gospel tried to improve on the first sketchy sermons. A second, a third, a fourth Gospel tried to complete the first. These and the other books of Scripture were proposed as authentic expressions of what she was trying to say. Later thinkers suggested further descriptions. She voiced no objection to some but insisted that others were not depicting what she actually saw. In ecumenical councils she explained these aspects of her knowledge in words whose accuracy she guaranteed. "Every teacher initiated in the mysteries of the kingdom of heaven is like the head of a household who produces from his store new things and old."[3] Clarifying, distinguishing, devising new ways to speak to new cultures, the Church has always known Christ but has always had the feeling that she could appreciate Him yet more and describe Him even better.

And yet, hearing the "Good News" and given the same insight by the same Spirit, men have been able to see through the words to Christ. Through the Mass and sacraments they too have entered into companionship with Him. They have known Him as one person knows another. Forced by sudden problems to notice one aspect of His revelation, led by experience or the accidents of history to appreciate another, they have reflected in their words and lives the answer to Christ's old question, "Who do you say that I am?"[4]

To study what Christ has revealed will thus be an experience of watching. And what we watch will not be a blueprint of abstract principles for a successful life or a photograph in which the dark world will stand out at last in clear detail. It will be a drama. It will tell us what life is about by showing us certain people who talk and do things. Revelation took place in time; and to understand it, we must watch it as it unfolds in time. These people have been taught by God, not only by His words but by His dealings with them in an amazing companionship. We who have been introduced to the faith ourselves by some of them and are sharers now in their union with Christ, will see more clearly how marriage appears in the light of this new knowledge if we observe these others who have had it.

What view of life accounts for that drama, for the actual history of the "Church," these people of God making their way together through the desert of this life to a Promised Land? What does this view of life show us about the influence of husband and wife on each other's companionship with God?

CONTENTS

The Theology of Marriage

PART I

"Yahweh God said . . ."

Gen. 2, 18.

THE OLD TESTAMENT

THE EARLIEST HINT of an answer to our question about the influence of husband and wife on each other is found in the Bible's oldest account of marriage.

Yahweh God said, 'It is not good that the man be alone. I must make him a helpmate of his own kind.' . . . Then Yahweh God made a deep slumber fall upon the man, and he went to sleep. He took one of his ribs and closed the flesh again over its place. Then, from the rib which he had drawn from the man, Yahweh God fashioned a woman and led her to the man. The man cried,

> 'This now is bone of my bones
> And flesh of my flesh.
> This one shall be called "woman,"
> For she was taken from man.'

That is why a man leaves his father and mother and attaches himself to his wife, and they become one flesh.[1]

Since God used the human being responsible for this passage as His means of communicating with us, what is this human author trying to say?

One thing must be remembered before we can answer. A man sets himself to compose because he wants to share an experience he has had of life and its meaning. He fashions a pattern of musical notes, a blend of colors, a certain arrangement of words because this is the best way he knows to make others see and feel as he has. Thus when an author, inspired this time in a special way by God, declares,

> The mountains leap like young bucks
> And the hills like lambs.[2]

it is important to know whether we are reading an eyewitness report or a lyric poem.

The book in which our passage about marriage occurs received its present form after the Jews had returned from Babylon. It takes poetry and prose from three ancient collections and weaves them into a single pattern. This narrative about the first man and woman derives from the "Yahwist" collection, so named from the word which its songs and sagas ordinarily use for God. Though the collection itself was assembled, and perhaps committed to writing, in the vicinity of Jerusalem during Solomon's time, the individual pieces had been circulating orally for generations. The land and the way of life they describe suggest the days when the Jews were becoming a single people.

No other Near-Eastern tradition derives the human race from a single pair,[3] and no earlier work known today contains this account of how woman came to be. It seems likely that, as the biblical author received it, it had a climax which he has suppressed in an effort to make it flow more smoothly into his next episode, the sin of the man and woman.

The treatment is therefore original, and yet certain details of both the action and setting are also found in Babylonian myths. There is no need to fear what this suggests.

We explain the world we see—clouds, the ice on rivers, spring, the darkness—by laws or mathematical formulas. These in turn lead us to philosophize about an ultimate cause which must at least be as personal as ourselves. Assuming that our formulas and philosophies are true as far as they go, the truths they deal with have no shape or color. They are somehow independent of time. Granted certain conditions, $e = mc^2$ is valid yesterday, today and always.

The people of the Near East were also aware of something behind the things of the world that we touch and see, something just as real, something that accounts for their being and motion. But their way of perceiving this transcendent reality was different from ours. We deduce its presence logically. They simply saw it at work in the world.[4]

Realizing its presence was not, however, the same as being able to describe it. Like ourselves they had to resort to symbols. Their idea of the transcendent reality was expressed not in formulas or combinations of scientific terms but in relationships between persons. They explained the world of shapes and colors and time by stories whose plots and characters were independent of time.

The stories were not expected to agree with one another. Where we try to extend our knowledge by analyzing reality, breaking it down mentally into constituent parts, they regarded wisdom as the ability to see that many things are really one, and merely looked at any one thing from different angles. Like the blind men with the elephant, each storyteller proposed a symbol for the whole of reality as it appeared in his limited contact with it.

Their myths may not be science or philosophy, but neither are they fiction. The symbols stand for something real. Wind and floods and thunder reminded them of the unpredictable actions of human beings. Not that the wind or thunder was a person. But if it were not for some personal reality, present and active but totally unlike the things we see and impossible to describe, there would never be wind or thunder.

The Jews had this same psychology and the same way of expressing it. But one thing about their stories was different. Yahweh was not a character designed to fit the demands of a world that had to be explained. The unknown reality was not entirely unknown. He had revealed Himself.

This meant that, if stories were going to be told, they would have to be told right. The old symbols did not fit the transcendent reality as He had shown Himself to be. The stories should still be relevant to every age, and yet the truths to be symbolized were no longer independent of time. For God had entered time to speak to us. Neither man nor the world would ever be the same. There had been a beginning, and there was now a goal, a Day of Yahweh, to look forward to. The symbols should explain what has happened between God and men in the past, because those past events themselves are symbols of the present.

This passage in Genesis is one attempt to correct the older stories. Is it a myth? It certainly has affinities to the Near-Eastern literature which goes by that name. Whatever we call it, we must recognize that the author's aim, and therefore God's, is to provide us, not with a newspaper report of how marriage came into existence, but with an explanation of what marriage is. This is a story, and though, like all Hebrew stories, it explains the historical dealings of God with men, every married couple who read it are supposed to understand that they are reading about themselves.[5]

The first thing it tells them about themselves appears in its opening words:

Yahweh God said . . .

The whole initiative is with God. It is His appraisal of man and His decision to help him which set the story in motion. It is He who presents the woman to him.

That feature in human beings which inclines them to pair off in a special relationship to one another would seem, then, to be something good. He has made them this way. When they live as husband and wife, they are living as He desires.

Now both were naked, the man and his wife, and they were not ashamed in each other's presence.[6]

Rather than ask what other truths are implied in this story from Genesis, it seems better to keep our attention on this one. We should trace it through later stages of revelation to see if it emerges any more clearly.

In the next chapter of Genesis the serpent is introduced. He leads the man and woman into sin. One detail with which the author describes this sin of theirs may be of special importance to us.

Much of the Old Testament can never be understood unless attention is paid to the pagan religions in and around the Promised Land. The conscious impulse which prompted so many Biblical authors to write was an anxiety to protect the Chosen People from ideas and practices which came so naturally to anyone living in that part of the world. In this particular author's association of sin with a serpent, more than one scholar has seen an allusion to the pagan fertility cult.

The serpent was used throughout the Middle East as a sexual symbol. Genesis may well be describing how woman's sexual attractiveness has ruined both man and herself, making men the slaves of a goddess and women the slaves of men.[7] The author is certainly trying to show that the sorrow and pain in life are not due, as the pagans claim, to some celestial principle of evil. The only God is Yahweh, and His will for the world is peace. If there is chaos and misery, it is because that will has been spurned. Impurity, so typical of all sin, attractive and yet defiling, would be an appropriate symbol of that rebellion.

But there is a difficulty with this interpretation. Since both the Jews and their neighbors used the serpent symbol, the presumption admittedly is that it had the same meaning for both. And yet this presumption is weakened by a fact. The serpent which the pagans associated with sex was a benign deity, whereas the Old Testament word for serpent is the same as that for a dragon and connotes an enemy of man.

Scripture scholars will have to settle the question. The point of the story, that the evils of life are due to some rebellion against

God, is the same in either interpretation; and what may possibly be implied in the author's treatment of the sin itself is suggested more clearly in his description of its consequences.

Then the eyes of both were opened, and they realized that they were naked. They sewed fig leaves together and made themselves coverings.[8]

When God calls for the man, the latter replies,

I heard your footstep in the garden . . . I was afraid because I was naked, and I hid myself.[9]

This certainly alters the impression gained from the previous chapter. There the two sexes were presented as the handiwork of God. Now it appears that there is something embarrassing about being male and female, something that cannot abide the presence of God.

A passage in the Book of Exodus gives the same impression. In its epic portrayal of the encounter with God at Sinai as understood by later Jews and reenacted in their worship, Moses tells the people,

Keep yourselves ready for the day after tomorrow. Abstain from relations with your wives.[10]

So too in the first book of Samuel, when David seeks food for his men from Ahimelek, the priest replies,

I have no ordinary bread on hand. There is only consecrated bread —provided that your men have kept themselves from relations with women.[11]

It seems taken for granted that sexual intercourse is somehow incompatible with nearness to God. The Dead Sea Scrolls are evidence that, by the time of Christ, one Jewish sect was even encouraging its members not to marry.

But these scattered texts must be read in a context that is especially clear whenever the Old Testament speaks of children. In the same Book of Exodus which has the people abstaining before their pact with God, marriage is so definitely expected of religious men that Yahweh is described as promising,

No woman in your land will have a miscarriage. None will be barren.[12]

These Mosaic traditions as they had evolved in the Northern Kingdom were brought to Jerusalem by refugees just before the fall of Samaria and put into some sort of unity. After the exile in Babylon they were edited again to form what we know as the Book of Deuteronomy. This second version of the events at Sinai also takes it for granted that the typical servant of God is married. It has Moses promise the Chosen People that, if they are faithful to Yahweh,

No one among you, man or woman, shall be childless.[13]

In the Book of Judges, also composed after the fall of the Northern Kingdom and reedited by the school which produced Deuteronomy, anecdotes about the early years in Palestine are arranged to show the meaning of Jewish history. The story of Jephte merits attention here. When he feels that his hasty vow obliges him to offer his daughter in sacrifice, she gives her consent but makes one request of him.

Leave me free for two months. I shall go off to wander in the mountains and in company with my friends shall mourn my virginity.[14]

It is a curse to live but not have children. Salvation histories, wisdom books, psalms—all repeat the theme again and again.[15]
There are still, of course, the two discordant themes which we have noted, an embarrassment at being male and female and

a sense of impropriety in approaching God after sexual relations. No attempt is made to resolve the discord.

But this is typical of Old Testament authors. They do not analyze and reconstruct. They simply note the different ways a subject appears as it is viewed from different angles. Granted the disturbing aspects of being male and female, it is still quite evident how this feature of human beings appears to them. It is from God. It is something good.

SECTION I: *Marriage and Sin*

1 *"DECEITFUL SPIRITS"*

THE WORD OF GOD, declared by prophets and Old Testament scribes, took final visible form in the person of Christ. One of the earliest references to marriage by those who saw life as He now revealed it is the Gospel parable of the guests who decline an invitation to a banquet.[1] One of them says,

> I just got married, and for that reason I cannot come.

There is no reason for taking this detail as a suggestion that it is morally wrong to marry. If the different excuses of the guests have allegorical meanings, the Gospel never explains them. The only certain message is that of the parable as a whole: Regardless of what men do, the Kingdom is coming. If the Jewish leaders do not care to enter it, others will take their place.

But there are some genuine signs of uneasiness about marriage among the earliest Christians. Paul's first Letter to the Corinthians includes a reply to questions which they had put to him, and we can judge from his declaration, what some of the questions must have been.

> If you marry, you commit no sin. . . .[2]

This does not seem like a momentous revelation, even to recent converts from paganism; and yet a warning that Paul addresses some years later to his young co-worker, Timothy, shows what he is confronting here.

13

Now the Spirit expressly says that in later times men will depart from the faith, by giving heed to deceitful spirits and doctrines of diabolical origin, propagated through the dissembling of liars who have a seared conscience. They will forbid marriage and enjoin abstinence from foods. . . .[3]

These will be religious men, earnest enough about their religion to be teaching others. There is a temptation, it seems, which appeals to that very earnestness, a tendency to ignore and despise the body.

Whether it comes from their own temperament or from the culture in which they live, one thing is clear. It is not Christian. Within twenty-five years of Pentecost and in an inspired document it is branded as a departure from the faith. The Letter to the Hebrews, whose author is steeped in Paul's theology, shows what orthodox teachers at this time are saying:

Let marriage be held in the fullest honor.[4]

But less than a century after Paul's death it is apparent that he has been all too reliable a prophet. Irenaeus, the bishop of Lyons in modern France, whose teachers had known the Apostles personally, relates how

Saturninus and Marcion, who are called 'the Continent,' preached that all should refrain from marriage. . . .[5]

Whether writing Latin in Rome or Greek in Alexandria, Christian authors of the early 200's insist that marriage is not a sin.[6] Both the cultural climate of Egypt at this time and the Church's reaction to it are reflected in a writer whom some have called the greatest intellectual in Christian history: Origen.

His self-castration as a young man in a mistaken idea of celibacy makes his comment on one of Christ's sayings[7] all the more impressive. As he sees it, "Those who are barred from marriage by an act of man" include all who are afraid to marry because of heretical teachings.[8]

But a century later a council of local bishops at Gangra, some fifty miles northeast of Ankara in modern Turkey, feels called upon to issue the following canons:

1. If anyone disparages marriage, shuns a faithful and God-fearing wife who sleeps with her husband, and speaks as though she cannot enter the Kingdom of God, let him be anathema. . . .

9. If anyone is a virgin or celibate but is avoiding marriage because he regards it as some moral disorder and not because of virginity's own beauty and holiness, let him be anathema.

10. If anyone of those who are celibates for the Lord's sake casts aspersions on those who take wives, let him be anathema. . . .

19. If any woman deserts her husband and wishes to be quit of him because she abhors marriage, let her be anathema.[9]

The bishops also note how those who have actually left their husbands or wives have invariably fallen into adultery.[10]

Farther south near the Euphrates, preachers of the same dour type who treat the body as something evil and speak of angels coming to earth to impregnate women[11] begin to draw fire from Ephrem, the most prominent of the Syriac theologians. Though never more than a deacon, he is listed among the writers whose learning and holiness have won them official recognition as Fathers of the Church, accredited witnesses of what the early Church was teaching. And he insists that, if there is any evil in a marriage, it is due to the particular husband and wife, not to marriage.[12]

I tell you, whoever casts scorn on marriage is an accursed growth, for he himself is cursing his own root.[13]

The Fathers of the Greek-speaking Church during the late 300's keep repeating this in sermons, essays, poems.

If marriage is impure, the living beings begotten from it are all just as impure; and therefore you too, not to mention human nature. How then is she a virgin who is impure?

Where shall we put you? With the Jews? They will not put up with you. They honor marriage and accept the creation of God.

With us? But you are not willing to listen to Christ when He tells us through Paul, 'Let marriage be held in the fullest honor.'

The only thing left for you, then, is to find a place with the gentiles, but even they cast you out as more impious than themselves . . . Do not be afraid, though. As fellow teachers you have the devil and his angels . . .

Do you forbid marriage? Why, you will not even receive the reward of celibacy. No; you will pay with pain and punishment.[14]

> Virtue raises all God-fearing men
> To the one degree . . .
> He who keeps the marriage laws
> Is ranked with the continent.[15]

> Christ, bestowing rewards on each,
> Will sit one at His right,
> The other at His left,
> And even this last is indeed great glory.[16]

It is at this time that the long-standing customs of churches in the East are codified by an unknown author and issued as the *Apostolic Canons*. The first forty, which will be translated into Latin and finally embodied in the papal *Code of Law*, include one canon censuring the cleric who repudiates his wife on the grounds of religion and another canon which declares it blasphemous to look with contempt on marriage.[17]

But the problem is not confined to the East. St. Philastrius, bishop of Brescia during these years, reports,

In Gaul, Spain and Aquitania there are so-called Abstainers, who are likewise following the pernicious sect of the Gnostics and Manichees and do not hesitate to preach the same notion, breaking up marriages by their persuasion.[18]

The reaction of the Latin-speaking Church may be gathered from the writings of St. Ambrose. Acclaimed bishop of Milan in 374, advisor to emperors, Father of the Church, he reflects the faith of his day in sermons and hymns which are classics. On the present question he is brief and to the point.

We have extolled virginity, but in such a way that widows are not spurned. We honor widows, but in such a way that due honor is kept for marriage. It is not our authority which teaches these precepts. It is God's.[19]

On another occasion he explains why these problems arise in the first place.

The human mind is inclined by very slight pressures and is frequently driven hither and yon by the tempter's cleverness. The devil sees . . . an unmarried man of stainless chastity and persuades him to condemn marriage in hopes of having him cast out of the Church and separated by his zeal for chastity from that Body which is chaste.[20]

Therefore, let no one who has chosen marriage find fault with virginity nor anyone who follows the way of virginity rail at marriage, for those who oppose this attitude have long since been condemned by the Church.[21]

Ambrose is representative of the generation which follows him both in the Latin Church and in the East.[22] St. Isidore of Pelusium, whose monastery in the Nile Delta was a center of Scripture studies and moral theology during the early 400's, reflects the common teaching during these years.

The Church . . . gives a middle rank both to marriage and to various kinds of food. He is really outstanding who is above the use of these things. He who enjoys a moderate use of them is not to be reprehended. But he who calumniates and foreswears them dwells outside the sacred camp.[23]

Through the invasions and cultural upheavals from 450 to 600, writers who are celibates themselves are notably careful in the way they speak of marriage.

Those who consecrate themselves totally to God are like holocausts. Others are like the victims which were only partly burnt—for example, those who have entered upon marriage and are giving their lives both to God and the world.[24]

But apparently there is still a need of more formal declarations. Among the questions asked of a bishop at this time before his consecration is "whether or not he belittles marriage or condemns second marriage."[25] Councils of bishops in some districts feel called upon to decree,

If anyone condemns human marriage and is horrified at the procreation of children, as Manichaeus and Priscillian were wont to be, let him be anathema.[26]

As a new social order emerges in the West with the crowning of Charlemagne, Christians are still assured that marriage is "very good and lawful."[27] One of Alcuin's disciples, Rabanus Maurus, who as abbot of Fulda and then archbishop of Mainz tried to bring to Germany the wisdom of classical times in books which simply paraphrase the Fathers, deems it a heresy to speak of marriage as evil.[28] For proof he turns to St. Paul. Just as in the Old Testament Lot thought of a little town that would save him from the fire that rained on Sodom, Paul

. . . points to one near at hand but secure enough to be safe. Married life is not far removed from the world, but neither is it estranged from the joy of salvation.[29]

Though this observation is repeated more than once during the wars and confusion of the next hundred years,[30] a new emergency is evident from the tone of the bishops who assemble at Arras in 1025.

They are deceived, then, who affirm that married people are to be banished from the Kingdom of God. We have a witness for what we say in the gospel, and this arrangement for human companionship is confirmed in many places by the teaching that has been handed down from the days of the apostles.[31]

The old pagan gloom which sees matter as evil and marriage as a sin has begun to settle on one French town after another. These are the days of the Cathars, the Pure Ones.

Theologians of the new wave of learning that courses through Europe during the 1100's find themselves compelled to refute assertions such as those condemned by a council assembled at Constantinople:

> Husbands must abstain from relations with the women joined to them in legitimate marriage, and also from meat and milk, fish and wine for three years. . . .
> Likewise, no layman will be saved, though he has found the road to every virtue, unless he becomes a monk.[32]

The most powerful voice of the century feels called upon to speak. St. Bernard of Clairvaux, who had persuaded his brothers and friends to join him in the austerities of Cistercian life and then almost ruined his health with penance, can hardly be called a lover of pleasure. But the eloquence that sent hundreds off to the Second Crusade turns on those who forbid people to marry. "Being heretics isn't enough," he fumes. "They have to be hypocrites."[33]

> Take honorable wedlock and the unsullied marriage bed from the Church, and will you not fill her with fornicators, practicers of incest, masturbators, perverts, homosexuals, men given to every kind of filth? . . .
> What? Shall turpitude be crowned? Nothing less becomes the Author of righteousness. Shall the whole human race be damned except for a handful who will not marry? This is no way to be a Savior.[34]

The dialectical methods just coming into fashion are applied to the arguments which the Cathars have fashioned from Scripture.

> I grant that 'It is good for a man not to touch a woman.'[35] But that does not force me to grant that it is evil and illicit for him to touch

one. Is it not just as true that, to avoid temptations, it is good for a man not to see a woman? . . .

If you grant that it is evil to touch a woman, since it is good not to touch one, grant also that it is evil to see a woman, since it is good not to see one. And if you grant that it is evil to see a woman, pluck out your eyes and never seen one.

You hypocrite! A man is allowed to touch his wife because each is allowed to have one, as we know from the words of the same Apostle.[36]

As the year 1200 ushers in the High Middle Ages, the profession of faith prescribed by Pope Innocent III for converted Waldensians states,

We do not deny that, according to the Apostle, marriage, with the intercourse it implies, may be contracted. . . . We also believe and publicly acknowledge that a man and his wife may be saved.[37]

And in 1215 the question is taken up by the bishops at the Fourth Lateran Council. With all the authority of an ecumenical council they declare,

Not only virgins and celibates but also married people who please God by right faith and good conduct merit to arrive at eternal happiness.[38]

Thus the Schoolmen, whose lectures in the new universities are making the 1200's a Golden Age of learning, can remark,

It is amazing how the heretics in their treason have been so foolish as to cast aspersions on conjugal chastity when it has been commended by so many unshakable testimonials.[39]

But in 1307 the archbishop of Cologne lists among his charges against the Beghards,

They also say: Unless a woman grieves at the loss of her virginity in marriage and by her grief deplores the fact, she cannot be saved.[40]

Other groups of this persuasion appear from time to time but are labeled at once as heretics.[41] The best known theologians of this and the following century insist that the saints in heaven will number people "in every walk of life,"[42] including "laymen who act according to God's will, not their own."[43]

As late as 1578 the Spanish Inquisition complains of the Alumbrados,

4. By their way of speaking they belittle the sacrament of matrimony. . . .

6. They persuade people that they should neither marry nor enter religion. They say that servants of God ought to shine forth in secular life.[44]

Though symptoms of this rigorism continue to appear among groups like the Jansenists, they are no longer so pronounced. Bishops do not seem as alarmed as before.[45] The stream of formal condemnations gradually peters out.

But one fact which emerges from these centuries of struggle cannot be ignored if we would hope to see marriage as Christ reveals it. Notice the groups who were condemned: Abstainers and Gnostics in the early days of the Church; Manichaeans and Priscillianists during the waning years of Graeco-Roman culture; Cathars and Waldensians, who, whatever be the source of their ideas, were ordinary men of the Middle Ages; Beghards and Alumbrados, avid for mystical prayer as were so many in the Rhine Valley during the 1300's or in the cloisters of sixteenth-century Spain. Each of these sects was a product of the times. Its theology was as new and distinctive as the age in which it appeared. And yet one doctrine is found among all of them: Marriage is evil.

This cannot be just a conclusion that happens to follow logically from a particular set of ideas. It is the expression of something much deeper: a vague, stubborn, temperamental suspicion which takes different forms in different times and countries as

it comes upon different theories about God and man which seem
to confirm it.

Whatever its origins, they are not Christian. Gnosticism is
older than the Church.[46] The Manichaeans took their rise in
Persia. And yet this uneasiness about the fact of being male and
female is part of the climate in which the Church has lived for
most of its history. Paul feels a need to warn Timothy against
it. The Greek and Latin Fathers have to take it into account
when they write on marriage. The next great period of theology,
the Middle Ages, responds with a new virulence of this perennial
mood. To understand what Christians have said about marriage,
we must remember this inescapable influence on all they said
and did.

Its power can be judged from the measures the Christians took
to oppose it: warnings in the New Testament, denunciations by
their greatest preachers, formal condemnations not only by local bishops but finally by an ecumenical council.

It has always appeared in the guise of religion. These men,
whatever name they take, are always a select few, more inter-
ested than most in the things of God. They are always the
"Pure Ones," who have the rest of the Church at a tactical disadvantage, being forced to defend what is easy. The Cathar
always smiles at those who associate God with marriage. Are
they trying to make a virtue out of necessity? Whether God
favors marriage or not, would they have the strength to live
without it?

However lofty and spiritual this attitude may appear, it is not
truly religious. In fact, the man who yields to it and insists on
treating marriage as something evil puts himself out of the
Church. He is refusing to see life as God has revealed it.

2 *WHY MARRIAGE IS GOOD*

SEEING MARRIAGE in the light of faith, the Church has been convinced that it is good. What has she seen in it that has convinced her?

One answer is apparent among Syriac-speaking Christians of the late 300's. Ephrem the Deacon, as we have noted, turned all the learning and eloquence that made him a Father of the Church against preachers who were claiming that marriage is evil. Time and again he reminds them that, since they themselves are the products of sexual intercourse, when they condemn it they are condemning themselves.[1]

This line of argument shows one aspect of marriage which has impressed him. It appears even more clearly in one of his hymns.

> Pure in the eyes of God is marriage.
> It has been planted in the world as a vine
> From which children hang like fruit.[2]

How should we look at marriage? How do we look at a human being? If he has dignity and value, so does marriage.

A few years later the Greek Fathers note how this should strike the man who is truly religious.

Marriage is good, for it brings many into the world who give pleasure to God.[3]

And Ambrose, whose preaching during these years is turning the eyes of scholars, popes and emperors toward Milan, remarks in his treatment of the different ways of life,

Someone will say, 'Therefore you dissuade people from marriage?' No; I persuade people to it, and I condemn those who have made a practice of dissuading people from it. . . . For he who speaks ill of marital relations also speaks ill of children.[4]

This view is typical, not only of Ambrose but of bishops in the West around the year 400. If a Christian simply looks at a child, he will see what to think of marriage. For children are "the reward of marriage,"[5] and those among them who will later dedicate themselves exclusively to God are even clearer illustrations of its value.

Fruit from a tree, grain from a stalk, virginity from marriage.[6]

This attitude does not change. During the centuries that follow one writer after another concludes that,

Marriage is therefore something great and to be loved, because its fruit is so precious. . . . If a field or a vineyard is considered of great value because of the grain or grapes it produces, how much more is marriage, which produces men?[7]

Marriage is good because of its issue. But early Christian writers also speak of the state itself. Irenaeus, the bishop of Lyons who could boast that his teachers had known the Apostles, observes in his book *Against Heresies,*

Saturninus and Marcion, who are called the Continent, preached abstinence from marriage, frustrating that ageold creation of God and implicitly finding fault with Him who made human beings male and female so that they could reproduce themselves. They introduced abstinence from what they describe as 'animal-like,' ungrateful as they are to Him who made everything, God.[8]

Clement, a resident of Alexandria at this time, whose school of theology will include no less a pupil than Origen, reacts to the same contempt with a similar observation.

If marriage . . . is a sin, I do not see how a person can say he knows God when he says that the law of God is a sin. But if 'the law is holy,' marriage is holy.[9]

During the "Little Peace" between 260 and 290 when Christians find themselves relatively free from persecution, St. Methodius, the bishop of Olympus on the southern coast of modern Turkey, takes Plato's *Symposium* as a model and presents his views on marriage and virginity in the form of a discussion by ten maidens in the garden of Virtue. Though the first participant in this celebrated *Banquet of the Ten Maidens* speaks of marriage in terms that later editors will feel obliged to soften, she is not allowed to go unchallenged.

Even now God is making man every day through this kind of marital intercourse. How then was it not rash to despise the process of begetting children when the Creator thinks it not at all unbecoming that His immaculate hands should have their part in it?[10]

To Syriac-speaking Christians of the following century Ephrem the Deacon addresses a similar observation,[11] and the common view of churches in the Middle East during the late 300's is apparent from that collection of usages which emerges as the *Apostolic Constitutions*.

If any bishop, priest, deacon or other member of the clergy abstains from marriage, flesh meat, and wine, not from a motive of asceticism, but because he detests these things, forgetting that 'all things were very good,' that God made human beings male and female, and blasphemously finding fault with creation, let him be corrected or deposed and ejected from the Church. The same applies to a layman.[12]

In the West at this time Ambrose cites Genesis as proof of his contention that marriage is good because it comes from God.[13] St. Chromatius, bishop of Aquileia on the Adriatic coast and one of the most respected theologians in Italy during these years, points to Christ's prohibition of divorce.

He commands that the chaste bond of marriage be kept by an indissoluble law, showing that it was He who in the beginning promulgated the law of marriage.[14]

Another bishop, in what eventually will come to be regarded as one of the best Latin commentaries of the period on St. Paul, draws a significant conclusion from the text, "As for virgins, I have no command from the Lord."[15]

He says he has not received a command from the Lord, because the originator of marriage could not impose any command against marriage without criticizing His deed of long ago.[16]

These bishops are not alone in their views.[17] The ordinary teaching given to the faithful of these years is apparent from the earliest known form of the Roman Missal, the *Leonine Sacramentary*. The work of an unknown author around the year 550, it is based on material one or two centuries older, and its rite for the veiling of a bride contains the following prayer:

Receive, Lord, we beg, the gift that is offered here in accord with the sacred law of marriage, and be the director of this work of which You are the creator.[18]

The declining years of Roman culture were dominated by a man who had been Prefect of Rome in 570, then later a monk, and in 590 was acclaimed as Pope. His success in both the political and spiritual care of Rome, his role in the missionary effort among the barbarians and the establishment of a church in England, and finally his *Moralia*, which would become the basic text in moral theology for the Middle Ages, have earned him the name Gregory the Great. There is more than ordinary importance, then, in his explanation of the Psalmist's plea, "Behold, I was born in guilt and in sin my mother conceived me."[19]

It is not as though men are conceived in sin because it is sinful for married people to have relations. That chaste activity involves no fault in one who is married. It is God who designed that there would be marital intercourse when He first created man and woman.[20]

Sentiments like these continue to be heard intermittently during the Dark Ages.[21] Hatto of Vercelli, writing around 960, declares,

We must realize that marriage is clean and holy. It is celebrated at God's command and involves nothing base, nothing dishonorable. If married people admit something shameful, dishonorable, indecent, the fault is not with marriage but with men.[22]

As Europe's intellectual life begins to quicken during the 1100's, theologians of the many new schools agree that marriage comes from God.[23] The point is made continually during these years of the Cathars,[24] and the Schoolmen of the following century find reason and faith converging on the same conclusion.

If bodily nature has been designed by a God who is good, it is impossible to assert that a thing which has to do with conserving bodily nature and which nature prompts one toward, is thoroughly evil.[25]

Marriage is something good in itself, formally good . . . because it has been established by God.[26]

Writers of the next two centuries take the connection with God for granted as they argue that, if marriage were sinful, God would be the perpetrator of sin.[27]

The typical instruction given to the faithful just after the rise of Protestantism may be gathered from two books, the first

of which is the *Summary of Christian Doctrine* by St. Peter
Canisius. This Jesuit and his catechism are two of the principal
reasons why the Church survived in Germany. His views on
marriage, though fortified with references to Scripture and the
Fathers of the Church, are brief and to the point.

If you look for the principal founder of this marriage union, it is
God good and great, who joined the first married couple and parents
of the human race in paradise itself and made their union an honorable
thing by His blessing.[28]

The other book, *The Perfect Wife,* made such an impression
in Spain that it is still selected as a wedding present. Its author,
Luis de Leon, who taught theology at the University of Salamanca, was respected for his doctrine as well as his style, though
he seems to have done his best work while a prisoner of the Inquisition.

In the opening paragraphs of *The Perfect Wife* he remarks
how highly a woman should esteem her marriage,

For truth to tell . . . it has always been much honored and privileged by the Holy Spirit in sacred scripture, and from scripture we
know that this way of life is the first and most ancient of all ways.[29]

During the early 1600's an Italian Capuchin, Lawrence of
Brindisi, won such acclaim as a preacher, diplomat, army chap-
lain and theologian that he has been canonized and named a Doctor of the Church. A passage in one of his Lenten sermons reflects the consensus of Catholics from his time till the present.

If a statue or picture is made worthy of esteem by the artist's name,
the age it has, the place in which it was fashioned and put on display,
its subject matter, its beauty, then obviously, for all these reasons, this
sacrament is noble indeed. . . . Therefore God wished to honor this
sacrament through all the patriarchs who married: Noah, Abraham,
Isaac, Jacob; through kings, prophets, even high priests of the Old

Law; and finally through the Incarnation of His Son, wishing Him to be conceived of a virgin who was espoused.[30]

The last remark touches on a special feature of the connection with God which is noted in the earliest Christian documents.

Two days later a wedding took place at Cana in Galilee at which the Mother of Jesus was present. Jesus and His disciples were also invited to the festivities.[31]

The Gospel ends this account of the miracle worked at Cana with the remark,

This is the first proof of his claims that Jesus gave, and he gave it at Cana in Galilee. He revealed His glory and his disciples believed in him.[32]

As a first gesture, this act of Christ is especially meaningful, and one meaning which Christians immediately saw appears in Ephrem the Deacon's protest against heretics of his day.

They have ridiculed the marriage feast at Cana, though the Lord judged it worthy of His presence.[33]

The presence of Christ at this village wedding should settle any doubts as to what God thinks of marriage. Around the year 400 both Greek- and Latin-speaking Churches take this for granted.

Paul promulgates laws on marriage and is not ashamed. He does not blush, and with good reason. For if his Lord brought honor to marriage, was not ashamed of it but enhanced it by His presence and His gift (Indeed, He brought the greatest gifts of all when He changed the nature of water into wine.), what could make the servant ashamed to proclaim laws on marriage?[34]

That the Lord, when invited, came to a wedding was intended, even aside from its mystical meaning, to confirm the fact that He is the one who designed marriage. For there were to be men whom the Apostle spoke of, who would forbid people to marry and say that marriage was evil and that the devil designed it.[35]

These views are shared by writers of the uncertain years before the Middle Ages;[36] and during the 1200's, theologians insist, not only in disputes with the Cathars but even when they explain why priests of the Roman rite do not marry, that Christ had all this in mind when He went to Cana. If there were anything sinful about marriage it would hardly have evoked such a gesture from Him who came to be the Savior.[37]

This refrain is echoed down to the present day.[38] The episode at Cana is symbolic. As the Father in the Old Testament, so Christ in the New presents Himself as the founder of marriage. It cannot be opposed to religion. God is the one responsible for it. It enters into that awesome design by which His will for the human race is to be accomplished.

But how? As something He positively favors or as a concession He makes to human weakness? It was not long before the Church was forced to realize that this is not an academic question.

3 *IF ADAM HAD NOT FALLEN*

ORIGEN, WHOSE SCHOOL at Alexandria and later in Palestine made the early 200's a new era in theology, ran the usual dangers of a mind that has neither an equal in its own day nor a model from the past. Though he insists that marriage is not a sin, his impresssion of it may be gathered from the way it appears in his general theory about matter and spirit. Every child, it seems to him, will find life a struggle between the soul's yearnings and the body's demands. Thus marriage does nothing but furnish bodies in which to imprison souls.

From this conclusion he and his followers went on to construct a theology of marriage which struck other thinkers as more expressive of Origen's personality than of the Christian revelation.

How can the Apostle Paul write, 'I wish the young widows to marry and beget children'? Is he commanding marriage so that bodies born of women may furnish prisons for angels who have fallen from heaven and are turned, according to you, into souls? Or is it rather to obey God's decree about the marriage union, and to preserve the human race?[1]

But more than a century after Origen's death marriage is again associated with evil, and this time by a theologian whom the bishops at the ecumenical council of Constantinople in 381 will acclaim as a "pillar of orthodoxy." St. Gregory of Nyssa, who all but took a bride himself before becoming a hermit and finally bishop of that city, sets out to study marriage in the light of the total Christian revelation.

> If, then, the life of those who are restored will be like the one which angels enjoy, obviously the life of man before the Fall was analogous to the life of the angels. . . . For although there is no propagation among the angels, as we have noted, their host is still in some sense infinite in number. . . .
> Therefore, if we had not fallen because of sin from the condition and rank in which we were equal to the angels, not even for us would there have been any need of marriage to increase our kind.[2]

Marriage, though not sinful in itself, is involved with rebellion against God. There would never be such a thing in human life were it not for original sin.

This cannot be dismissed, like Origen's view, as the random thought of a private theologian. The "Fathers of the Church" are the acknowledged witnesses to what the early Church taught and believed, and Gregory of Nyssa is numbered among them. What is more, his view is shared by another of the Fathers, St. John Chrysostom.

Bishop of the imperial capital, Constantinople, in 398, John of the Golden Tongue was one of the Church's greatest preachers. As an authority in matters of practical Christian living, he has few equals. And he affirms with even more conviction than Gregory that marriage is due to original sin.

> That age demanded it, with human nature raging and neither standing firm against the attack of sensuality nor having any port to flee to for safety in the storm.
> What was commanded? That they live in continence and virginity? Why that would have caused a greater fall and a more vehement flame. . . . That is why virginity was not given in the beginning; or rather, that is why, though virginity did exist in the beginning—even before marriage—marriage thrust itself on the scene and seemed neces-

sary; whereas if Adam had remained obedient, there would have been no need of it.

'But who,' he says, 'would have begotten so many thousands of men?'

Since this anxious fear haunts you, I ask in turn where Adam came from and where Eve came from when there was no marriage?

'What then? Is that the way all men were to have been born?'

Whether in this way or some other way is not for me to say. The point is that God did not need marriage to fill the earth with men.[3]

The school of Scripture scholars in Chrysostom's native Antioch, then the capital of Syria, had its last great moment some fifty years after his death in the work of Theodoret. A personal friend of Nestorius, with whom he had gone to school, this bishop of Cyrus, not far from the Euphrates, had both personal and intellectual problems with the Nestorian heresy but spoke against it and died in communion with Rome. In a celebrated commentary on the book of Genesis he notes that God was not moved to punish Adam and Eve by any burst of regret that He had created them.

Foreseeing and foreknowing that Adam would be liable to death because of the violation of the command, He already fashioned a nature of this kind beforehand and formed it into a male and female body. The reason, of course, was that this is the design of bodies that are mortal and need the procreation of children to conserve the race.

An immortal nature has no need of a female sex. This is why the Creator produced the entire number of bodiless creatures at the same time but, when it came to creatures which had bodies and could die, created two of each species, male and female, and later gave them the blessing of increase, 'Be fruitful and multiply.'

Thus He also designed human nature as male and female and gave them the same blessing.[4]

This view of how marriage originated does not appear in the West until the early 500's. The monk in Rome who gives it expression, though not a Father of the Church, is of no small importance. It was Dionysius Exiguus, Denis the Insignificant, as he styled himself, whose attempt to calculate the year of Christ's birth gave us our present system of dates. His collection of the laws of different churches is the most important canonical work of its time, and he devoted himself to translating the thought of the Greek-speaking Church into Latin.

In the spirit of Chrysostom or Theodoret he reasons that, since there will be no marriage in heaven, there was none before the Fall.

The grace of the resurrection promises us nothing else than that we shall be changed from our fall to the ancient state. . . . If therefore restored men will be like the angels as far as number and relationship to one another are concerned, it is clear that man before the fall was regarded as a kind of angel. . . . Logically, therefore, if no sinful excess had removed us from the angelic dignity, the means for us to multiply our race need not have been marriage but whatever that natural process is by which angels are multiplied—perfect indeed, though it cannot be imagined by any conjecture of man's.

Why, then, did God create the two sexes? Dionysius replies,

He knew in His all-powerful providence that the choice of the human will would not be moved to the right things and that, as a consequence, man would withdraw from those family ties with the angels. Lest the number of human souls be diminished, since theirs was the same process by which angels are multiplied . . . in the design of human beings, in place of the sublime power of the angels, He included the process by which beasts and irrational things receive life from one another.[5]

Though Dionysius seems to have few disciples in Western Europe, the idea continues to appear in the East.[6] During the early 700's, when Islam is flooding over one province after another, St. John of Damascus, the last of the Greek Fathers and the one whose special concern is to summarize their teaching for his beleagured fellow Christians, echoes Chrysostom and Gregory of Nyssa. Human beings were to have been produced by some other means than sexual union. This is why Genesis has woman fashioned later than man.[7] Marriage is due to original sin.

Since God in His foreknowledge realized that he would violate the law imposed on him and fall into corruption, He fashioned a woman from him. She was like him and was a helpmate for him—a helpmate, I say, to preserve the human race by begetting one generation to take the place of another.[8]

But all through the centuries in which these views were being voiced by such eminent names in the Church, there was a cross current of opinion, older, and also found in the East. A generation before Gregory of Nyssa, Ephrem the Deacon takes it for granted that marriage is not the result of original sin. Commenting on Genesis, he remarks that Eve

. . . would not have abounded in so numerous a family as has since come into being, because she would not, on the other hand, have begotten one that could die.[9]

This is the sentiment which prevails in the West, due principally to a North African who in the year of Ephrem's death was a non-Catholic keeping a mistress in Carthage but by the year of Chrysostom's ordination had been so affected by the preaching of Ambrose that he finally entered the Church. Returning to North Africa, the thirty-four-year-old Augustine became a priest in Hippo, then bishop of that city in 396. For the next thirty-four years he poured out sermons, letters, commentaries on Scripture, treatises on points of theology, classics like the *Confessions*. The most celebrated of the Latin Fathers, he rivals Origen and Aquinas as the greatest mind in the Church.

His view of how marriage began is evident from more than one passage in his writings.

You are entirely mistaken when you think that marriage was instituted so that the passing of the dead would be compensated for by the
succession of those who were born. Marriage was instituted so that
the chastity of women would make sons known to their fathers and
fathers to their sons.

True, it was possible that men be born of promiscuous and random
intercourse with any women at all, but there could not have been a
bond of kinship between fathers and sons.[10]

We read that they were already expelled from paradise when they
had relations and conceived children. Still I do not see what could
prevent their having honorable marriage and an immaculate marriage
bed even in paradise. When they were living faithfully and justly,
serving Him with obedience and holiness, God could have arranged
that, without any restless ardor of sensual desire, without any labor or
childbirth pain, children would be born of their seed.

The idea would not be that the children take the place of their
parents when they had died. The parents would remain in some bodily
state and draw bodily strength from the tree of life which had been
planted there. The children too would be brought to the same state,
until the predetermined number was complete.

Then, granted that all lived justly and obediently, the final stage
would come. Without any death, animal bodies would be transformed
into another kind in the sense that they would bow to every wish,
even the slightest, of the spirit that ruled them, would live merely
because of the lifegiving spirit without nourishment from bodily food,
and would be called spiritual. . . .

'Why then did they not have relations until they had left paradise?'
We can answer at once. Because that sin took place soon after the
woman was created, before they had had relations. . . .

It can also be argued that God had not yet commanded them to
have relations. For why would they not await His authorization for
this when there was no concupiscence like the goad of disobedient
flesh to keep prodding them? God had not given this command because He was arranging everything according to His providence, and
by this He knew in advance beyond all doubt that they would fall
and that the human race would already be mortal when it was propagated.[11]

Therefore, when the Lord said with regard to the resurrection, 'Neither do they marry nor do they take wives, for they do not die,' His intent was not to show that marriage was instituted because men were mortal, but rather that, with the number of the saints complete, there was no need of anyone's being born, because in that land no one had to die.[12]

Augustine takes it for granted that this is the Christian view. He has heard the claim that marriage is a result of original sin, but unaware that Chrysostom and Gregory of Nyssa are among those who have made it, he remarks,

Those who hold this opinion think perhaps that all sexual intercourse is a sin. For it is difficult for men, when they avoid vices in the wrong way, not to run willfully into their contraries. . . . As long as men do not know what it is that the law of God condemns in adulteries and fornications, they detest sexual intercourse in marriage even for the sake of having children.[13]

He is convinced, therefore, that marriage is not simply a means of preserving a race of creatures who must die. There was a certain good which God envisaged in the fact that all men, whether mortal or immortal, would be descended from an original pair. Even if there had never been an original sin, there would be marriage.

Though Dionysius Exiguus around the year 500 will follow the Eastern view, it is Augustine whose theology on this point, as on so many others, appeals to the Church in the West. The teaching given to the faithful is apparent from the liturgy which gradually develops around the veiling of a bride. The nuptial blessing in the missal known as the *Gregorian Sacramentary* illustrates the Roman rite around the year 600.

O God, through whom man is joined to woman and the society established in the beginning is endowed with that blessing which alone has not been taken away either by the punishment of original sin or the sentence of the Flood, look down with favor upon this woman your servant. . . .[14]

The theologians of the Dark Ages, whose intent is simply to echo what has been taught by the Fathers, share Augustine's view of marriage,[15] sometimes adding refinements of their own. Eve's being fashioned from Adam's rib is a detail intended to teach us that the world was to be filled by means of their union.[16] Marriage was to be part of their life in Eden so that new beings could replace the fallen angels.[17]

The revival of learning after the year 1000 does not occasion any change in this view.[18] In 1150 Peter Lombard's four books of *Sentences* prove to be such an agreeable synthesis of the Christian revelation that theology courses are soon little more than commentaries on them. And the second book echoes Augustine. There would have been marriage even if man had never sinned.[19]

Robert of Melun, an Englishman whose school of theology in that city numbered St. Thomas à Becket among its pupils, concludes that Adam and Eve would indeed have sinned by abstaining from sexual intercourse.[20]

During the early 1200's when one of the professors of theology at Paris tells his students that marriage is a consequence of original sin, Pope Innocent III finds the idea "not so heretical as insane."[21] Popular writings as well as theological treatises reflect a common conviction that there would have been sexual intercourse regardless of original sin so that men could beget the predestined number of saints.[22] In fact, to facilitate marriage among Adam's descendants, there would have been an equal number of men and women.[23]

One of the leading spokesmen for the age which follows the Schoolmen is Thomas of Strasbourg, who taught at Paris before being elected Prior General of the Hermits of St. Augustine. In his writings the general outlook of Augustine blends with the best ideas of the Schoolmen. His remarks on marriage are typical. To him it is inconceivable that the reason why there are many human beings in the world today is original sin. The ability to generate offspring is a sign of a being's perfection, and man is surely no less perfect than the animals.[24]

Not only during the years which immediately follow the outbreak of Protestantism[25] but as the energies of the Counter-Reformation reach their climax during the early 1600's, Catholic writers are more emphatic than ever. A representative spokesman for the age is St. Lawrence of Brindisi, the Italian Capuchin whose sermons and writings have, as we remarked, won him the title Doctor of the Church.

If man had not sinned, human nature could have been permanent in that couple in whom it was first embodied. Since God made them eternal, so that, though mortal by nature, they still could not have died, the power to reproduce themselves was not necessary to preserve the species. And yet they still would have begotten children to the glory of God in order to communicate that nature to the many whom God had selected beforehand for grace and glory.[26]

Theories like Chrysostom's of an angelic type of increase for the human race have by this time disappeared from the discussion. Toward the end of the nineteenth century an encyclical by Pope Leo XIII gives official expression to the common conviction that in God's design, whether the first two human beings would sin or not, all others were to be descended from them.

We recall what is known to all and doubted by no one, that after ... God had formed man ... , He wished to give him a helpmate ... and in so doing, our ever-provident God desired this model of all marriages to be the natural source of all men.[27]

Thus, despite the suspicion with which some eminent Christians have looked on marriage, it is the considered view of the Church that marriage is neither a sin nor the result of sin. Even if the first man and woman had lived an ideal life, one feature of that life would have been marriage.

But the very Christians who saw this from the beginning had suspicions of their own. In the earliest days of the Church we find, not marriage, but the sex instinct traced to original sin.

4 *LIBIDO*

JUSTIN THE MARTYR was born in a village which pagan colonists had just built in Palestine. At the nearby well Christ had stopped some seventy years before to talk to the Samaritan woman. After studying philosophy and finding it unsatisfying, Justin became a Christian himself. Seeing how few of his fellow believers were able to discuss religion with educated pagans, he opened a school of philosophy and even addressed two defenses of Christianity to the emperor, Antoninus Pius.

His criticisms of pagan vices eventually led to his martyrdom. One of them merits attention here. Contrasting pagan sexual practices with those of the Christians, he explains,

> Either we marry with only one thought, to have children, or if we avoid marriage, we keep ourselves continent at all times.[1]

Christians "marry with only one thought." Sexual intercourse, even in marriage, appears as something evil unless the motive is to have children.

It appears this way a generation later in the writings of Athanagoras, another "Apologist" for Christianity, and indeed one of the greatest.[2] And during the early 200's, Clement, bishop of Alexandria and head of its celebrated school of theology, writes,

... the man who has taken a wife in order to have children should also practice continence, not even seeking pleasure from his own wife, whom he ought to love, but with honorable and moderate desire having but one intention, children.[3]

What is there about sexual intercourse which seems to demand this avoidance?

An answer is suggested by Clement's most eminent pupil, Origen, who cautions married people against having relations once the wife has conceived.[4] This and similar warnings which are voiced as late as the 1400's seem to be prompted by a concern for the child.

For then are conceived monstrous offspring, lame, blind or defective in some other way, as Jerome says.[5]

The man whose authority is cited here was born in what is now northern Italy. A hermit in the Syrian desert when Ambrose became bishop of Milan, a priest at Antioch eight years before Chrysostom's ordination, an acquaintance of Gregory of Nyssa, secretary to Pope Damasas, a hermit again in Bethlehem, where in 390 he began a Latin translation of the Bible whose adoption by the West for private reading and the liturgy itself would make it the common version or Vulgate, Jerome was a man to be listened to.

But he seems concerned with something more than the welfare of the child.

The activities of marriage itself, if they are not modest and do not take place under the eyes of God, as it were, so that the only intention is children, are filth and lust.[6]

In another place he calls them a desecration of God's temple,[7] and even these strong terms are not as significant as a passage in his translation of the Book of Tobit. When young Tobias is afraid to marry Sara because her seven former husbands have died on their wedding night, the angel tells him,

Listen. I am going to show you those whom the demon can conquer. Those who at the time of their marriage banish God from their thoughts and give themselves over so completely to their instincts that they have no more intelligence than a horse or a mule, the demon is stronger than they. But you, when you marry her, spend three days in continence having no concern but praying with her . . . After the third night, in the fear of the Lord take the maiden, prompted not so much by instinct as by love of children. . . .[8]

If this is the inspired word of God, it cannot be passed over lightly.

But is it?

Jerome himself did not think so. Aware that the Jews were not including the Book of Tobit in their official Old Testament collection, he told the bishops Chromatius and Heliodorus, who had urged him to translate it: "I've satisfied your desires, not my own taste. I've done my best with it."[9]

This last remark touches on a fact that is also important. The text he had worked from was in Aramaic. Mistrusting his knowledge of that language, he had had a Jew translate it aloud into Hebrew which he would recast into Latin and dictate to a scribe. Even with so complicated a procedure he had finished the book in a day.

The text which resulted from this treatment of a work which did not seem to merit greater care is often too strongly colored by Jerome's personal feelings to be an accurate rendering of the original. The advice quoted above is not found in any other version of the angel's words to Tobias.

But it thus occurs in the only one which the vast majority of Christians in Western Europe will use for over a thousand years. Since, contrary to Jerome, they will number Tobit among the inspired books of the Old Testament, his version of the angel's words will affect their attitude toward sexual relations. And it leaves no doubt about his own conviction, a conviction which links him, not only with earlier writers like Justin and Clement, but with Augustine.

Energetically serving as leader of the North African bishops while Jerome, with whom he had a somewhat nervous friendship, was working on the Vulgate, Augustine was forced to speak often on marriage. His own early years, with their sad blend of Manichaean contempt for matter and yet surrender to the allurements of life with a mistress, had given him an unusual concern with this aspect of human life.

He speaks his mind clearly and often. For a husband and wife, the virtue of purity consists in desiring only children.[10] To seek relations for any other motive is a sin, though only a venial sin since they are married.[11]

Typical is his discussion of marriage among holy men and women of Old Testament times.

Obedience compelled them to marry, so that the people of God . . . would be propagated, since those people . . . were nothing less than a prophet of Christ and from them would even be born the flesh of Christ. . . . Thus even holy women were inflamed, not with the desire of intercourse but with a faithful concern to have children. Indeed, it is by no means incorrect to suppose that they would not have sought intercourse if they could have had children in some other way.[12]

Just as that wise and just man (St. Paul) who yearned to be dissolved and be with Christ . . . took nourishment in order to remain in the flesh, since it was necessary for the sake of others, so the holy men of those days regarded intercourse with women as an obligation of the marriage law.[13]

Not long after Augustine's death in 430 there are signs of the same outlook in the Greek-speaking Church. Theodoret, whose commentaries establish him as the last great name in the Antioch school of Biblical scholars, urges restraint in marriage and warns that the proper motive for having relations is not pleasure but children.[14]

The idea is still current in the East a century later.[15] As for the West, after the Vulgate translation of Tobit and the many statements of Augustine, it is not hard to guess the thought of writers during the 500's.[16] What is remarkable is the consistency with which, through the Dark Ages and the rise of medieval culture, the same idea is repeated. Sexual intercourse for any other motive but children is sinful, though only venially sinful since the couple are married.[17]

A thousand years after Augustine's death his words are still being echoed.[18] Sixteenth-century theologians reflect his point of view.[19] And the catechism issued for priests by order of the Council of Trent quotes Jerome's translation of Tobit to show the proper attitude for the use of marriage.[20] Though it seems to be the conservative theologians who write in this vein during the 1600's,[21] Pope Innocent XI formally condemns the proposition that there is no fault whatever in having marital relations from the motive of sheer pleasure.[22]

What is the view of marriage which inspired this conviction of so many thinkers through so many centuries?

Justin, intent on showing the pagans how badly they need the new religion, is one of the earliest to answer.

Either we marry with only one thought, to have children, or if we avoid marriage, we keep ourselves continent at all times.[23]

In other words, Christians do not imitate the Graeco-Roman world with its impulsive swings from a philosophical contempt for the body to an all-permissive license in social customs. Sexual relationships as Christians actually find them in such a culture suggest nothing so much as evil. It cannot be right to abandon oneself in this way. Personal values must be respected. There must be a better reason for marriage.

The most obvious one is children. This is surely God's purpose. Marital relations were never intended to be what the pagan world makes them, an exercise in pleasure.

A century later, when Clement of Alexandria dissuades a husband from desiring even his wife, "whom he ought to love,"[24] he seems to imply that using a human being as a mere source of personal gratification is the thing that is wrong. Augustine gives the same impression. By having relations only when he wants to beget a child a husband pays his wife the honor which is her due.[25]

Too ardent a lover of his wife is an adulterer, if pleasure in his wife is sought for its own sake.[26]

These sentiments are voiced continually during the following centuries[27] and suggest themselves in Pope Innocent XI's condemnation of the statement that there is no fault in having marital relations from a motive of sheer gratification.[28] A modern expression of this attitude is found in a remark of Pius XII:

Some have the notion that happiness in marriage is in direct proportion to the pleasure they bring each other in marital intercourse. No; happiness in marriage is in direct proportion to the respect they have for each other even in their intimate relations. Not that they regard as immoral or look with disdain on what nature offers and the Creator has given them. This respect, however, along with the mutual esteem it begets, is one of the strongest elements of a love that is all the more tender because it is pure.[29]

This is certainly one aspect of the thinking which prompted those repeated warnings that children should be the reason for marital intercourse. But it is not the only one. A remark of Origen's that the bedroom is not a fitting place for prayer[30] betrays an embarrassment about sexual activity itself, a sense that it involves some intrinsic evil. Though Latin-speaking Christians disagree with his contention that it merely provides bodies in which to imprison souls, they seem to share his embarrassment. In Origen's own day they describe this activity as "so frivolous, so impure."[31] During the late 300's the sex instinct is regarded as a weakness, a sickness, a defect. Young people trying to choose between marriage and celibacy are told, "Decide what you prefer, a cure or health."[32] Ambrose bids his people,

Show Him that Adam who existed before sin, that Eve who existed before she drew in the serpent's deceptive poison, before they were brought to ruin by his wiles, in the days when they still had nothing to be ashamed of. For now, although marriage is good, it includes something that makes even married people blush at themselves.[33]

Augustine, as has been noted, was convinced that marriage does not derive from original sin. And yet,

Ever since that day it has remained for married people . . . to avoid the observation of men during this activity and thus to admit that it is shameful, since no one should be ashamed of what is good. Two things are thus implied here: the good of praiseworthy relations from which children are begotten, and the evil of the sex appetite which causes their shame . . . Consequently, those who use the shameful sex appetite licitly are making good use of evil; those who use it illicitly are making evil use of evil.[34]

During the centuries which follow, voices in both East and West agree that even the children who result from sexual intercourse cannot make it something noble, for they cannot be conceived without "the stain of carnal pleasure."[35] This attitude is still apparent around the year 1000. Burchard of Worms, whose celebrated collection of Church laws from earlier ages reflects his own opinions, quotes a directive of bishops in the neighborhood of Milan.

In a first marriage the priest should celebrate Mass and bless the couple. Afterwards let them keep themselves away from church for thirty days.[36]

Later in the same century St. Bruno of Asti, friend and advisor of several popes and the best Biblical scholar in Italy from the sixth till the twelfth century, feels that Paul's reason for advising married couples to abstain at times is to make them purer when they pray.[37]

One of the outstanding theologians of this period is St. Anselm of Canterbury, who entered the abbey of Bec in Normandy six years before William the Conqueror sailed for England. Abbot of Bec some years later and the father of Scholasticism by his technique of blending revealed truths with the discoveries of philosophy, he was eventually named archbishop of Canterbury by England's new Norman kings. As for the present subject, he feels that it was "cleaner and more honorable" that Christ was born of one human being rather than from a man and woman.[38] And his argument against incest is based on the assumption that sexual intercourse is extremely shameful. In a good Christian marriage the desire of children covers over, as it were, this shamefulness, but members of the same family are not pardoned by "love of generation" for inflicting it on each other.[39]

As the new wave of learning reaches its crest in the twelfth and thirteenth centuries, the feeling persists that, since nature does not err in these matters, man's instinctive embarrassment proves that "To God all carnal pleasure is an abomination."[40]

With the gradual decline of theology during the 1300's, most writers simply repeat the statements of those who have gone before.[41] St. Antoninus, the archbishop of Florence whose *Summaries* of dogmatic and moral theology remained popular long after his death in 1459, remarks that for forty days after the birth of a child both husband and wife are excused from going to church.[42]

The same general outlook is apparent during the 1500's.[43] Alfonso Salmeron, a Spanish Jesuit who was one of the papal theologians at the Council of Trent, repeats Augustine's comments on "procreation, which would take place in a much more honorable way if it could be had without intercourse."[44] And the fact which seems to have the most influence on his attitude is the inborn embarrassment. A man who does not feel this is lower than every beast. Hence, with nature his guide, Adam fled to the fig leaves and God furnished him with garments of skin.

Thus the foolish Cynics among the philosophers . . . although they had an apparent reason for spurning modesty (the fact that nothing natural would seem to merit shame) can still in no way be excused, for they are refuted by nature itself, silently speaking, even finding fault with them. This preaching of nature has had its effect on all men. As soon as the use of reason is opened in boys they feel the censure of embarrassment.[45]

It seems clear that these many writers sense the presence of evil, not just in a selfish use of marriage but in any use at all. We have seen that a similar feeling existed before Christianity, outside of it and even in opposition to it. It is too much to expect that this cultural context has no bearing at all on what Christian writers have said about marriage. True, the Gospels show the matter-of-fact attitude toward sex that is typical of the Old Testament, and St. Paul warns his flock against the mentality which will produce Gnostics and Manichaeans. But Paul, who was proud to have sat at the feet of Gamaliel and describes himself as more zealous than the Pharisees for the Law, came with an Old-Testament background to the revelation of Christ. Later Christian writers did not. Once the Church moved out of Palestine, all thinking and preaching took place in an ancient pagan culture which brutally demanded its pleasure and yet had a deep suspicion and contempt for this whole area of human life. If Christians in one century after another were even leaving the Church for sects whose rigorism was more congenial, it can hardly be that those who remained were temperamentally neutral when they asked what revelation said about marriage.

And yet the reasons they give for their conviction are from revelation. In the third chapter of Genesis, Adam and Eve, after eating the forbidden fruit, are ashamed of their nakedness.[46] Some of the Greek Fathers concluded that marriage derives from original sin. Augustine denies this but does see a connection between the two.

'Increase and multiply and fill the earth.' Although it seems that this could not happen without the intercourse of man and woman . . . still we may say that in immortal bodies there could have been another process in which, by the mere emotion of pious charity, with no concupiscence, that sign of corruption, children would be born.[47]

For who denies that there would have been intercourse even if no sin had gone before? But it would have taken place with the generative organs moved by the will like other members, not excited by the sex instinct—or if you insist, by the sex instinct itself, not as it is now but subject to the direction of the will.[48]

He finds confirmation of this in the fact that even now there are cases where the will has an extraordinary control over the body. Some men can make their ears move. Other can stand fire without flinching.[49]

No turbulent heat would stir those parts of the body. A free control would make use of them when there was need . . . Just as it is not the cry of pain but the impulse of a completed process which releases the female organs to bring forth a child, so it would not be the cravings of *libido* but an act of the will which would bring the sexes together to conceive one.[50]

The Latin term *libido* is the key to his thinking. The sex instinct, sex pleasure and a tendency to rebellion are all packed into it, because he sees a unity among them.

Human nature is beyond all doubt ashamed of this *libido*, and deservedly ashamed. For in its disobedience, which has subjected the genital organs of the body to its impulses alone and snatched them from the power of the will, it is all too evident what man's punishment is for that first disobedience. It was most important that it appear in the part which generates the nature which was changed for the worse by that first and terrible sin.[51]

Adam and Eve were never ashamed before their sin because they had no experience like this to be ashamed of.[52] True, *libido* is a sickness, not a sin.

That sickness, however, is the punishment of sin; and human nature cannot exist without it, since it is not yet entirely restored to health.[53]

To have relations for any motive but children would be a surrender to this lawlessness and therefore a sin.[54] For *libido*, the sex instinct as it exists today, is a wounded nature's perennial cry of rebellion, a reminder of where we came from, and an incentive to desire the new love we will know in that life where there is no more death or corruption.[55]

These are the sentiments which prevail during the century which follows the death of Augustine.

It is not propagation but sexual pleasure which transmits original sin to succeeding generations.[56]

Because the first man by sinning fell from the state of righteousness to ruin, he handed the punishment of sin down to his children. For the sex appetite is the punishment of sin, and it is so sprung from the root of sin that no one is begotten into the world without its operation.[57]

The new era that begins in 800 A.D. with the coronation of Charlemagne brings no change in this view of marriage. Halitgar, the bishop of Cambrai and a moving spirit among the reformers of the Church in France, declares that there would be no pleasure in sexual relations were it not for original sin.[58] A spurious letter of Pope Gregory the Great to St. Augustine of Canterbury, which will receive considerable attention from later theologians, calls sexual pleasure "sin," i.e. the effect of original sin, and forbids married couples who procure it for any reason except children from coming to church for a time.[59]

What man's embarrassment already suggests is made clear beyond all doubting, they feel, by Scripture. The sex instinct has a direct connection with rebellion against God.[60]

For if man had not sinned, never would he be spurred on by the ardor of pleasure. Just as we turn the eye here and there . . . so we would use the genital organs, not for pleasure but for begetting children.[61]

As the science of theology begins to take on greater precision during the 1100's, Rupert, the controversial abbot of the monastery of Deutz near Cologne, independent, but usually more daring in style than in content, presents this view in more detail.

When He said to the other animals, "Increase and multiply . . ." they did not understand what God wanted or realize that any breed among them could be propagated by the commingling of male and female. For this reason they had to receive a prompter, the burning goad of their flesh . . . But man is rational, and thus if he had loved the Creator and been willing to build up his house with the charity due from him, he would have needed no other prompter. As an informed and prudent citizen-soldier, he would have furnished new citizens for the heavenly commonwealth and devoted the service of his flesh to this task with the same sense of duty with which the priest or prelate makes use of his tongue or voice to give those who are born in sin to this world a good new birth to God. . . .

Thus the avenging God did as He should by rising up against him when he deliberately rebelled and hurling the weapons of a bestial sex instinct at this adversary of His, so that bound and chained like a slave, he would beget children in punishment and shame, when he could have begotten them to God in honor and the delights of charity.[62]

Others agree with this analysis.

If anything in the flesh is a corruption due to sin, it can be known by its effect, just as we know that there is a flaw in a vessel from the fact that it makes the wine sour.[63]

One center of the revival of learning that grew ever more noticeable as the century progressed was the parish of St. Victor in Paris. Its school was soon known far beyond the city, thanks especially to Hugh of St. Victor, a professor who by the time of his death in 1141 was being called a saint as well as a theologian. The mind of the period is well expressed by his description of the sex instinct.

By God's mercy, and in order that man could survive, it has been arranged that the other parts of the body are quiet or move at the bidding of reason. But as a sign of the transgression, one part does not obey reason. I mean the generative organs. The reason is that the entire propagation of the human race was to pass through that part. Written on it, as on a doorway, is the sign of the parents' disobedience: the disobedience inflicted on the members.[64]

As the intellectual current reaches its crest with the arrival of the thirteenth-century Schoolmen, Alexander of Hales, an English lay professor at the new University of Paris who became a Franciscan and one of their most influential theologians, asks whether there would be such a thing as sexual pleasure were it not for original sin. His answer:

Pleasure is of two kinds: carnal, or pleasure of the flesh, and spiritual, or pleasure of the soul. There is greater pleasure (and it is spiritual) . . . in works of virtue, or those which take place under the impulse of virtue, than in works of sin, or those which take place under the impulse of sin. And thus it can readily be granted that the pleasure of the spirit in the union of male and female in the primal state would have been greater than in the present condition . . . It is not so, however, with regard to carnal pleasure but just the opposite.[65]

It agrees better with the words of Augustine and the evidence presented to human reason that . . . there would have been some pleasure, but moderate and measured by what man's rectitude demanded. Therefore it was not as great as it is at present. For now, because that power has gone completely beyond the rule of reason . . . , with the reins on it left slack, it hurls itself toward the pleasurable object presented to it with all its thrust and striving, not because of the intensity of the power that moves it, but due to the feebleness of the power that hold its in check.[66]

Thus he explains the custom noted in the letter mistakenly attributed to Pope Gregory of forbidding husbands and wives who had recently had relations from entering a church.

This is not because of any sin but because of a certain bodily or carnal uncleanness contracted from intercourse.[67]

He assumes, of course, that having marital relations simply in response to this prompting would be a sin.

It does not follow that, if it is natural, it is not to be classed as sin. It is from a nature that is corrupted.[68]

In 1252, seven years after Alexander's death, the University of Paris was stirred by a young Dominican from Aquino in southern Italy who, in accord with the requirements for a doctorate in theology, was beginning to lecture on the Bible. The stir that Master Thomas caused has lasted to this day. No single theologian since his time has had such an influence on Catholic thought. Though he died before completing the section on marriage in his masterwork, the *Summa Theologica*, his allusions to marriage in other sections are in the same vein as his earlier writings, and in these he stays close to Augustine. Marital intercourse is not evil in itself;[69] but as man's embarrassment shows,[70] this is not true of *libido*, a term which designates "venereal pleasure . . . as Augustine says."[71]

This feature of man's fallen nature is not like his appetite for food, which, though likewise corrupted by Adam's fall, is not infected as well, since it does not transmit original sin. The generative power, which does transmit it, is both corrupted and infected.[72]

The friend and fellow professor of Aquinas at Paris was an Italian Franciscan who had taken the name of Bonaventure. Minister General of his Order, a cardinal, eventually a canonized saint, he dominated the age along with Aquinas. Insisting as did the other Franciscans that sexual pleasure has not been diminished but rather caused by original sin,[73] he agrees with his friend Thomas that,

Some have erred by saying that in the act of generation there is no fault unless there is some excess, just as in the act of nourishment.[74]

Thus the Schoolmen describe the sex instinct with Augustine's terms and in Augustine's spirit.[75] As a period of decline sets in, others are content to repeat them;[76] and little change is apparent until the time of the Council of Trent.[77]

This conviction that the sex instinct is a product of sin and made evil by this association seems to condemn marriage almost as effectively as did the claims of the Gnostics and Cathars. Augustine was quite aware of this.

I also wrote two books to the illustrious Count Valerius after hearing that the Pelagians had written something or other to him about me claiming that I condemned marriage by relating it to original sin.

The title of these books is *Marriage and Concupiscence*. I defended the goodness of marriage lest it be thought that concupiscence of the flesh and that law in the members rebelling against the law of the mind was a vice inherent in it, when, really, married chastity puts the evil sex appetite to good use in order to have children.[78]

He thus calls attention to a central feature of this view of marriage.

Incontinence is evil, but it does not follow that marriage is too, or that the act by which the incontinent have intercourse is not something good. No, this good is not to be blamed because of that evil. Rather, because of this good, that evil is rendered harmless. For the good that marriage has, and that makes marriage good, can never be a sin.

Now, this good is threefold: fidelity, offspring, and the sacred pledge. In fidelity, the main concern is that there be no relations with another man or woman outside the marriage bond; in offspring, that they be received with love, raised with kindness, educated to religion; in the sacred pledge, that the marriage be not severed and the banished husband or wife united to another for the sake of children.

This is the rule, as it were, of marriage. By it either the fertility of human nature is enhanced or the baseness of incontinence held in check.[79]

Augustine's three headings for the good that there is in marriage are adopted at once by later writers, and his explanation of the sense in which marriage is good becomes the accepted view of the early Middle Ages.

Because human beings by their transgression incurred carnal concupiscence, without which man and woman cannot have intercourse, that act has become evil and reprehensible unless it is excused because of the assets of marriage.[80]

But as the movement of more independent thought begins which will reach its height in the thirteenth century, writers begin to detect certain flaws in this picture of marriage.

Intercourse of this type does not and cannot take place, even among the just, without a disordered pleasure which is a sin and the effect of original sin. What Augustine says, that relations for the sake of having children are blameless and are the only truly marital relations, seems to contradict this.

Solution: Relations of this last type, although they are a sin, are not imputed, nor does one who has relations with his wife for this motive alone need any satisfaction.[81]

Alain de Lille, a monk in the newly founded Cistercian order who not only published poems and prose but taught theology in

Paris and took a leading role in the struggle with the Cathars, finds that the inherent evil of the sex instinct actually proves the goodness of marriage.

Through the sacrament of matrimony it happens that carnal intercourse is either not a grave sin or is no sin at all.[82]

Oh, how great is the dignity of marriage! It had its beginning in paradise. It removes the vice of incontinence. It embraces in itself the symbol of something heavenly. It preserves the fidelity of the marriage bed. It binds the spouses fast in joint society for working out their lives. It frees their offspring from infamy. It excuses carnal intercourse from fault. In this state the patriarchs were saved. In this state some of the Apostles were called. Oh, how great is the power of this sacrament![83]

As the thirteenth century begins, the conclusion implied here is stated more explicitly. If sexual relations are not sinful when compensated for by the three assets of marriage, they must even be meritorious.[84]

William of Auvergne, though he followed no school of thought exclusively and had no religious order to propagate his ideas, made such a name for himself at the University of Paris that he was named archbishop of that city. Besides the astrologers and Arab philosophers who constantly drew his attention, the Cathars made him give thought to the theology of marriage. While admitting the presence of some inherent evil in the sex instinct, he shows how they have followed this fact to the wrong conclusion.

That consent, even if given from a love of sexual pleasure, is none the less a consent to marriage, not to fornication or lust; for he consents, not only to sexual pleasure but to all the burdens of marriage.[85]

But his Franciscan colleague at the University, Alexander of Hales, states the assumption which still underlies these claims that marriage is good:

The generative power has a greater corruption than the others. Because of it, sexual intercourse itself is evil if a proper circumstance is not added—just as it is obvious that the act of swearing is evil from the lack of a proper circumstance, as when a person swears without need.[86]

Bonaventure, the most celebrated of this Franciscan school, states their opinion bluntly.

Were it not for that remedy which is marriage, there would be disorder, not only in the feelings but also in the reason, and thus there would always be sin . . . The generative act is a sin unless it is excused.[87]

He insists that it is not marriage which is evil but this disorder. Thanks to the three assets of marriage, children, fidelity, the sacred pledge, a couple who have relations for the proper motive are not yielding to it. In fact, they are curing it. But a person whose motive is pleasure does not really have marital relations and thus can find no cure. In fact, he increases the disorder.[88]

His friend and fellow professor, Aquinas, whose influence on subsequent thought would be even greater, notes that an act is made good either by the virtue which prompts it or by the circumstances which shape its distinctive form. And the three assets of marriage are to sexual intercourse what circumstances can be to another act. Because of them, it becomes an act of virtue.[89]

He thus assigns marital relations to the class of things which are useful; and,

A useful thing (such as acquiring money) is only good in itself to the extent that it is related to something honorable. Therefore by the same token, it is not enough for an act of virtue that its cause be some pleasure. It must end in something morally good.[90]

Not only the other Schoolmen but theologians of the period between the Middle Ages and the rise of Protestantism reflect this point of view.[91] St. Antoninus, the noted fifteenth-century moralist and bishop of Florence, uses it to explain man's natural embarrassment about sexual intercourse.

Embarrassment arises not only from the shamefulness attached to a fault but also from whatever has the appearance of a fault. And such is the marriage act. In appearance it is of the same nature as the act of fornication but is excused because of the assets of marriage.[92]

He also suggests a more weighty reason for this embarrassment.

That prompting of sense pleasure which is called a stimulus has simply the function of a law in other animals . . . But in men it does not have the function of a law. It is a deviation, in fact, from the law of reason.[93]

This view appeals to theologians of the 1500's. Early in the following century Lawrence of Brindisi summarizes the thought of those who have gone before him.

Although not taught this by another human being, . . . a person is compelled to blush. . . . For he seems to expose the baseness and sin that lies hidden in these members.[94]

The words are reminiscent of Augustine, and yet the view of these theologians is not really the same as his. It seems that from the earliest years of the Church there were cross-currents of opinion. Before examining them, however, it may be useful to recall the salient features of the view which we have found expressed for more than a thousand years after Augustine's death. Sexual intercourse is permitted between husband and wife because the three assets of marriage, offspring, fidelity, and the sacred pledge, give it a distinctive quality which makes it morally good. But it is not good in itself; it is good only in this setting.

The sex instinct is an effect of original sin and indelibly tainted by its origin. To allow such an evil force to express itself would be to perpetuate the primal rebellion. Sexual intercourse needs some excuse. The pleasure it involves may be tolerated but never desired.

5 *THE INSTINCT OF THE FAITHFUL*

A SIGNIFICANT FACT about these norms of conduct is alluded to by Augustine himself. There are Catholics who find it easier not to marry than to live by them.[1]

St. Fulgentius, the bishop of Ruspe on the North African coast who, though born a century after Augustine, became his most ardent disciple, makes a more sweeping statement.

If anyone, intent on good works, has kept such moderation in intercourse with his wife that he has relations with her only to have children, such a man is undoubtedly deserving of great praise—if anyone is capable of such conduct in this age of ours.[2]

This may be a sigh of weariness from a bishop whose territory is in continual upheaval from the struggles with Vandals and Arians. But he does make the statement. There are apparently grounds for claiming that few if any married Catholics are living by the rules that a theology like Augustine's would demand. And toward the end of that embattled century Pope Gregory the Great, whose works would be the Bible on moral theology for the Middle Ages, goes so far as to declare that married couples always sin in having intercourse. The reason is not that "something illicit is done" but that "what is licit is not kept within the bound of moderation."[3]

Through the dying years of Roman culture and into the Dark Ages, in other words, during the period when the great concern is to preserve and repeat the teachings of the Fathers, a continuous line of writers admit that few if any married couples are putting Augustine's principles into practice.

When we say this, we do not think marriage is a sin. But since the legitimate intercourse of the married cannot take place without the pleasure of the flesh, they must refrain from entering the sacred place, because the pleasure itself cannot exist without sin.[4]

Halitgar, who as bishop of Cambrai is one of the leading reformers of the Church in Charlemagne's new empire, is no more optimistic about the practice of Frankish Catholics. Though the use of marriage is legitimate in itself, there are always sins of excess.[5]

As a new age of learning begins to emerge, the feeling appears even more widespread. A survey of twelfth-century theologians will show why one of them can say,

More convincing and more esteemed is the opinion that sexual intercourse cannot be completed without sin.[6]

Typical of the period is a popular textbook, the *Sentences* of Robert Pullen. The author, besides helping Oxford to develop, made such a name for himself at Paris that St. Bernard sought his counsel for a monk of his who had become Pope Eugene III. According to Pullen,

There are some actions which it is easy to complete without fault, such as sitting down or walking, and some that are shielded from sin but not easily, such as eating or speaking. Some, however, simply do not occur without fault. An example is sexual intercourse.[7]

The book of *Sentences* which became the standard textbook is the one which emerged in 1150 under the authorship of Peter Lombard. In one of its chapters on marriage the student is told,

Scarcely any can still be found today among those who experience sexual intercourse who do not seek relations from time to time for motives other than having children.[8]

By the following century so many are convinced that married couples rarely if ever avoid sin during relations[9] that Alexander of Hales tries to reconcile this conviction with another just as widely held.

Some are convinced that every act of intercourse involves venial sin and yet that one of them is still meritorious, just as preaching, when vanity insinuates itself, can be meritorious.

Others, however, explain the phrase 'without sin' to mean 'without the taint of shamefulness which proceeds from the fault of our first parents, in whom the generative power, which is a power of human nature, was corrupted.'[10]

Though this latter interpretation of Peter's text implies that a couple is not automatically guilty of some moral wrong, the judgment of the Schoolmen on the actual practice of married Catholics is illustrated by Bonaventure. Marital relations are good, he feels, when the motive for them is children,

but only if this motive lasts from beginning to end, so that the mind is not turned aside to anything else, which is very difficult.[11]

This attitude survives the decline of Scholasticism.[12] During the 1400's Denis the Carthusian, whose writings on every aspect of theology made the Charterhouse at Roermond known far beyond Flanders, is convinced that married people "always or inevitably sin."[13]

A century later the Council of Trent makes a significant pronouncement in the course of rejecting Luther's explanation of why Paul refers to concupiscence as "sin."

The Catholic Church has always understood that it is called sin, not because, in those who have been regenerated, there is sin in the true and proper sense, but only because it derives from sin and inclines to sin. If anyone thinks the contrary, let him be anathema.[14]

Though nothing in this definition either identifies concupiscence with the sex instinct or pronounces on the actual practice of married couples, Denis Peteau, a Jesuit who was much quoted after his lectures on theology at Paris during the early 1600's, reads it in the light of Augustine's ideas on *libido*.

The marriage act is not performed without concupiscence or sex pleasure, which is a kind of stain and disease of sinful nature. In fact, it is even designated in the writings of the Apostle by the name of *sin* —not in the proper sense of the word, but because it is the effect and cause of sin. For sin can scarcely be avoided in the use of marriage, though it is venial in that case, as Augustine explains in more than one passage.[15]

This general impression of the actual practice of married couples is still evident toward the end of the century. Blessed Claude de la Columbière, though best known as the guide of St. Margaret Mary Alacoque during her mystical encounters with the Sacred Heart, also directed laymen, and in a book on marriage he cites Augustine's conclusion that it is easier for many Christians not to marry than to use their marriage rights without sin.[16]

It seems more than a coincidence that, once Augustine's theology of *libido* is accepted, and all through the centuries during which it prevails, there are also these continual assertions that marital relations in actual practice always involve sin. The general—and some said universal—practice of Catholic couples was evidently at variance with the moral principles that flow from Augustine's analysis.

If we hope to discover how marriage has appeared to those who have seen it in the light of Christ's revelation, this counter-trend cannot be ignored. These married people were the Church.

They were the majority of its members. True, they were not official teachers, but baptism gave them a genuine share of that insight which is faith.

Of course, their conduct appears in the documents just quoted as a case of the same human weakness which also leads to continual sins of anger, gossip, lying. This was undoubtedly true of some. And the others, raised in a cultural climate which had helped to make Augustine a Manichaean and still kept spawning rigorous groups who would even leave the Church, were hardly immune from feelings of guilt.

But certain impressions of human life as the faith reveals it tended in the other direction. There was Genesis with its revelation of who it is who established marriage. The Gospel account of a God who had real human flesh, who ate and drank and made good wine and called attention to the beauty of lilies, jars any suspicion of matter and pleasure.

Then, too, although they heard about Adam and Eve, married couples were completely unaware of what theologians were writing about the sex instinct and original sin. Most of them actually could not read. Saxon villagers and recently converted Lombards knew little more of Augustine than his name. The liturgical cycle gave them a view of life. They lived by their general Catholic instinct and rarely felt the need of anything else. Without any special thought on the matter, they married and then made use of their marriage rights.

And no one told them they were wrong. They cannot be compared with Catholics today who practice contraceptive birth control. Whatever be the reason, the fact remains that, from Augustine's time till the Middle Ages, their ordinary conduct may be lamented in books, but nothing is said to them directly. Adulterers are castigated from the pulpit. Neo-Manichaeans are condemned. But there are no sermons on this theme, no prayers in the liturgy. The books of penances compiled by bishops like Halitgar of Cambrai for the instruction of priests give no impression that people are including each use of marriage in their confession.[17] The whole discussion on the origin of the sex instinct took place among a relatively secluded group of professionals using Latin in an age that could not read.

And the way in which these scholars react to the situation merits attention. What they know of Augustine's theology and what they know of the married life of Catholics in their day seem to converge on one conclusion: These couples are continually guilty of sin. As long as they merely read Augustine, this is what they conclude. But then they start their own investigation. By the 1100's certain precisions begin to appear. Both theologians and canon lawyers agree with a passing remark of Augustine[18] that, even when there is no question of having children, one married person does not sin in acceding to the other's desire of intercourse when the latter would otherwise be tempted to seek satisfaction elsewhere.[19]

Theory thus begins to justify at least some incidents in the practice of the faithful. A couple's motive here is not children; and yet, for one of them at least, there is no sin.

Peter Lombard's *Book of Sentences* indicates that this is the common teaching in his day and helps to establish it as the position of the Schoolmen.[20] Their views are given summary form by John Duns Scotus, whose lectures both at Oxford and Paris during the early 1300's had a shrewdness and originality that rank him with Bonaventure for his influence on later theologians.

Justice requires that one grant the other what is his by right. And a person is bound to grant it, not only when there is question of a basic aim such as the good of having children, but also when a less basic aim is involved, protecting married chastity by keeping him from seeking illicit intercourse and acting against the good of fidelity.[21]

Because of the second aim, avoiding illicit intercourse, it is praiseworthy, but only in the second way, in other words, as an act of justice. That just fulfillment of duty, however, would not be just, nor would the person be bound to accede to the petition, unless God had given a dispensation because of man's tendency after the fall.[22]

The general feeling from this time until after the Council of Trent is illustrated during the early 1600's by a moralist whose best-known work is on marriage, Thomas Sanchez.

The meaning of the second asset, fidelity, is obvious. Husbands and wives are bound in justice to grant what they owe each other in marital relations. Therefore one who has relations with the other to satisfy this obligation is so far from sinning that he or she is rather performing an act of virtue and duty.[23]

The theologians who first agreed on this had not detected some new fact which altered their conviction that the sex instinct is evil. The demands of that instinct are satisfied in this case to avoid a greater evil. But if one of the partners may thus avert this evil from the other, some begin to surmise that he may do the same for himself.[24]

They are clean of heart but not of body who do not crave this for pleasure, as we have said, but from need, to avoid offending God by illicit intercourse. These people will also be among the saved and will not lack the vision of God.[24]

A certain vagueness in their notion of sin extends to the judgment of this case by theologians. Some speak rather ambiguously of a fault which God overlooks.[25] Peter Lombard remarks,

Marital intercourse which takes place because of one's incontinence is permitted, that is to say, tolerated, in the sense that it is not forbidden.[26]

One of his most prominent pupils and the first to write a commentary on his *Book of Sentences* was Peter of Poitiers. Chancellor of the University of Paris during the late 1100's he completed his own five books of *Sentences* and tries in the last of them to clarify the issues in this case with a distinction. Marital relations are sinful if a person's motive gradually changes from allaying concupiscence to "satisfying sexual desire."[27]

One of the most popular of the many commentaries on Peter Lombard's *Sentences* during the early 1200's was a *Golden Summary* by William of Auxerre. A professor at Paris with a strong bent toward Augustine's way of thinking, it was he to whom Pope Gregory IX entrusted the project of "purifying" the text of Aristotle for the use of students.

The man who seeks marital relations "in order to avoid incontinence" reminds him of the preacher who is praised for one of his sermons. There is no moral wrong unless "the pleasure involved pleases him to a certain extent," in which case he is guilty of venial sin.

If the pleasure which is there in no way pleases him, in fact is hateful to him, that intercourse is without any sin at all. But this rarely happens.[28]

His colleague, Alexander of Hales, and later in the century both Thomas and Bonaventure, disagree with this entire school of thought. The very need of having relations to avoid serious sin seems to them to betray a certain excess. Thus there would always be venial sin.[29]

Pierre de la Palu, Patriarch of Jerusalem and one of the best regarded theologians of the early 1300's, tries to reconcile the two opinions.

If the person's condition is such that there is the usual possibility of having children, he commits a venial sin by acting against the order of reason, putting a secondary aim ahead of the one that is first and foremost. . . . But when he is an elderly man and cannot beget children, and on the one hand there is no hope of offspring but on the other a fear of fornication, then there seems to be no sin. Otherwise elderly men cannot contract marriage without sin.[30]

Thomas of Strasbourg, the most distinguished pupil of the Thomistic school founded during these years by Giles of Rome, extends this concession even to those who can have children.

If . . . he petitions, either he does so because of his need or he does so without need in order to satisfy sexual desire. In the first case he is still excused from sin inasmuch as, after the fall of the first parents, that sacrament was not only instituted for the role of parenthood but also as a remedy against fornication.[31]

But he adds an afterthought.

Although they are excused from sin by reason of the sacrament, they still do not merit by that act, inasmuch as they do not intend either offspring, the good which is the first asset, or fidelity in granting what is owed to the spouse who petitions.[32]

This more permissive trend continues into the 1400's. St. Antoninus feels that if a person could avoid adultery in some other way, there would be venial sin in having relations simply for this motive. Otherwise there is no sin at all.[33] Denis the Carthusian, whose books on every subject from mysticism to marriage were being quoted throughout northern Europe, first recalls Thomas's opinion that there is always venial sin and then observes,

To others it appears that, since marriage was instituted as a remedy against sin, if the intention of the husband or wife in the case mentioned above is not pleasure but merely the avoidance of adultery or other personal stain, he or she does not sin.[34]

By the 1500's this is the accepted view. Dominic Soto, confessor to Emperor Charles V and imperial theologian at the Council of Trent, lists the authorities who hold the more rigorous opinion and admits that it is "quite probable."

Still it seems that the one which follows is more benign and perhaps more in accord with the idea of marriage. Nor is it opposed to the words of the apostle. When a married person thinks it necessary to avoid a personal sin of impurity, he is allowed to petition.[35]

He grants that, if some other way of avoiding impurity were possible, the person would be guilty of venial sin, since his motive would really be pleasure. But in other cases he finds no sin,[36] and after listing those who support this opinion, in his own and in earlier centuries, he quotes the advice of St. Paul, "For fear of fornication let each have his own wife."

If each then is allowed to take a wife to avoid fornication in his own person, in other words, because he sees that he cannot contain himself and that it is better to marry than to burn with desire, obviously the use of marriage for that purpose will also be allowed. If the ability to achieve some purpose is good, surely the use of that ability for the same purpose will also be good.[37]

This is clearly the common opinion after the Council of Trent.[38] Though married couples do not always have children in mind, their actual practice is still blameless in many cases because they are trying to avoid adultery or solitary sins.

The theologians who draw this conclusion do not ignore older thinkers, but neither are they afraid to rely on their own personal observation of life in the Church. This is evident in a remark by Soto. Though he feels, along with writers of earlier times, that intercourse is blameless only if the motive which prompts it is one of the aims of marriage,[39] he adds,

It is not required that married people actually have these aims in mind when they come together. It is enough if there is a virtual relation, in other words, if they introduce no evil circumstance.[40]

They need not be thinking explicitly of one of the aims of marriage. Soto is not alone in this opinion. Alfonso Salmeron, one of the Holy See's theologians at Trent, gives it a theoretical justification.

It would be wrong to consider enjoyment as the aim to which the act of procreation is related here or because of which it is desired. It is simply the cause which moves and impels them not to forego having children.[41]

By 1602, when the treatise appears which will give Thomas Sanchez his reputation, it is apparent that this has become a clear and recognized feature of marriage as seen by Catholics.

Those who contract marriage for morally indifferent reasons extrinsic to marriage are usually excused from venial sin, because they usually choose them, not as their aims in marriage but as the reason for bethinking themselves of marriage, or of marriage to one particular person. The aim of their marriage is still the proper one even if they do not give it any thought. Unless they expressly exclude the proper aim, they intend it virtually and implicitly by the very fact that they intend to contract marriage.[42]

Nor in the marriage act itself is there any need to recall some one of the permissible aims. It is enough if the act is habitually related to them, just as, according to the common opinion of theologians, this is sufficient for merit. . . . Thus it is enough if in the beginning the couple enter upon marriage with them in mind and have no contrary aim in the act itself . . . This is why Ledesma says that married people are excused from many venial sins . . .

From this we deduce that a husband making use of marriage and neither expressly intending nor excluding children but simply unmindful of them and intent solely on having relations with his wife because she is his wife, in no way sins. Granted that he does not intend children formally, he does intend them virtually, since that act, by its own very nature, is designed for the procreation of children, and the performer's intention is not directing it to any other aim.[43]

Only seven years later a book appears which will come to be regarded as the classic guide for laymen who wish to be saints, *The Introduction to the Devout Life*. Its author, St. Francis de Sales, bishop of Annecy near Geneva, converted literally thousands of Calvinists by his personal charm. It would be difficult to name his equal as a spiritual director for laymen, and the theology embodied in his books, conferences, and thousands of letters has won him the title Doctor of the Church.

The Introduction to the Devout Life seems to take it for granted that a couple's conscious motive for having relations may simply be the fact that they are husband and wife.

The duty of marriage should always be performed faithfully, frankly, and always as though there were hope of having children, even though for some reason there is no such hope.[44]

Once again theologians are directing their attention, not to a concept or a quotation from some ancient authority but to a complex experience of actual life. And once again the actual practice of married couples in many cases is declared to be blameless.

This reappraisal of the norms for the use of marriage does not necessarily presuppose a new concept of the sex instinct. As a matter of fact, it can be noticed how carefully the more lenient principles were integrated with the old supposition that venereal pleasure is inherently evil. Intercourse is permitted only when other factors are compensating for that evil.

This was the basic assumption of all studies of marriage once Augustine had expressed it so cogently. And yet at the same time and in the same studies, conclusions begin to appear which are actually at variance with that assumption.

During the 1100's more than one theologian is careful to point out that pleasure is not necessarily sinful. It proceeds from a nature which is still essentially good despite the damage done by original sin. Some note that this is just as true of sexual pleasure, provided of course that it is not excessive and that the motive for the intercourse which gives rise to it is one of the two which all by this time are accepting as blameless, viz., the procreation of children or helping the other spouse to avoid sin.[45]

Notable among those who take this position is Peter Abelard. Though his reputation was twice shattered, once when it was found that his pupil, Eloise, had been seduced, and later when twelve propositions from his writings were condemned by the Holy See, still the man and his talents have continued to be respected from his own day till ours.

Abelard insists that both intercourse itself and the pleasure which accompanies it are good, since both are from God. Of those who attack this position, he remarks,

They seem to be constraining us more by authority than by proofs to admit that sexual pleasure itself is a sin.[46]

Other writers make a distinction. Part of the pleasure in sexual activity is due to original sin, but part is as natural and good as the pleasure of eating.[47] Peter Lombard, though convinced that intercourse always incites that rebellion of the flesh which began with Adam, concludes that,

Concupiscence is always evil because it is tainted and a punishment of sin. Still it is not always a sin. A holy man is often delighted according to the flesh in one thing or another such as resting after work or eating after hunger, and yet such pleasure is not a sin unless it is immoderate.[48]

William of Auxerre, who edited Aristotle for students of the early 1200's, asks in the popular *Golden Summary* of Peter Lombard's *Sentences* whether sexual pleasure would exist if there had never been an original sin.

We must realize that the instinctive appetite in man is twofold. There is an animal appetite which only craves what the senses can perceive, and a human appetite which craves what is perceived by both the senses and the intellect, good things and evil as well . . . As far as the animal appetite is concerned, there is neither virtue nor vice; and as far as it is concerned, Adam, before his sin, would have found pleasure in marital relations. For he had an animal body needing the nourishment of food.

Thus he would have experienced sense pleasure and would not sin, but this does not imply that, since there was pleasure, there was also *libido*. *Libido* is a tendency toward illicit pleasure.[49]

And yet William is still suspicious of that pleasure as it exists in reality.

The higher appetite takes pleasure only in God and the things of God. Therefore as long as that other pleasure remains within bounds, in other words, on the animal level, not involved with the human will, it is not a sin no matter how intense it may be . . . There is sin . . . when the lower appetite draws the higher appetite to itself.[50]

This approach is followed by a Schoolman whose method of utilizing science as well as faith and Aristotle as well as Plato won him the name Albert the Great and inspired one of his students, Aquinas, to change the entire course of theology. Albert agrees with William of Auxerre that Adam experienced pleasure but not concupiscence.[51] He moves on, however, to a different conclusion. Sexual intercourse is now a reminder of original sin, not because it involves a certain pleasure, but because that pleasure is not as great as it would have been.

I readily concede that there would have been a greater and more sincere pleasure in the act then; and yet it would have been under the control of reason. For reason was then strengthened by the grace of innocence. Nothing inferior to it, no matter how intense it might have been, would have turned it from contemplating the changeless First Good.[52]

Thus if there is any sin in sexual relations, it is due, not to the pleasure but to some disorder in the way that pleasure is experienced.[53]

Aquinas shares his professor's opinion.

There would have been a sense pleasure, and it would have been as keener as the nature was purer and the body more sensitive. . . . A temperate man who takes his food in a moderate way experiences no less pleasure than a glutton. His instinctive appetite is simply less absorbed in this kind of pleasure.[54]

Duns Scotus, whose lectures at the turn of the century combine the brilliance of the Schoolmen with the spirit of a new age, stresses a point which is important here.

What is formally good of itself does not need other good things to excuse it. If it were good only because of these other things, it would not be formally good.[55]

His principle applies to sexual pleasure if the latter is intrinsically good; and during the early 1300's Thomas of Strasbourg, Prior General of the Augustinians and one of their best known Thomistic theologians, is careful to note that mere intensity does not make sexual pleasure evil.

Although that pleasure or passion is immoderate comparatively speaking, in other words, because it exceeds all other bodily pleasures, still it can be properly moderate in its own sphere when it has proper circumstances associated with it; and these it finds in the above mentioned assets of marriage itself.[56]

A few years later the subject appears in a completely new light as it is viewed from a different angle. Demetrius Cydones, secretary to the Patriarch of Constantinople, was converted from schism, studied Aquinas extensively and translated his works into Greek. As though this were not unusual enough, his views on sexual pleasure are found in a work entitled *Despising Death*. Remarking that some may rebel at the thought of no longer knowing the joys of marriage, he reminds them of why these things exist.

He devised them for parents so that men would be more prompt to see that there were children to take their place. Pleasure tends to make them forget the inconveniences which result from having a family. We see . . . doctors, even harsh ones, . . . mix certain sweetenings with their bitterest preparations so that people, intent on the sweet, will more easily take the medicines as well.[57]

Though regarded as perfectly orthodox after his conversion and imbued by his studies of Aquinas with the spirit of Latin theology, this writer is not so strongly affected by it because of his background. And not long after his death in 1400, it becomes apparent that he is not as different as might be expected from Latin theologians of the time. In Flanders Denis the Carthusian explains that,

Pleasure cannot be avoided in sexual intercourse, and yet it is not a sin when it is not sought after and the act itself is performed as it should be. In the same way the pleasure in food and drink, natural as it is and related to a spiritual goal, is not a fault.[58]

In another passage he distinguishes four kinds of love: spiritual, natural, social, and finally carnal, "by which two human beings love each other because of sensual delights or personal and earthly advantages."[59]

The difficult question is whether married people ought to love each other with a carnal love. And it appears that they should not, because carnal love is entirely unclean and tainted with sin, as the theologians say. Some theologians, however, say that married couples can love each other blamelessly with carnal love.

We must reply, then, that they should not love each other with carnal love if that meant a love tainted with evil. But since a husband and wife can have relations without sin and virtuously, as has been said, there is a legitimate carnal love. They love each other because of the pleasure they have in and from each other to the extent that that pleasure is natural, joined to the marriage act by God's providence, and related to a proper aim.

As Aristotle says and St. Thomas repeats, our moral evaluation of an act and the pleasure joined to an act is the same. Therefore the

pleasure from a good and virtuous act is good; and to the extent that
it is good, it can be desired.[60]

By the following century it is apparent that this view has
blended with that of Cydones. According to Charles V's theologian at Trent, Dominic Soto,

Nature has wisely attached pleasure to that act because of the need
to conserve the race. . . . Therefore just as taking one's food and
drink with pleasure is no sin, neither is marital intercourse.

And certainly those who say the contrary, in other words, that it is
a sin unless a man abhors the pleasure involved, are trying to deprive
men of their natural feeling. The mind is simply not able to elicit displeasure in that situation.[61]

Alfonso Salmeron, one of the pope's own theologians at Trent,
not only shares this view[62] but tries to settle a difficulty which
had bothered so many. If this pleasure is good, why is there an
instinctive embarrassment about sexual relations?

He answers with earlier writers that it indicates, not a sin but
a punishment and then observes,

Christ the Lord has not taken away the embarrassment about this
matter so that the embarrassment itself would be a restraint on intercourse.[63]

It is not a proof that the sex instinct is evil. It is a protection
against an evil more basic than the sex instinct, the lawlessness of
fallen human nature.

In 1602 Sanchez deals with another notion of earlier thinkers,
the comparison between pleasure in marital relations and vanity
in preaching.

Vanity is evil in itself and therefore to be completely rejected.
Pleasure is not something base in itself. In fact, it is nature which has
wisely attached it to the act with an eye to that asset of marriage,

children, so that men would be more eager to devote themselves to begetting them.[64]

A few years later St. Francis de Sales reflects on the problem of pleasure and addresses his solution directly to laymen. To go to excess in the use of marriage, he tells them, is wrong. To have relations

> simply to satisfy the appetite is something tolerable and yet not worthy of praise.[65]

From this time on it is clear even from those who write in the spirit of Augustine that Catholics no longer see the matter as he did. Jean Grou, a spiritual director whose books have been translated into five or six languages, declares,

> In itself concupiscence is something shameful and humiliating to man and with more reason to the Christian. It is a purely animal instinct which, in the marriage act, is only intent on sense pleasure and makes this its goal. Reason disavows this instinct and blushes at it. Religion reproves it and does not permit man to yield himself to it, for this would upset right order.[66]

The ideas are those of Augustine, but Grou moves on to conclusions which reflect the more nuanced view of later generations.

> The pleasure which God has attached to the union of the sexes is a means and not an end. It is not permitted to seek the means for its own sake to the exclusion of the end. . . .
>
> As for the marriage act in particular, man would naturally have some aversion for it and would never be borne by pure reason to take up a state so enslaving, so hard to bear as marriage were it not accompanied by some pleasure attractive to the senses. The Creator's arrangement is, therefore, very wise. In one sense it is even necessary.[67]

Any lingering doubt that sexual pleasure is something more than a residue of the primal revolt against God seems to have dis-

appeared by this present century. An encyclical of Pope Pius XII
includes the most authoritative description yet of what is due to
original sin and what is not.

We should not take a stern view of this type of pleasure which
arises without any sin from marriage. But by the same token we must
admit that the lower powers of human nature, after the deplorable
fall of Adam, keep resisting right reason and sometimes even drive
man on to do evil.[68]

What this implies about sexual pleasure is clear from one of
his discourses.

It is the Creator who, in His goodness and wisdom, wished to use
the activity of man and woman to conserve and propagate the human race. It is He who united them in marriage. And it is He Himself who has also arranged that in this role the couple experience
pleasure and happiness in body and spirit. Married people, therefore,
are doing nothing wrong when they seek and enjoy this pleasure.
They are merely accepting what the Creator has designed for them.

Nonetheless, here too the couple must be sure to stay within the
bounds of due moderation. As in the enjoyment of food and drink, so
in sexual enjoyment, they may not abandon themselves without restraint to the impulse of the senses.

This, then, is the true norm: The use of the natural generative
powers is morally allowable only in marriage, in the service of the
aims of marriage, and in agreement with the relation of those aims to
one another.[69]

The couple therefore may seek and enjoy what God has provided for them. Gone are the suspicions of earlier times. In fact,
long before Pius XII, a change even more profound begins to
appear in Christian writings on marriage.

So much of the world's effort to understand the relationship
between man and woman has been an attempt to evaluate a certain pleasure which every human being finds available. Why
does this pleasure exist? May a person seek it or allow it? This

is how pagan thinkers had approached the subject in the lands where the Church began, and from what we have seen it is evident that Christian writers followed their example. The answers may be different, but the questions are still the same.

During the early 1200's, however, that mysterious episode in human experience which is sexual intercourse is described in entirely different terms. William of Auvergne, eclectic in his theology but so respected as to be named archbishop of Paris, observes that,

> Intercourse, although it is carnal, can involve a spiritual pleasure. Every act of virtue involves pleasure, or at least is able to. . . . So if the marriage act results from a concern to grant the other what is due or from a charitable anxiety to keep oneself or one's wife from the stain of sin . . . no one should doubt that from that act there can sometimes arise a spiritual delight in the heart of the one who performs it.[70]

That activity is simply the outward manifestation of some virtuous feeling toward another. There is pleasure, but it is the satisfaction which virtue feels in being able to express itself, the delight that comes from being able to bring the other some good. All concern and attention are on that other.

> Nothing so dominates the human soul as love. It dominates it to the point where the soul can do nothing against it, so completely does it bear a man on to his beloved until it is neither enjoyable nor possible to think of anything unless it be the beloved or for the beloved's sake.[71]

These observations are not presented by William as novel or original. And yet they are typical neither of him nor of the Schoolmen. Bonaventure, for example, declares that the principal aim of a man who marries should be "having children or something similar." Beauty, charm, wisdom, virtue—in other words, the woman herself—may be no more than a secondary motive.

The love these inspire is permissible only if it is not intense. Jacob's feeling for Rachel as described by the Old Testament, a love that impelled him to work so many years to win her, leads Bonaventure to suspect him of venial sin.[72]

But William's idea appears again during the 1400's. Denis the Carthusian remarks that,

Since charity is the highest virtue and the commander and mover of all the virtues . . . the marriage act can be an act of charity or spiritual love. For all good works ought to be done from a spiritual and divine love. [73]

It gradually becomes apparent that these are more than chance observations of a few scattered thinkers. In 1566 under the seal of Pope Pius V there appears a catechism for the use of parish priests. Entrusted by the Council of Trent to a commission headed by the bishop of Milan, St. Charles Borromeo, it summarizes, among other things, what the faithful are to be told about marriage. As reasons why a man should enter that state, it offers those that the Schoolmen had agreed upon but then reflects the same view as later writers like Soto or Salmeron.

If to these reasons are also added others which induce men to enter marriage and, in making the choice of a wife, to prefer this one to that—the desire of leaving an heir, wealth, beauty, the prominence of the family, similar tastes and habits—these reasons are certainly not to be condemned, since they are not opposed to the holiness of marriage. In sacred scripture the Patriarch Jacob is not reprehended for being allured by Rachel's beauty and prefering her to Lia.[74]

What this would imply about intercourse itself is stated clearly some years later by Sanchez. Love for the other is a perfectly licit motive, not only for marrying in the first place but for having marital relations.[75] St. Francis de Sales explains this directly to laymen.

To eat with no thought of preserving life but simply with a view to maintaining the companionship and affability we owe one another is something very just and honorable. By the same token, the reciprocal and legitimate satisfaction of the partners to a holy marriage is called by St. Paul a debt, and a debt so great that he does not want one of the partners to exempt himself from it without the free and ready consent of the other, not even for the exercises of devotion. . . . How much less, then, can one exempt himself for capricious claims of virtue or fits of anger and disdain?[76]

This attention to sexual intercourse as an expression of a married couple's whole attitude toward each other and a help to keeping it unchanged is evident toward the end of the eighteenth century in the works of Jean Grou, whose popularity as a spiritual director is not due to any laxity in his opinions. Discussing whether a couple should abstain from the use of marriage if the wife is pregnant or has no hope of children, he warns,

This is a counsel, not an obligation. It can only be done by mutual consent.[77]

During the nineteenth century, seminarians, who will eventually be directing married couples, are taught,

If they have relations to foster their love for each other, to ease any suspicions that love is growing cold, or for other such reasons, these aims are not alien to the use of marriage. They are reducible to fidelity, which is a distinctive asset of that state.[78]

Moralists of the present century agree.

Intercourse may honorably be sought . . . to show one's love.[79]

An authoritative statement of how the matter appears to Catholics is furnished by Pius XI's encyclical on marriage.

Both in marriage itself and in the use of marital rights there are also secondary aims such as . . . fostering mutual love . . . which married people are in no way forbidden to seek, as long as the intrinsic nature of the act, and hence its right order to the primary aim, is always secure.[80]

Thus the very fact which gave rise to all the difficulty, a distinctive pleasure of the senses, emerges as almost incidental to the intercourse of husband and wife. For them the experience is more than a biological mating. It is the response of a person to a person. There is tremendous satisfaction, but its source is noble, distinctively human, and emphatically Christian: a sincere and unselfish love.

6 *MALE AND FEMALE*

WHAT, THEN, DOES REVELATION actually say about that orientation toward the other sex which is so notable a feature of human nature?

This is more difficult to answer than the question about the goodness of marriage. There is no series of ideas which were condemned. Neither popes nor councils have articulated the Christian view in detailed and explicit dogmas. Much more attention will have to be paid to the ordinary process by which the Church has learned and taught what it knows.

Two peculiarities of that process should especially be noticed. First, it did not take place in a vacuum. The Apostles received their insight into the meaning of life at a definite time in a particular place amid a swirl of concrete events which had a continual influence on them. This is no less true of later Christians. To see what they have seen, we must notice how they have reacted to the actual historical world in which they have lived.

A second fact to be noted: the Church is not only the theologians nor even the clergy. This is important in view of the type of knowledge which faith involves.

Our ability to detect truth in a concrete situation is not the same as our skill in dealing with abstractions. An eminent physicist may be a very poor judge of men. A politician cannot solve every moral problem by simply recalling the seventh commandment. One final type of knowledge must come into play, an insight into the truth behind a particular constellation of facts.

Though principles can guide this final insight, they cannot supply it. It is a new act, frighteningly unique because no two combinations of evidence are the same; frighteningly personal since no other mind has the same background against which to set the evidence; frighteningly autonomous because it can always misinterpret what it sees. This is why the prudent man must always notice the practice of other prudent men. Their insight is one more help for his.

If this is true of every human being, it is especially true of one who has been given, not a philosophy but a companionship with the unique living Christ in a concrete historical world. Among members of the one Mystical Body there is a continual action and reaction. Each one's knowledge of Christ is formed by that of others who teach him. Each has his own confrontation with Christ. Each in some way shares his personal store of knowledge with others.

Some are divinely commissioned to provide the rest with the knowledge they need of Christ and to protect them from doubts and distortions. But these teachers themselves are still men. Grace has not dispensed them from the need to consult other men.

"Custom is the best interpreter of the laws." This axiom of canon law is no less true of the law of God. Laymen too have that insight of faith which enables them to judge concrete events in the light of Christ's revelation. Though their judgment can err—and this is why Christ has provided them with authoritative teachers—it is not ignored, even by those authoritative teachers. There is a constant dialogue between the professional theologians, who alone have the training which a genuine progress demands, and the laymen, who are actually immersed in the life which the professionals are trying to evaluate.

Thus, though it would be excessive to claim that, since the theologians have usually been celibates, they are incompetent to speak on marriage, it would be just as great an excess to discount the views of the only Catholics with experience of the subject. Each Catholic reacting to life on the basis of what he knows and all Catholics acting on one another—not only in a single age but down through the centuries—this is tradition. This is the process by which Christ reveals Himself to the eyes of our faith.

What the Church has known about human sexuality will thus be apparent from the way it has reacted to an historical situation, or rather to two historical facts: the culture of the lands in which most Catholics have lived and the awareness felt by each adult Catholic of a tendency deep within to have no regard for God, other persons, anything but himself. This experience has been complicated in individual cases by a past habit of surrendering to that tendency.

Confronted with that twofold situation and appraising it in the light of Christ, how has the Church reacted?

As for typical married couples living as they thought they were expected to, the signs of that contempt for the body which was part of Graeco-Roman culture have grown steadily less pronounced. In fact, from the very beginning the practice of Catholic couples has been lamented by more rigorous theologians. Little variation can really be noted in it from early times till the present. Apparently they have been acting from stable principles based on a stable view of life.

But these have been principles of prudence, that ability to judge a concrete situation on evidence which, though valid and compelling, is not always easy to identify. Although moral decisions are not irrational, we have ways of knowing which cannot be described. Professional moralists and ordinary laymen agree, for example, that lying is wrong; and yet no expert has ever framed an explanation of why it is wrong that all the other experts will accept.

In the same way, the understanding of marriage on which these couples have based their conduct has been unformulated, as prudential knowledge usually is. They may not always have been able to explain to others, or even to themselves, why they were acting as they did. But the consistency of their practice down through the centuries is evidence of a common settled conviction.

Turning, however, from practical judgments to explicit statements about the sex instinct, it is obvious that there has been a tremendous change. Only a sleight of hand with the documents can make Augustine, Aquinas and Pius XII say the same things. But before constructing a theology of sex from what Christians have said about it, we must always ask whether a writer's words reflect the insights of faith or the prejudices of the world in which he lives.

It is easier to baptize a man than a culture. It is easier to teach him a set of conscious ideas than to change that unreflective view of life, that complex of attitudes and values, which he has absorbed as a child from the world around him. These attitudes and values are now almost instinctive. Instead of being reflected on, they are the setting in which all formal teaching is studied. Instead of appraising these cultural impressions in the light of Scripture, he is more likely to be impressed by the passages from Scripture which seem to confirm them. On two levels of the same mind there can often be two conflicting sets of ideas.

Once the Church had moved out of Palestine, all study and speculation took place in an ancient pagan culture which had an ingrained suspicion of matter and pleasure. Augustine not only grew up in this atmosphere but for several years was even a Manichaean. And his was the theology handed down to Western Europe. The Schoolmen received it hallowed by time, enhanced by the absence of any comparable body of thought since his death, and strengthened by a few spurious documents which gave it more official sanction than it really had. Blending with the Graeco-Roman concept of man which they were discovering in the pages of Aristotle, it could not help but affect their view of what Christ had revealed.

During all this time, however, there were forces pulling from the opposite direction. Cultures change with glacial slowness, but the more the Christian view of life actually dominated the age in which they lived, the more Christian writers seem to have changed. And the more they modified what they read by what they saw, the more pronounced the change appears.

The Church's intellectual life depends, as we have noticed, on a continual dialogue. The faithful receive a general set of values which they apply to practical daily living, and the theologians keep refining general theories to fit the life they see, not among those who persist in doing what they continually hear is wrong, such as couples today who use contraceptives, but among the great mass of "good Catholics" who assume that they are doing all they should.

When we speak of traditions we must consider both participants in this dialogue; and if we do, it becomes apparent that the Catholic tradition on human sexuality has been an ever-growing appreciation of insights possessed from the beginning.

The same prudential knowledge from which the faithful were acting told the theologians that the faithful were right. Since they were obviously not on a pagan quest of pleasure and yet were not always thinking of children either, there must be other reasons which justified their conduct. These other reasons gradually find their way into the books—keeping the other from sin, rendering the debt, allying concupiscence, fostering mutual love. As formulas are gradually modified to express what is right, the descriptions of marriage gradually change to show why it is right. Pius XII's description, though different in so many ways from Augustine's, would not cause any radical change in the practice of Catholics of other centuries. On the other hand, it is to the basic intuitions of Augustine and the struggles of later theologians, by whom they were gradually refined, that the Church owes the clarity and depth of these recent papal pronouncements.

This evolution does not show the traits of a moral relativism whose principles change with every change of culture. Nor do Catholics give evidence of living by a situation ethic, relating each decision of conscience to nothing but the concrete event which has occasioned it. All the signs point to some fundamental insight which has gradually become more explicit, more refined, more influential on the general culture.

Few things are more basic to a culture than its concept of the relationship between man and woman. Since the deepest emotions and the most intimate details of life are involved, the thought of many generations has usually been expended on the subject, and few convictions are more impatient of any disturbance. The change in what Christian writers say from the second till the twentieth century reflects nothing so much as a struggle between two cultural views of human sexuality with the Christian view gradually prevailing.

This Christian view discloses certain truths about human life as Christ reveals it. First, the tendency that each of us feels to make himself the axis around which the rest of the world revolves, to use other men and even God to his own advantage, is the result of a primal sin which has made us inheritors of a damaged human nature. But though sexual intercourse is one occasion when that unruly tendency displays itself, the sex instinct is not the result of original sin. Much less is it the continuation of that rebellion. Both the instinct and its expression in marriage are features of human life as God designed it.

Nor is there any warrant for thinking that this part of human nature has been more severely damaged than the rest. The orientation of man and woman toward each other is not simply "man's lower nature." If revelation shows that this orientation has been affected by original sin, the reaction it suggests is not shame but modesty: an impulse to protect what is good, a fear of desecrating something holy, a reserve about a part of life as personal as prayer. If a human being has dignity or value, sexual pleasure shares it, for it is the means God has devised to set a process in motion which terminates in human life.

Granted that husband and wife as a rule have their whole attention on each other, this does not mean that God's design is thwarted. The process has a built-in purpose. It follows logically that they may never frustrate that purpose, but it does not follow that they must have it in mind. Since the term of the process is not an animal but a human being, God may conceivably intend that this term result from a certain psychological state of two other human beings.

As a matter of fact, this is the distinctive feature of human sexuality. The rigorist errs as badly as the libertine when he describes the intercourse of husband and wife in terms of pleasure. That particular activity of a human being is supposed to say something. It is essentially a gesture. Just as words are designed to convey thought, this gesture has been devised by the Creator as the expression of a unique attitude toward another human being. As real and essential as the connection with life is its connection with love.

Perhaps this is why so many cultures have felt ashamed of the sex instinct. The way it has been permitted to express itself among them has really been shameful. When a man separates it from love, classes it with hunger and thirst as a mere prompting to develop himself, the woman involved is desecrated and cannot help but know it. Her response will range from toleration to disgust.

The man is no less aware of being degraded, even when society does not condemn him. Since the ideal life can hardly include this degradation, the ideal man, it seems, must be purely spiritual. The body is extrinsic, confining, hostile. It is not he but the body which craves that experience, and he treats it as he would treat a pestering child, spoiling it, terrorizing it, or granting it occasional concessions to keep the peace.

Asia with its phallic processions and its fakirs, Greece and Rome with their permissiveness and their ethereal concept of human nature, Gnostics and Manichaeans and Cathars desirous of intercourse but not children, seventeenth-century France with the debauchery of Versailles and the prudery of the Jansenists, the United States with its movie ads and its nervous cult of frankness—so many civilizations seem to bear witness that excessive indulgence and excessive rigor are always found together and always come from a single source: the separation of intercourse from a distinctive kind of love which it has been designed to express.

Christians too have felt this shame, because they too have experienced a tendency, not to love but to enjoy love. Just as in the old pagan times, marriage customs have often been based on personal advantage, either to the individual or to his family. Nothing else was considered important.

But one may not simply use a human being, even to have children. Experience has shown what other institutions besides marriage arise in any Christian country that tries.

Thus, in addition to being the source of human life, a fact which calls for certain restraints, sexual intercourse has another function, no less intrinsic, no less designed by God; and this too demands certain restraints. The expression of love must never become an expression of selfishness.

But the good man is not the one who is insensitive to sexual stimuli. He is the one who makes a reasonable effort to avoid them outside of the proper time. If his instincts happen to be weak, this is no more an asset than if he had no taste for food, no appreciation of music. Both marriage itself and the instinct which prompts it are from God and need no apology.

As a matter of fact, the passage in Genesis with which this investigation began relates them with a man's success in life.

PART II

"It is not good that the man be alone."

INTRODUCTION: PART II
SALVATION IN PAIRS

MUCH OF WHAT the Old Testament says about God and man is a reaction to ideas that were current in Syria and Mesopotamia.[1] This is especially true of the early chapters of Genesis.

According to the Canaanites, the interplay of sun and rain, seed and soil is the reverberation of a cosmic battle between a benevolent god and Chaos, a monster. Though the god has subdued Chaos and fashioned the world we see from its remains, the change of the seasons indicates that the struggle has not yet ended. The god is attacked again and killed by the monster. Winter begins.

But he rises from the dead, slays his adversary, and then has sexual intercourse with his consort. This makes the earth bear fruit again.

Thus the unpredictable changes of nature, even its regular cycles, are a great celestial drama. To insure that spring and summer, rain and sun will always keep returning, man must reenact the drama in the fertility rite. The activity which makes him most like the life-giving gods is sexual intercourse, and woman exists solely to provide this experience. A goddess when she does, for the rest of the time she is a beast of burden. Man is the one for whose comfort everything else in the world exists, including women.[2]

The early chapters of Genesis are a rejection of this Canaanite myth and all it stood for.[3] The story of the world must fit what

95

Yahweh has shown His People. Good and evil are not two equal forces. Yahweh is supreme, and the world He made is good. Whatever evil appears in it is man's fault.

Nor does Yahweh have any consort with whom he produced it. No one is like Him. If human beings are male and female, this is due solely to His good pleasure.

Why then has He decided that these images of Himself should have two forms? In the chapter with which our investigation began, only one reason is given:

> It is not good that the man be alone.

In other words, it is a mistake to conceive religion exclusively in terms of an individual man and God. Whatever a man is here on earth to do he is not to do alone but in a unique type of companionship with a woman. God has so arranged the world that typical human beings work out their destiny in pairs.

In the first chapter of Genesis, an independent and somewhat later effort to explain the origin and meaning of life in the same imaginative way, this theme appears again.

> God created man in His own image,
> In the image of God He created him.
> He created man and woman.

God blessed them and said to them, 'Be fruitful, multiply, fill the earth and subdue it.'[4]

What God says is said to both of them. They are given a goal in life, a certain work to do, and the implication is that they are to do it together.

Among the Jews, to be wise meant to work at your trade with the skill that results from talent and experience. Since there is also an art of living, this most valuable skill of all was simply called wisdom. As a master craftsman shows his apprentice all the tricks of the trade, the authors of the Old Testament wisdom books offer a young man the accumulated insights of his elders.

In the Book of Qoheleth, composed between 300 and 200 BC and read each year at the Feast of Tabernacles, the sage recasts a couple of lines from a celebrated pagan epic to express his own melancholy wisdom.

> Enjoy life along with the wife you love,
> All the days of this fleeting life of yours that God
>   gives you under the sun.[5]

Human life is a thing that passes. This is his message throughout the book. But he takes it for granted that human beings should confront it in pairs.

The book of Ben Sira, composed a century later, represents the reaction of Hebrew wisdom to the Greek view of life, which had pervaded the entire Middle East. A collection rather than an original work, it voices the traditional sentiments of the devout Israelite:

> The man who acquires a wife has the beginning of good fortune,
> A helpmate like himself, a column of support.
> Without a hedge the grounds lie open to pilfering.
> Without a wife a man groans and aimlessly drifts about.[6]

This is the most emphatic statement yet. A life-companion is not merely useful but necessary. A man is not himself without a wife. Exposed to misfortune, he wanders through a life that has no purpose.

This notion of salvation in pairs seems to assume that marriage as God designed it is between a man and one woman. How reconcile this with the polygamy which Biblical authors attribute even to Abraham and David?[7]

The answer does not seem to be in individual texts but in the whole tenor of the Old Testament. Patriarchs and kings are described as having more than one wife, and a prophecy mentions polygamy as an example of how desperate things will be if Israel does not obey God.[8] In other words, the Biblical authors record a fact, and one which is passing out of existence. It forms no part of Jewish social life as portrayed in the wisdom books. By the time of the New Testament Christ apparently feels that there is no need to comment on it at all.

But when they intend to impart some explicit teaching on marriage, describing how it began, giving advice, commenting on married life, there is no passage which does not take it for granted that a husband has but one wife.[9] The idea that first appears in Genesis is a constant refrain. This is not a man's world. To be all he was made to be, a man needs a wife. Typical human beings are designed by God to do His will in pairs.

In the New Testament the first thing we confront is a startling change.

7 *A SPECIAL GIFT*

WHEN THE APOSTLES observe that, if divorce is forbidden, a man would do better not to marry, Our Lord replies,

Not all master this lesson, but only such as have received a special gift: as there are those barred from marrying by a natural defect, and those barred by an act of man, so there are those who bar themselves from marrying for the sake of the kingdom of heaven. Only a strong soul should try to master this lesson.[1]

He had told them on another occasion that they, as Apostles, had been given a special gift which enabled them to know God's hidden designs for the world.[2] Now again there is mention of a gift. The question of whether a man should marry is fully appreciated only by those who see it in the light of God's hidden designs, and these notice that there are advantages in going on without a life-companion.

He concludes with an invitation. Let one who has been given such a deeper sense of values study these advantages and consider whether this celibate life is for him.

The Old Testament had never claimed that God intends literally all men to marry. Some are simply unable to. Now it appears that even those who are able should not think of it at once.

The suggestion is tantalizingly brief. The only reason given is "the kingdom of heaven." But what this means begins to appear in the letters of St. Paul.

To the question of the delegates from his young church at Corinth, "May a Christian marry?", Paul gives a definite yes but adds,

I think that it is excellent, in view of the present distress, yes that it is excellent for a person to remain in this state of virginity.[3]

Marriage is good, but "the present distress" makes it ill advised. Christians are beginning to learn from personal experience the strain of living in a pagan world. It is difficult enough to face it alone. Watching a wife or husband suffer would double the anguish.

But this is only part of a more general situation which Paul seems to have in mind. The one great Old Testament figure who never married was Jeremiah, and the reason was his unusual role in life. Celibate, with no offspring to perpetuate his name, he was to be a prophet and a prophecy, a living symbol of the Kingdom that was dying and of a new relationship between God and His people.[4] In Scripture a symbol usually does more than explain some reality. It is a first stage. In it the reality itself is making its first appearance.

The Jewish sect at Qumran by the Dead Sea not long before the time of Christ regarded celibacy as the ideal state for its members. Once again the reason is the times in which they lived. The old order of things, they felt, was drawing to a close. Yahweh was about to intervene in history and bring the world to its final stage. An extraordinary age called for an extraordinary preparation, a celibate life.

It is against this background that we should read Paul's words about "the present distress." Life is no longer what it used to be. The day on which Christ will come again may still be far in the future, but the last age of the world has already begun. Calvary was the dividing point. The risen Christ is even now enjoying the life that will soon belong to all of us.

It remains that those who have wives be as if they had none; and those who weep, as though not weeping; and those who rejoice, as though not rejoicing; and those who buy as though not possessing; and those who use this world as though not using it, for this world as we see it is passing away.[5]

Since the whole human race must be brought to realize what has happened, Christians are invited to be living reminders, living symbols of the world that is dying and the new life that man is living now.[6] By foregoing marriage they can help married couples to recall that our old human worries and concerns are unimportant now compared to the tremendous things that are happening as God brings history to its climax.

We know from Paul's epistles how eagerly men were longing for the change to be complete and for Christ to come a second time. Significant, then, is a letter written around the year 200 by a married Christian to his wife.

A brilliant Roman lawyer who, though only five years in the Church, has recently been ordained, Tertullian, its author, will ultimately join the Montanist heretics because of his stern views on marriage. Yet it is he who is coining the terms by which Christian theology can now express itself in Latin, and the quality of his work during these years of his as a Catholic may be judged from the fact that a man like St. Cyprian of Carthage will claim that he has read Tertullian daily.

In this letter he asks his wife,

Why are we anxious to have children when we want to leave them once we have them for fear of the impending trials? Are we not eager ourselves to be quit of this sinful age and received into the presence of the Lord as even the Apostle desired? Offspring are hardly needful to the servant of God. . . .

Why did the Lord prophesy, 'Woe to the pregnant and nursing' except to bear witness that the baggage of family cares will be an encumbrance on that day of departure that is to come?[7]

The ideal is no longer to symbolize the meaning of the age but to be practical in adjusting to it. Granting Tertullian's rigorism and his habit of making a point as forcefully as rhetoric will permit, this view of marriage as now an indifferent factor, if not an obstacle, in God's plan for the final glory of man is not peculiar to him. It reappears two centuries later.

St. John Chrysostom, whose sermons as bishop of Constantinople show the Greek-speaking Church in its finest hour, sees marriage as one of the fleeting satisfactions of a life which is only a prelude to our real life with Christ.

We may have left many children. We may have had a beautiful wife, pleasure, all the other things I have just enumerated. We may have arrived at a ripe old age. But what help in true and eternal assets will all these bring us for that day of judgment? None at all.

So these things are a shadow, a dream. For in those endless ages which will then engulf us, no fruit is to be hoped for from them, no comfort. The one who had them is destined to be in the same situation as those who were without them.[8]

The unknown bishop who is responsible for one of the finest Latin commentaries of this period on St. Paul shows that Christians in Italy are still reading Paul in the spirit of Tertullian.

Since the end of the world is almost at hand, we should not be anxious about begetting children. . . . For there will be pressures upon us such as have never been before.

After all, none of us wants these things to happen in his own time. . . . Let us be mindful of others too and abstain from having many children. Let us give ourselves more to prayer and the service of God, looking ahead to the day of judgment. Thus we for our part will not be weighed down by the baggage of earthly concerns, and they will not be faced with something that we ourselves are afraid of.[9]

These sentiments are by no means uncommon. St. Jerome, acquainted with the most eminent churchmen of the late 300's and acclaimed himself for his work in Scripture, asks,

What is the necessity (to which Paul is referring)?

'Woe to the women that are with child or nursing in those days.' The forest grows thick to be cut down someday later. The field is sown to be harvested. The world is already full. The land does not hold us. Daily wars cut us down. Diseases remove us. Shipwrecks swallow us up. . . .[10]

It is not harlots who are threatened here with doom, not houses of prostitution, which no one doubts will be condemned, but swelling wombs and crying babies and the fruits and works of marriage.[11]

This same line of thought bears Augustine on to conclude that it would be better now if no one married.

But I know some will complain, 'What if all men wished to abstain from sexual relations? How would the human race survive?'

If only all men would have such a wish! . . . The City of God would be filled much more quickly and the end of the world made to come sooner.

What else does the Apostle seem to urge when he says on this point, 'I would wish that all were like myself,' or in that passage, 'I say this however, brethren: the time is short. It remains that those who have wives be as though they did not have them. . . ?' From all this it seems to me that in this present age only those who lack self control should marry.[12]

None of these men intend to belittle marriage. They are quite aware that the greatest event in history has depended on it. The chain of marriages and births that has stretched down from the moment when the first husband and wife conceived their child has led to a woman who is the mother of God. But the greatest of men has been born and the race redeemed. It no longer has the same needs. Marriage has lost the meaning it had before the birth of Christ.

As the age of the Fathers comes to an end, the Church in the northern countries begins to express itself. By the year 700 the faith has been accepted by the great mass of the people in England, and the ideas of the Fathers are explained to them by an Anglo-Saxon scholar named Bede. Bishops and kings seek his advice, priests read his works to the people at Mass, and the whole country will canonize him after his death with the title of Venerable.

His words on marriage echo Augustine.

Marriage is not to be condemned. The grace of a blessing from on high has established it for propagating the human race and filling the earth. But more to be honored and worthy of a greater blessing is virginity, which, now that the earth has been filled with men, . . . desires to follow the Lord Jesus in heaven and sing the new canticle which no one else can sing to Him.

For God and Our Lord, who in the first age of the newborn world formed a woman from the side of the man to teach us that the earth was to be filled by their union with each other, has Himself in the last age of history taken manhood from the flesh of the Virgin . . . to prove that He loves the glory of virginity more than marriage.[13]

On the continent, whether they share Jerome's opinion that the end of the world is near or Augustine's hope that, if all were celibates, the day would be at hand, writers of the next few centuries agree that

the need presses on all men to prepare themselves for the coming of the Judge, and married couples are less able to do this.[14]

During the 1200's the Schoolmen come to this question when they discuss God's command in Genesis, "Be fruitful and multiply." Bonaventure feels that there is no more need and therefore no more command to have children. In these New Testament times the command has become an "indulgence."[15]

Albert the Great, whose erudition and use of Aristotle will affect scholarship for centuries to come, agrees with Bonaventure's conclusion but for a different reason.

This command is from nature due to the lack of a very large number, and therefore I readily grant that it does not oblige once a sizable number exists.[16]

Thomas, his student, explains this in detail. In the beginning all who could were obliged to have children. Now they are not —except for those designated by civil authority to meet the need of a certain district.[17] The command to marry is like the command to give alms. It is intended for every age and is just as valid today as in Old Testament times. But it binds the human race as such, not a given person. A man is bound to give alms or marry only when he finds himself in a concrete situation which demands it.[18]

In the following century Thomas of Strasbourg sees Mary as the dividing point of history. Before her time marriage was better. Virginity was neither commanded nor advised. But since her time the better way to God is virginity.[19]

As a new period of reflection begins with the 1500's, the distinction is made again between the Old Testament and the New. Now that Christ has come, it is better not to marry.[20] But Dominic Soto takes issue with earlier writers who had gone so far as to claim that the ancient command, "Be fruitful and multiply," has terminated with the birth of Christ. To accomplish God's design for the world, marriage is still as essential as ever.

The time when the end of the world is to occur has not been included in the sum of man's knowledge. 'That hour no one knows, not even the Son of Man.' And therefore, unless a special revelation made it clear, the natural and common law should be kept.

Thus if need should arise (which does not seem possible), even those who have bound themselves by a vow of chastity would be held by law to marry, for vows always include the proviso: unless this conflicts with the obligation from natural law to conserve the human race.[21]

Salmeron finds it idle to worry about preserving the race when men are so prone to marry.[22] But on the level of theory he differs from Soto. God's original command was abrogated, he feels, in the fullness of time when Christ came. With Jerome and Augustine he concludes that there is no more need of marriage. If the race died out, it would not be a catastrophe. The City of God would be at hand.[23]

Others agree with him;[24] and Canisius finds time amid the labors that will have him acclaimed a second founder of the Church in Germany for a series of meditations in which, like Chrysostom centuries before, he urges Christians to see marriage against the background of this brief human life and the unending life that is to come.[25]

Around the turn of the century St. Lawrence of Brindisi remarks that God's so-called command was not really a command at all but a permission and a blessing on the human race.[26] Leonard Lessius, a professor at Louvain and one of the leading Jesuits in the theological wars that rage over the problem of grace and free will, adds that, if the human race were in danger of extinction,

It is not improbable that there would then be a command. . . . So feel the majority of experts.

Perhaps, though, it is truer to say that this would not be commanded, especially in this age of the gospel law. For the Lord advised celibacy without reservation and did not make any case an exception.

Then too, since the safety of the human race is not the responsibility of each individual man but of God's providence, it seems more plausible that, if such a case would arise, God would be wishing to put an end to the world.[27]

Though moralists of later years have turned their attention to problems which seemed more urgent, the underlying conviction which prompted this entire discussion should not be ignored. Reappearing periodically since the days of Paul, it draws attention to a fact that is most important. Further revelation has modified the insight first recorded in Genesis that typical human beings are intended to work out their destiny in pairs.

We should not exaggerate the change. It does not seem as evident as some Christian writers have claimed that man is now free of all obligation to preserve the race. Though the New Testament makes it clear that all the events of history are parts of a plan by which Christ will be "all in all," revelation has given us very few details of the plan. Until it learns differently, the human race should assume that it is still to take all necessary means to insure its survival.

But in the midst of our well-founded fear today of the end of the world or of a titanic struggle between the Church and its enemies, we are reminded that marriage is no longer the ideal way to God. In every age the Christian is a martyr, a living proclamation that Christ has come and that the world is different now. Some are invited to bear witness by foregoing marriage.

One aspect of this truth has not always been appreciated, though it is basic to Christian thought on virginity. The documents we have noted have all dealt with that way of life, not in the abstract, as it might have existed in any age, but in the concrete, historical situation of the world since the birth of Christ. In that setting and that one alone, it appears as something to be desired. Before Christ, to go through life unmarried was, as the Old Testament so often avers, a misfortune.

To the Christian, history has a meaning. Each moment of time has its importance. It is a unique stage in the progress of the world toward the goal God envisioned when He created it. For there is no waste in creation. This progress toward the goal is part of a plan. The forces of nature, the free will of man? These are not obstructions. They are the very agents He has devised to bring the plan to completion.

Therefore to understand marriage, it is not enough to philosophize about it as though it were simply a universal concept like human nature or justice. Marriage has been affected by history. It is no longer as urgent as it was when its ultimate issue was to be Christ. He has come now. History is in its final stage. And in this new situation there is a new way to God. A man may be wiser now to do without a life-companion.

This, we say, is due to the state of the world in which he is living. But Paul also points to a reason in marriage itself.

8 *THE CARES OF MARRIED LIFE*

MARRIAGE IS NOT A SIN, Paul tells his converts at Corinth,

But the married will have their human trials, and I would like to spare you that.[1]

What these "human trials" are he does not say. They must be experiences that are somehow part of married life, since the Corinthians would escape them by not marrying.

We find the Greek Fathers showing Christians of the late 300's that "marriage is a heavy weight"[2] by listing the day-to-day cares of a typical couple. As soon as a child is conceived, you worry about the mother. If she survives, there is the anxiety of raising the child. The more children she has, the more pain and sadness she sees them suffer, and it afflicts her worse than her own.

When her husband is home, she is under his orders. When he is not home, she worries about him. If he dies, she is left a widow longing for death herself, lonely if she has no children, troubled if she has.[3]

St. John Chrysostom looks at married life from the husband's side.

It is a serious thing to be married to a poor girl and serious to be married to a rich one. The one lessens a man's wealth, the other his authority and freedom.

It is a burden to have children, a greater burden not to have them. In the first case you are subjected to a bitter slavery, in the second you have taken a wife in vain.

The boy falls sick. No ordinary fear. He dies young. A grief beyond consoling. At every stage of growth, anxiety for them, worries and labors. . . .

This is the life, Theodore, in which one soul is divided among so many cares, serves so many, lives for so many and never for itself.[4]

Commentators in the West during this period read Paul's words about "the present distress," which we have just considered, as an allusion to the cares of married life.[5] Ambrose describes the bride's veil as a symbol of the clouds that will surely come to darken her home.[6]

Who is so adverse to truth that he condemns marriage? But who is so far removed from sense that he does not realize the burdens of marriage?[7]

Jerome feels that others have described these burdens well enough.[8] He does remark that

Women grow old quickly, especially those who have husbands.[9]

Augustine reflects on Paul's apparent reticence.

As for his stating that he spares those who are to have human trials, nothing more plausible occurs to me at present than that he was unwilling to reveal and list in detail the precise human trials of which he was forewarning those who choose marriage: The suspicions of a jealous husband or wife, bearing and raising children, the fears and sorrows of a widow at the death of the other. Which among all these feelings does not pull and chafe a person once he has bound himself by the chains of marriage?[10]

Through the rest of this period the same view is evident in both Greek- and Latin-speaking Churches.[11] Writers of the

Dark Ages echo the Fathers.[12] Lanfranc, whose reputation is not only drawing scholars to the Norman abbey of Bec but will eventually prompt William the Conqueror to secure him as archbishop of Canterbury, feels that "the present distress" which Paul has in mind is

The want of this world's goods, which married people frequently suffer as they provide for their sons and daughters and support each other. To escape this, he says that it is good for a man to be without a wife.[13]

Other medieval writers include this problem of support among the worries that come to a man with marriage.[14] Bonaventure adds that a wife must bear the curse of Eve. Only those who have suffered a difficult childbirth know how hard it is to bear. Scripture uses it as the symbol of terrible pain.[15]

During the years of transition the same views are heard,[16] and even the new spirit of the 1500's seems to bring little change. Some repeat the usual list of cares.[17] Salmeron declares that conscientious married couples bear "an almost perpetual cross."[18] Luis de Granada, the leading Dominican spiritual writer of the time and one who addresses himself to laymen, tells them,

The sun has two periods: the one from its rising till noon, during which its light keeps increasing, the other from noon till its setting, during which its light is on the wane.

The life of married people has two similar periods: the first when the two spouses love each other tenderly, when little children are playing and babbling under the eyes of their parents. It is delightful.

But when the children have grown up . . . the worries of the parents increase. Then the sun begins its decline. The early brightness of happiness begins to darken. It is then that the heart is pierced, wounded by a horde of distresses. The needs of the children must be provided for. Unforeseen accidents befall them. Then one of the two partners reaches the moment of death.[19]

Others call special attention to this last misfortune,[20] and St. Francis de Sales, kindly though he is and concerned about married couples, declares,

The state of marriage is one that requires more virtue and more constancy than any other. It is a perpetual exercise of mortification.[21]

Alas, those souls who have a completely one-sided inclination to marriage find so many opportunities for patience and mortification in it, however happy it be, that only with great difficulty can they bear its burden.[22]

These repeated warnings are obviously not meant as appeals to selfishness. If the Church directs this continued attention to the cares of married life, they must have repercussions on a couple's religion. As early as the year 200 we find this explicitly stated. Tertullian, married himself and respected as a theologian, though his rigorism led him out of the church, insists that marriage is good but also insists that it distracts a person from God.[23]

A century later the noted Church historian Eusebius of Caesarea reveals his own impression of married life as he tries to answer the charge that Christians, by praising those who do not marry, contradict the Old Testament, which they themselves claim was inspired by God.

There was nothing to prevent those men of old, who lived a more relaxed and freer life, from caring for their home and children and at the same time being free for the service of God. They were able to give assiduous care to religion as well as to their wives and children and household and were never pulled away from the better pursuit by outside concerns. But our business includes countless affairs which bear down on us from without, draw us from all sides into other concerns, and distract us from our careful attention to pleasing God.[24]

As a bishop in Italy expresses it toward the end of the century, the work and worry of married life slow the pace of the runner like weights on his feet.[25]

St. Ambrose finds this difficulty symbolized in Genesis by the sleep into which God cast Adam before He fashioned Eve.

What is that sleep for a short time except the fact that, when we turn our soul to being united with someone in marriage, we seem to lower and close eyes that were intent on the kingdom of God for a kind of slumber here in the world and are asleep to divine things for awhile as we rest in the fleeting affairs of earth.[26]

Jerome comments on Paul's remark about "human trials."

Do you think the same way of life can combine spending days and nights in prayer and fasting with freshening up at the arrival of your husband, mincing your step, devising flatteries? . . .

Babies cry, the servants set up a racket, children are watched and spoken to, accounts are added up, money is put aside for this and that. The cook with sleeves rolled up is grinding meat. The girls are chattering at their weaving.

Meanwhile word arrives that the husband has come with some friends. She flies like a swallow through every room of the house. Is everything in order? Have they swept the floors? Is the table set? Is dinner ready?

Now tell me, among all these things where is there any thought of God?[27]

Augustine and Fulgentius of Ruspe, his disciple, see the same problem.[28] During the early 600's St. John Climacus, the abbot of the monastery on Mt. Sinai whose last name derives from his classic *Steps To Paradise*, observes,

Those whose feet are in chains can still walk, though they constantly trip and hurt themselves. A single man given over to the cares of this life is like one who has his hands in chains but can go wherever he likes . . . A man bound by marriage is like one with chains on both hands and feet.[29]

Early medieval writers agree that

> Worry . . . and the obligation to provide for a wife and children separate a person from God.[30]

Peter Abelard, whose arrival in Paris makes the year 1100 a notable date in the history of theology, explains why, in the second chapter of Genesis, Adam names the animals and birds but not the reptiles.

> We think that this is an excellent passage for its sacred symbolism. The celibates in the Church today . . . may be compared to birds, and good married couples to the beasts, which partly touch the earth, with their feet, and are partly separated from it, since their bodies do not crawl upon it. For the man who is joined in wedlock is divided, partly serving God, partly intent on the world, due to the ever-present demands of married life.[31]

Not only Abelard's contemporaries but the Schoolmen of the following century agree that these concerns make married people "less prompt for good."[32] Bonaventure finds the advantages of marriage hopelessly intertwined with the cares that married life involves.[33] "And all these things keep us from entirely tending toward God."[34] Albert the Great goes so far as to call that way of life a hindrance to salvation because of its burdens.[35] This, he feels, may be a reason why some have denied that any grace is conferred by the sacrament of matrimony.

> For it confers one, not to bring the person a good but to help him avoid an evil.[36]

Aquinas concludes that the decision to undergo these "human trials," which he understands as worries over temporal things, is not in accord with our purpose in life unless the trials are compensated for by other good effects.[37]

During the 1400's Denis the Carthusian wonders why Paul

mentions only these annoyances and discomforts as reasons for deciding not to marry.

He could have alleged a worthier reason, that the married state, due to the cares that are joined to it, withdraws a person very far from the purity and fervor and stability of contemplation and love of God.[38]

Cajetan in the following century is sure that Paul does mean to speak about spiritual disadvantages.[39]

Nor is Paul contradicting the declaration of God . . . "It is not good that the man be alone." . . . As far as the existence of the species is concerned, it is not good for man to be alone, because it takes away nature's means of increasing the species. But Paul is speaking of man with regard to his spiritual life, and here it is good not to take a wife. For something of a hindrance to spiritual life arises from marriage.[40]

Theologians of the Counter-Reformation are convinced that marriage makes it difficult to find time enough for God.[41] In the face of Protestant attacks on clerical celibacy they explain that priests in the Western Church do not take a wife

because of the hindrances and worldly concerns which necessarily follow in the wake of marriage.[42]

Time and again they insist that this is more than a question of avoiding certain discomforts.

More harm is done by slavery of the mind than that of the body and by the loss of good thoughts than the loss of money.[43]

We see very many who, bound by the chains of marriage, are so busy and anxious about earthly concerns that they can hardly have a serious thought about their salvation.

True, they arrive on time once or twice a week for divine service, but their attention is whisked away by their usual worries to thoughts of this world. In body they are present at the affairs of God, in mind they dwell amid the affairs of earth, for they are so distracted by them that they can scarcely pay attention to what is going on in front of them.[44]

As late as this present century and by no less an authority than Pius XII, this is seen as one of the lessons of Matthew's Gospel.

The statement of Jesus Christ implies that this type of perfect abstinence from marriage unburdens people from the weighty responsibilities and duties which it entails . . . The society which gives them their obligations as husband and wife clearly commands that 'The two shall be one flesh.' For in good times and bad a husband and wife are bound by many chains . . . and distracted by worrisome cares which make it difficult to find time for prayerful reflection on the things of God because of their responsibilities now.[45]

But if a married man will have a greater struggle to serve God, will not his steadfastness in the face of these trials win him a greater reward?

During the late 300's Chrysostom replies,

And who, pray, forced him to take up so heavy a burden?
If by entering marriage a man fulfilled a command, if he violated a law by not entering it, this would probably be true. But if a man who has been free not to take on the yoke of marriage wishes, beyond all duty, with no one forcing him, to place himself in the midst of those difficulties, this means nothing to the promoter of the contest. He ordered him to do only one thing, to engage the devil in combat and seek a victory over vice.[46]

Writers of the Dark Ages consider this the mind of Paul.

Here we see that a maiden does not commit sin if she marries but does enter upon something which involves the hardest toil and which, as far as God is concerned, has no reward just as it has no punishment.[47]

The principle implied in these conclusions is stated explicitly during the Middle Ages:

It is not true that where there is greater labor, there is greater merit.[48]

In virginity, with less toil, there is greater progress and therefore greater ability to merit. In marriage, there is great toil and small progress, for in this state of life it is a great thing just to hold your ground.[49]

During the 1500's Salmeron adds a reason why, in some cases at least, the greater struggle should not be expected to bring a greater reward.

Oftentimes imprudent men enter marriage against the advice of the Lord and in response to the flesh and its concupiscence. As a result, those tribulations and annoyances tend to lessen merit rather than increase it.[50]

Men have always known about the worries and cares of married life, but Christians have seen a new dimension in them. Every human being, with his need of food and clothes and a home, his liability to pain, his association with others who must be answered and helped and loved and competed with, feels a tendency to live absorbed in this world so keenly real, not going to excess perhaps but not giving God much more than the occasional attention which decency seems to require. Anyone who undertakes to share life with another will feel this tendency as he never has before. However great his good will, however high his ideals, he is starting down a road which will keep confronting him with what might be called urgent trivialities.

His first problem will be time. Even less of it will be available than he had before for exclusive attention to God.

And even during this limited time he will find that the calm of prayer is an emotional vacuum which will be filled at once by an onrush of plans and questions and anxieties, more numerous now and more urgent, since more will be at stake than there was before marriage.

True, he can see his new work as a new way of serving God. But no matter how he sees it, it has to be done. And it lends itself all too readily to being done for its own sake. It is so demanding or fascinating or painful or tiring that he will find it hard to think of anything else.

This should not lead to exaggerated conclusions. On the other hand, it discloses an occupational hazard which a couple must frankly acknowledge if their relationship with God is not to suffer. A gradual erosion of old ideals by the cares of married life can leave them willing to settle for small gains, content with being "good Catholics."

God must remain as real as the world around them. Spiritual things must be as compelling as the demands of "common sense" and "practical" life. Together, early, learning by experience, they must work out different methods of insuring this.

The first modification of the idea of salvation in pairs is due, we have seen, to the period of salvation-history in which a couple are living. This second one derives from marriage itself. And Paul's advice to the Corinthians brings a third one to light, which has its origin in the two people who marry.

9 *ABSTINENCE AND PRAYER*

WE HAVE SEEN how the Jews abstained from sexual intercourse when they felt that in some unusual way they were in
the presence of God.[1] Paul continues this tradition.

So, the husband has no right over his own body; that right belongs
to his wife. Of this right do not deprive each other, except perhaps
temporarily by mutual consent, that you may be free for prayer.[2]

Both Greek and Latin Fathers echo Paul,[3] though they are
careful to insist that,

We are not proclaiming a law. We are giving advice. Our wish is
that absolutely everything which is yours be for your profit and for
the wellbeing of each of you.[4]

Theologians and bishops and popes from that day to this reflect a conviction that, although marital relations are certainly
not evil, a couple will find it helpful to abstain from them at
times.[5]

By the early 200's this general advice has taken on a certain
precision. Origen tells married people that they should have relations only at "stated and legitimate times."[6] Though there is no
Church law on the subject, there seem to be occasions during
the year when Christians feel that they should abstain. As Theodoret explains in a comment on Paul's advice,

It is fitting to honor a time of fasting by holiness.[7]

During the Dark Ages Lent is named as one of these times,[8] then Advent.[9] The books in which, during the 800's, priests, who have little formal theology, are shown what penances to impose for sins confessed to them, mention the three forty-day periods of fasting observed in some places and also Wednesday and Friday, long regarded as days of penance every week.[10]

Medieval theologians usually restrict themselves to more general expressions such as "fast days," but the obligation itself is taken for granted.[11] Late in the 1400's Denis the Carthusian adds,

A person should not indulge in sexual pleasure during a time of general tribulation. And therefore, according to Catholic and Jewish experts, Noah and his sons and the brute beasts abstained in the Ark.[12]

Writers who propagate the reforming spirit of the Council of Trent associate sexual abstinence with Lent,[13] and from the *Apostolic Canons* of the fourth century, which forbid weddings during that time, up to Trent's prohibition, still in force today, of a solemn ceremony during Lent and Advent,[14] the same spirit is apparent.

The important point here is not the obligation involved but the attitude which these documents reflect. And this attitude may be inspired by nothing more than the obvious principle that during a time of penance it is fitting to do without the ordinary enjoyments of life.

But during the early 400's a different spirit is evident in a document which will have a tremendous influence on the Church in the West. We have already discussed St. Jerome's treatment of the Book of Tobit. At the point in the narrative where young Tobias protests that he dare not seek the hand of Sara, the angel, in Jerome's version, replies:

When you marry her, spend three days in continence, having no concern but praying with her. . . . After the third night, in the fear of the Lord, take the maiden, prompted not so much by instinct as by love of children, so as to obtain for your sons the blessing of the race of Abraham.[15]

The passage is not authentic; but whether it derives from Jerome himself or some previous translator, it suggests that a custom of abstaining for a time after their wedding exists among some Christians of the period.

A writer in southern Gaul, perhaps St. Caesarius, whose achievements as bishop of Arles from 503 to 543 will have him acknowledged as a founder of the Church in France, is responsible for a collection of 104 canons which illustrate the practice of that area. As for weddings,

When the bride and groom are to be blessed by the priest, let them be presented by their parents or the bridal party. When they have received the blessing, let them remain in virginity that night out of reverence for the blessing.[16]

During the following century a letter spuriously attributed to one of the early popes shows the influence of the Vulgate.

And let them devote themselves to prayer for two or three days and keep their chastity so that they may have good children and please the Lord in all they do.[17]

The same directive appears in the books of penances[18] and collections of ancient canons which emerge during the next two centuries.[19] Around 1100 Raoul Ardent, a native of Poitiers, tells young couples in one of his sermons that,

When they have received the nuptial blessing, they should not have relations at once but should give honor to the sacrament and on the first night keep vigil in the church with torches and spend the time in prayer.[20]

This feeling does not die with the Middle Ages. Though Denis the Carthusian in a commentary on the Book of Tobit remarks,

They are not obliged to remain continent for the three nights after their marriage begins,[21]

Salmeron claims a century later,

The Church is accustomed to demand . . . continence on the first night out of reverence for the sacrament.[22]

And St. Charles Borromeo, attempting as bishop of Milan to conform his diocese to the new spirit of earnestness that has emerged from the Council of Trent, tells his priests,

The pastor . . . should first take care to advise them with serious urging to prepare themselves for entering upon it with fasts and prayers, and also, once it has been properly celebrated, . . . to abstain for three days out of reverence, devoting themselves during that time to very frequent prayer, and with this strength against spiritual evils and the impulsiveness of the flesh, to set their minds on winning themselves salvation and more abundant grace from that sacrament.[23]

Once again, the important question is not the binding force of this custom but the attitude it reveals. Abstinence from sexual intercourse is associated with nearness to God.

This is even more evident in another practice of those times. During the early Middle Ages, Sundays, the greater feasts of saints, and the octave of Easter are cited as occasions when married people should practice continence.[24] Peter Lombard's *Book of Sentences* shows that this is the mind of theologians during the 1100's,[25] and the Schoolmen a century later feel that it would be a venial sin to urge one's marriage rights on these occasions.[26] Later writers agree,[27] though Denis the Carthusian explains,

It is not forbidden by law but dissuaded by doctrine . . . In other words, it is not becoming.[28]

Post-Reformation theologians still advise this abstinence on holy days[29] but mention, like Denis, that it is not required by any law of the Church. In fact, they doubt that there is any real obligation.[30] As time goes on the subject is no longer mentioned.

But Jerome's comparison of married couples with David's men when they ate the altar bread discloses a still more significant custom.

Near the cleanness of the body of Christ all intercourse is unclean.[31]

If there is doubt about what this might imply for the daily life of Catholics, the doubt is not long allowed to remain. Writers of the 800's rail at husbands and wives who have relations and later,

irreverently coming into church, are not only so indiscreet as to come up as far as the holy altar but even think nothing of receiving the body and blood of Christ. Let them understand that they should only enter Christ's church and receive His body and blood with a clean body and pure heart.[32]

A more benign attitude is evident by the 1100's, and the Schoolmen treat the matter as a counsel, not a command.[33] According to Thomas,

Jerome's statement should be understood not of every married person without exception but only of those who are ministers of the Church, as in the Greek church . . . The rest of the faithful, as long as they are otherwise properly disposed, should not be kept from holy communion for having performed their marriage duty toward their partner. In this matter they are to be left to their own devotion and conscience.[34]

Though abstinence still continues to be encouraged, a decree of the Holy Office in 1587 forbids priests from restricting married people to communion on certain days. Each individual is simply to follow the advice of his confessor.[35] This is emphasized by another decree a century later.[36]

But meanwhile Catholics have begun to receive communion more frequently, and this affects the advice that is given to married people. St. Francis de Sales assures one of his clients that, since Christians in the early Church received every day and yet were warned by Paul not to deny a spouse's marriage rights, there is never any sin in consenting to the other's desire either before or on a communion day. As for petitioning,

The sin would only be very venial and slight due to a little irreverence which would result from it.[37]

Even this last caution is no longer heard as the trend toward frequent communion gathers momentum.[38] In 1902 Leo XIII affirms that married people are in no way prevented from approaching the altar and indeed can well use the help of the sacrament.[39] Pius X, who succeeds him, censures anyone who would exclude husbands and wives from frequent, even daily, communion.[40]

Before attempting to see what it was that prompted these customs of abstinence, one final trend should be noted: the gradually growing feeling in the Church that those with holy orders should not marry.

Up to the year 300, celibacy among the clergy appears to be honored but not imposed. Then the practice of different churches begins to differ. In the East, the general custom and eventually the law requires that bishops be unmarried. As for priests, a man is forbidden to marry once he becomes a subdeacon, but one who is already married may receive major orders and continue to live with his wife.

In the West, a significant directive emerges from a council at Elvira, not far from Granada in Spain. Bishops, priests and deacons are forbidden to have relations with their wives. Offenders will be deposed from clerical rank.[41]

The custom which this decree suggests keeps growing ever more widespread. By the late 300's not only is celibacy demanded by bishops and local councils, but the popes themselves are imposing it on the clergy of North Africa and Western Europe. If Paul desired married laymen to abstain occasionally for prayer, they argue that a priest, who is saying Mass or baptizing every day, should make no use at all of marriage.[42] Though this demand for celibacy was not uniformly promulgated or heeded at first, it has been made ever since of the Latin clergy.[43]

Some of these customs just described were never universal, and most have not lasted till the present. Still there has obviously been a certain uneasiness among Christians about making use of marriage and then approaching God in prayer. What is the reason for this feeling?

10 *"WHERE YOUR TREASURE IS . . ."*

ONE REASON immediately suggests itself when we recall the cultural climate into which the Church moved when it left Palestine. The growth and decline of these customs parallels the growth and decline of the conviction that the sex instinct, and not merely its unruly quality, is a product of original sin. A person who feels that he has recently yielded himself to this perennial experience of the rebellion against God cannot but be uncomfortable in His presence.

There seems little doubt that the advice given to married Christians was often based on the assumption that the less they have of this experience, the better. St. Jerome tells them that, by abstaining at times for prayer, they will acquire a taste for continence.[1] Some medieval priests draw protests for forbidding marital relations on five days out of the week and "bestirring themselves by oblique means to destroy marriage."[2] Alexander of Hales feels that even couples who are justified in using their marriage rights on a communion day should do so

with anxiety of mind because of what is there due to the sickness of concupiscence.[3]

But this cannot be the whole explanation. Whatever implications men may have read into the New Testament, it does advise abstaining at times for prayer. We have seen the practice

127

of sexual abstinence on extraordinary religious occasions mentioned in the Old Testament. Paul may simply be taking a Jewish custom for granted. Or is he aware of something in sexual
intercourse which affects a person's life with God?

According to St. John Chrysostom, abstaining from relations
is not a requirement for prayer, but it is a help.

Through continence prayer is made more earnest.[4]

Augustine explains how

they will give their prayers more appeal by this abstinence just
as by fasting.[5]

Other prelates in the Western Church agree that,

Marriage is pure, but a person should still abstain even from what
is permitted so that his prayer may more easily lead to results. . . .
When he does not touch even the things he is allowed, he shows that
he wishes to receive what he prays for.[6]

Then too, this abstinence is a sign of his sorrow for things
in his life that were not allowed.[7]

From early medieval commentators[8] to Jesuit writers of the
1600's who are trying to increase a couple's confidence so that
they will dare to climb the "mountain of myrrh" like Moses,
David and the married saints,[9] Catholics of different ages have
put sexual abstinence in a class with fasting. It is simply one of
many ascetical practices which a person is free to adopt according to his needs and preferences. There is no suggestion that
marital intercourse is an obstacle to union with God.

But such a suggestion does appear in a reason which Ephrem
the Deacon proposes to Syrian Catholics of the late 300's for
dedicating themselves to the celibate life. Alluding to sexual desire, he advises,

See that you pull it out of your heart roots and all, my brother, so that it may not keep growing and bearing fruit every hour of the day.[10]

Giving it expression can make it stronger and harder to cope with. Some of the Greek and Latin Fathers go so far as to say that it would be easier for certain people not to take a wife than to avoid sins of excess in marriage.[11] As Graeco-Roman culture wanes, through the Dark Ages, and as a new intellectual current begins to stir after the year 1000, similar ideas keep reappearing.[12] During the 1200's William of Auvergne is sure that married people need special help from God because

There is no one who doubts or does not know . . . how strongly our generative power moves and incites the common run of men, not with measure and modesty nor by the law and tempering power of reason but by a brutal onrush and excitation.[13]

As Aquinas explains,

The more use a man makes of pleasurable things, the more the craving for pleasurable things grows in him. The concupiscences are weakened by abstinence and the other bodily exercises which are appropriate for those who have a fixed intention of foregoing marriage.[14]

Through the decline of Scholasticism and the surge of Counter-Reformation theology this same conviction persists.[15] Preachers give voice to it as French eloquence enters its Golden Age in the 1600's.[16] Though the exaggerations of individual scholars or of particular centuries are gradually sifted out by the passage of time, Pius XII tells our own age,

We should not take a stern view of this type of pleasure. . . . But on the other hand we must admit that the lower powers of human nature, after the deplorable fall of Adam, keep resisting right reason and sometimes even drive man on to doing evil. For as the Angelic

Doctor writes, the use of marriage 'draws the soul back from giving itself completely to the service of God.'[17]

The conclusion is not that no one should marry. Those who have emphasized this problem most strongly have been careful to make it clear that only certain individuals would find moderation in marriage more difficult than celibacy.

But their words reflect a conviction, and one that is not restricted to such extreme cases as husbands and wives who use contraceptives rather than abstain. No couple can escape a certain struggle. The very instinct which is designed to express one of the most selfless kinds of love will, if not checked, become the most demanding, calculating, unsympathetic force in human nature. No one is less concerned about others than the person who lets it have its way. This area of married life, if not kept under surveillance, does, therefore, involve rebellion against God and is then incompatible with His presence.

Origen finds this incompatibility even when there is no moral wrong.

Legitimate marriage, for example, is without sin, and yet the presence of the Holy Spirit will not be given during the time of marital relations, even in the case of a prophet fulfilling his duty of begetting children. There are many other things as well in which human strength is sufficient by itself and the matter does not require the presence of the Holy Spirit nor would it be fitting.[18]

It would not be fitting. Both the remark and its connotation appear again in one of the most important productions of the 1100's, the *Decree* of Gratian. A professor of canon law at Bologna, this author does not simply collect ancient canons but arranges them into a treatise, citing the authorities who have spoken on a problem and then proposing his own solution. Though never official, his collection will become the basis of all subsequent canon law.

On one point he sides with Origen,

Marriage, when according to law, is indeed without sin; and yet during the time when marital relations take place, the presence of the Holy Spirit will not be given.[19]

Although his authority alone would be enough to give this notion currency during the 1100's, it is also espoused by Peter Lombard.[20] The Schoolmen accept it, though they cite another dictum from the Book of Sentences, "He does not cease to pray who does not cease to do good,"[21] and insist that marital relations never conflict with prayer taken in this sense.[22]

As Thomas explains,

We are joined to God in two ways, by the habit of grace and by the act of contemplation and love. What breaks the first union is always a sin, but not what breaks the second.[23]

During the 1300's Thomas of Strasbourg adds that, if Origen meant anything else,

then I would say that we should not stay with Origen in this, just as the faithful take him to task for many of his other assertions.[24]

Theologians of the following century feel the same,[25] and in the *Third ABC of the Spiritual Life*, which numbered Theresa of Avila among its avid readers during the 1500's, Francisco de Ossuna denies Origen's statement even if it only implies that married people cannot reach the higher forms of prayer. Admitting that eminent men have explained how the Holy Spirit never inspired the prophets while they were making use of marriage, he observes that he is trying to form friends of God, not prophets.[26]

St. Robert Bellarmine, whom Clement VIII will force to become a cardinal in 1599 "because he has not his equal for learning in the Church," finds Gratian quoted by Protestant theologians as proof that marriage is not a sacrament. After observing that Gratian is citing Origen, "who does not enjoy such authority in the Church that we must necessarily agree with his opinion," he rejects the whole idea. Origen's supposition is that no special presence of God is needed because sexual intercourse is something natural. But it is the motive of the husband and wife which makes it morally good, and this good motive requires grace.[27]

Leonard Lessius, the embattled professor at Louvain, whose talents were much esteemed by Bellarmine, concludes,

> It cannot but follow that the Holy Spirit is present during this activity inasmuch as it is an act of justice or charity or religion or some other virtue. For the will cannot intend the goals of these virtues without the help of the Holy Spirit.[28]

With this, Origen's remark is laid to rest. He himself might have had no objection to the precisions of these later theologians. At any rate the mind of the Church is clear. The unique presence of God which is the privilege of men who are acting virtuously while in the state of grace is no less real or abiding when they are using their rights in marriage.

But Origen's remark, "it is not fitting," may reflect an idea about human sexuality which was taken for granted by Greek and Roman philosophers. As Aristotle put it,

> The pleasures are a hindrance to thought, the more so the more a person delights in them. Take sexual pleasure for example. No one would be able to think of anything while absorbed in that.[29]

Origen may or may not agree. Augustine certainly does. Whether he has gotten the idea from Aristotle or from Cicero's *Hortensius* or from his own experience, he is convinced that this pleasure

> stirs the whole person. The affection of the mind is joined and blended with the craving of the flesh, and no greater pleasure of the body exists than the one which results. In fact, at the precise moment

of time at which it reaches its climax, almost all the keenness and alertness of our thinking process are overwhelmed.[30]

He assimilates into his own theology of marriage an idea from Cicero's *Hortensius:*

The greater the onrush of this pleasure, the more inimical it is to the love of wisdom. For great pleasure of the body can in no way coexist with thought. When he is experiencing the greatest pleasure there is, who can keep his soul attentive, take up a line of reasoning, or think of anything at all?

But the religious soul, making good use of this evil, makes the following its thought: It will merely endure the pleasure of intercourse, since it cannot think while it is enduring it, just as a man thinks of his health and lends himself to sleep, knowing that he cannot think while he is sleeping.[31]

During the early Middle Ages, this line of thought reaches the point where impurity is regarded as sinful precisely because of that dominion of the soul by the body.[32] Rupert, abbot of the monastery of Deutz in the Rhine valley, whose extremely personal thought and style are making his books a target, though he is basically quite orthodox, shows how this notion is applied to marriage during the early 1100's.

In married people, however holy and just they may be, the flesh wars with the spirit. However religiously they may live the rest of the time and subject their flesh to the spirit, the flesh is superior while they are having relations, the soul inferior; and all the mind's keenness is so overwhelmed that there is no possibility of reflecting on God or devoting themselves to prayer.[33]

"Entirely flesh." This phrase which Peter Lombard used to describe a person during intercourse is repeated by others,[34] though Alexander of Hales notes that it applies more to sinful intercourse than to marriage, where the flesh "is partly subject to reason."[35]

Bonaventure finds this difference rather slight. Sexual intercourse, even in marriage, seems to him like deliberate drunkenness. The reason is in control beforehand when the decision is made to act, but not during the act itself.[36] For then,

The submerging and absorbing power of pleasure subdues the captive mind.[37]

Every act in which the allurement of sexual pleasure rules to such an extent that the reason is absorbed and man becomes entirely flesh is a disordered act, an act which, as far as it itself is concerned, overturns the kingdom of the soul and that directive power which is part of the soul's strength.[38]

Albert the Great agrees that, although the intense pleasure cannot destroy the prudence which set the act in motion, it does suspend the prudence that normally accompanies any virtuous deed.[39] To submit to such an overpowering experience would thus be sinful were it not conpensated for by other effects.[40]

Through most of the next five centuries this description of sexual intercouse is repeated in either Aristotle's terms or Augustine's.[41] During the 1800's there is still mention of

a certain clouding of the reason because of the vehemence of passion, which somehow absorbs the reason.[42]

Although the list of those who have spoken in this vein includes so many who are eminent in the Church, it should be noted that they regard themselves as dealing with a fact of common experience. Their source is Aristotle, not revelation.

Is the mind really stupefied, as it were, during marital relations? Only married people are qualified to say. But one remark does not seem out of order. Practically none of the theologians who have written on this question· could speak from personal experience. Augustine, on whom they rely so heavily, was admittedly not a celibate at first, but neither was he married.

It should not be assumed without proof that the experience of a man and woman who feel they are doing wrong is the same as that of a husband and wife. The same is true when a society like that of Aristotle and Cicero tolerates extra-marital intercourse. Two people whose aim is simple gratification without any permanent commitment are not automatically to be compared with two who are giving themselves to each other for life. The role of passion is hardly likely to be the same. Aristotle and Augustine notwithstanding, there are Catholic married couples today who deny that the reason is so overwhelmed by this experience.

But whatever be the truth of the matter, the same theologians call attention to one aspect of the experience which is within the ambit of revelation. Commenting on the First Epistle to the Corinthians, Jerome declares,

> If we must always pray, it follows that we must never use marriage, because as often as a man renders the debt to his wife he is unable to pray.
> Peter the apostle has experience of the chains of marriage. See how he instructs the Church and what he teaches Christians: 'Similarly, you husbands, under the guidance of wisdom lead the common life with your wives, the weaker sex, and honor them as joint heirs of the blessings the Christian life imparts, so that nothing may diminish the efficacy of your prayers.' Notice how in the same sense, because also in the same spirit, he says prayers are hindered by the marriage debt.[43]
>
> The love of a woman is always insatiable. After abundance it is needy again. It makes a manly spirit effeminate and will not allow it to think of anything but the passion it bears.[44]

Whatever be the result of one particular experience, the habitual lovemaking that is part of married life does, he feels, have an effect on a couple's relationship with God.

Augustine leaves little doubt about his own opinion.

Make her as attractive as you will. Heap every good quality upon her. I have still determined that for me nothing is to be shunned so completely as sexual relations. I feel that there is nothing which so plunges the soul of a man down from the heights as a woman's blandishments and that bodily intercourse which is implied in having a wife.[45]

Fulgentius of Ruspe takes up the theme a century later,[46] and Isidore of Seville, the last of the Latin Fathers, passes it on to medieval writers.[47] According to Bonaventure, not merely the abuse but the legitimate use of marriage is as great an obstacle to prayer as venial sin.[48]

Though most of Thomas's views appear in his earlier works, he does not seem to have changed his opinion that concentration on God "is especially hindered" by the sexual aspect of married life.[49]

Engaging in pleasurable experiences makes the mind cling with special force to things that concern the flesh, since delight causes the appetite to find rest in the enjoyable object. Thus it is especially harmful to those who are intent on the contemplation of divine things—and of any truth for that matter—to be given to venereal pleasures and especially useful to abstain from them.[50]

Scotus feels that a married man needs special grace because of this pleasure, "which distracts his mind vehemently from God."[51] During the 1400's the popular *Summary of Sacred Theology* by St. Antoninus, archbishop of Florence, notes this difficulty,[52] and Denis the Carthusian affirms that

intercourse of the flesh, although legitimate, is no ordinary hindrance to prayer.[53]

Even after an act of this kind, the senses remain less suited for awhile for spiritual activities.[54]

The very pleasure of the flesh begets boredom and distaste for the things of God and makes a man powerless for deeds of virtue.[55]

The same conviction is apparent in Biblical commentaries of the 1500's.

The removal of a rib from the man to form the woman, inasmuch as the rib is bone, is a symbol of the diminution of strength from a man's spirit because of a wife.[56]

That habit seems to make a man unfit for spiritual things. This is doubtless the reason why Paul advises married people that for the sake of prayer they should abstain for a time.[57]

Others cite Augustine,[58] and St. Charles Borromeo asks,

How is it surprising that impurity, an utterly detestable sin, tears us away and separates us from God, when holy matrimony . . . distracts us considerably from the contemplation of God, as Paul warns?[59]

As the Counter-Reformation reaches its climax during the 1600's, others are even more emphatic.[60] St. Lawrence of Brindisi, who spent some time in German-speaking regions, declares that

Luther . . . was wise according to the flesh . . . when he claimed that marriage is a most spiritual thing which rouses a man to the heights of piety. Paul says that it is an impediment to piety toward God and, therefore, that a man should abstain from the use of marriage for the sake of prayer.

This is so evident from experience that even Cicero said he could not pay due attention both to philosophy and to a wife.[61]

Pius XII makes a similar reply to similar claims in our own time.

This sacrament does indeed confer God's grace on the spouses to fulfill the duties of husband and wife in a holy manner. It strengthens the bonds of mutual love by which they are reserved to each other. Nevertheless it was not instituted to make the use of marriage an instrument more suited by design for joining the souls of the spouses with God Himself by the bond of charity.

Why, in fact, does the Apostle Paul acknowledge the right of married people to abstain for a time from the use of marriage to be free for prayer? Is it not precisely because abstinence of this kind affords greater freedom to the soul which desires to devote itself to heavenly things and prayerful union with God?[62]

In appraising these indications of what Christians have seen in this aspect of married life, we must again be careful to distinguish a cultural inheritance from the data of revelation. Would an experience which so involves the entire person be the same in a Christian culture as it was in Greece and Rome? Would it have the same effect on a husband and wife as on two people who are not married? The general nature of their statements and the fact that they are usually quoting more ancient authors suggest that many of those who wrote about the effect of marital relations on a person's conscious union with God had not asked these questions.

But on the other hand, it must not be forgotten that men usually see the truth better than they express it. Somerset Maugham once remarked that philosophy is the bad reasons people give for what they already know by common sense. This is certainly true at times of theology. The Christian revelation should not be confused with the rhetorical aids that Christians have often seized upon to make others see what was obvious to them. The Graeco-Roman influence is not enough to account for what so many, and at least one pope among them, have for so long been saying.

Among those who have seen life as Christ reveals it there has been a perennial conviction that the habitual sexual intercourse of husband and wife makes it more difficult to achieve a union with God in prayer. The yearning to repeat the experience or the keen sense of its loss takes forceful possession of the mind and emotions. Though this need not lead to any selfish excess, it does tend to dull the taste for spiritual things. In comparison with the vivid life enjoyed here and now, the supernatural world can seem very unreal.

But a previous part of this study has shown that it would be slighting the truth to discuss this activity of husband and wife as a quest of pleasure. It is essentially a gesture. It symbolizes and expresses the entire relationship they have to each other. This more important feature of the experience must be taken into account, since it involves a still more basic difficulty that Christians have seen in having a life-companion.

11 *"FOR BETTER, FOR WORSE . . . "*

IN MATTHEW'S GOSPEL Our Lord tells the Pharisees that the man who takes a wife acquires a relationship with her which no human authority can sever. The impact of this statement may be judged from the comment it evoked—and not from the Pharisees.

'If that is the predicament of a married man,' the disciples said to Him, 'then one had better not get married!'[1]

The man who marries loses the autonomy that he has always known. His life has now been joined with that of another person and will continually feel the pull of that other life. To the disciples, at least, this is not an attractive prospect.

Nor does it seem any more appealing to Christians of the Middle East during the late 300's. Chrysostom, in fact, goes so far as to say that Paul, when speaking against divorce, is really persuading his readers not to marry.

For anyone who hears that, after marriage, he will no longer be his own but will be subject to the will of his wife, will try to free himself without delay from that most bitter slavery—or rather, will not even take the yoke upon himself, since once he has done so, he must be a slave as long as it pleases his wife.[2]

The mind of the Western Church at this time is evident from Ambrose's remark about the bridal dowery.

The girl who is married is sold into slavery with her own money.[3]

The chain of love is indeed good, but it is still a chain. A wife cannot release herself from it when she likes. She cannot have free disposal of herself. . . .

If the one who is stronger does not have power over himself, how much less the weaker? The wife is not exempted from this mutual slavery. In fact, she is the one more closely bound.[4]

Since both Jerome and Augustine speak in the same vein,[5] it is not hard to predict the statements of writers in the West during the decline of Rome and the first stirring of medieval culture.

Jerome understands that this is the slavery which the Apostle has in mind when he says: 'Have you been called as a slave? Let that not disturb you.'

For the man who, after being married for some time, is converted to the faith of Christ is, by God's inspiration, called and drawn as a slave.

What should be called a greater slavery than the fact that husband and wife do not have power over their own body and may not abstain from the use of the flesh or devote themselves to prayer except by agreement?[6]

Alain de Lille, though so many of his lectures at Paris during the late 1100's assail the Cathars who are claiming that marriage is sinful, still declares,

In that state a wife is placed under the power of her husband, even a violent husband . . .[7]

During the 1400's Denis the Carthusian concludes,

The wise young girl does not consent to a husband without great fear.[8]

St. Antoninus looks at it from the man's side.

What is the dominion of women like? Listen to Cicero in his paradoxes.

'Is a man free when he is under a woman's orders? She imposes laws, prescribes, commands, forbids whatever seems good to her; and as for refusing when she gives a command, he cannot or dare not.

'In my opinion he should be called, not a slave but the most wretched of slaves, though he be born of the noblest family.'[9]

Theologians of the Counter-Reformation agree. In fact, a celebrated commentary on Genesis has Adam refer to marriage as a trap.[10] Bourdaloue asks the Parisians who flock to hear him during the late 1600's,

Is not a state which makes you subject without really knowing the one to whom you are giving yourself and takes from you all freedom to change, the state of a slave? . . . By the priesthood I have been bound only to God and myself. . . . By marriage you transfer that dominion which you have over yourself to someone else.[11]

These warnings may seem to be pointing to nothing more than the irritation that arises, partly from selfishness, at never being able to act without giving thought to the feelings of another. But by the time of the Greek Fathers it is evident that this "slavery" is something more serious. Chrysostom, for example, explains why Our Lord's disciples felt that, without divorce, it is better not to marry.

It seemed really burdensome to have a wife full of every wickedness whom you must endure and to be harboring an untamed beast in your home.[12]

The difficulty is not just being bound, but being bound to someone hard to live with. As Jerome puts it,

He who is not arguing is not married.[13]

He describes the problem as it appears to him.

We may cite that golden book of Theophrastus, *Marriage,* in which he asks whether a wise man takes a wife. When he has carefully stated the conditions, . . . he adds at once, 'It is rare that all these things are found in a single marriage. Therefore, a wise man should not take a wife.

'First of all, his study of philosophy would be hindered. No one can dedicate himself at the same time to books and a wife. There are many things which are necessary to the daily life of women, expensive clothes, gold, jewelry, purchases, slave girls, a dress for each occasion. . . .

'Then throughout entire nights the long-winded complaints: "That woman has nicer things to wear outside. . . . This one is looked up to by everybody. . . . Poor little me. When the girls get together, they laugh at me. . . . Why were you looking at that woman next door? . . . What were you saying to the smart young slave girl? . . . What did you bring back with you from the forum?"

'No friend may we have, no companion. She suspects that love of the other is hatred for her. . . .

'Then too, there is no chance to try a wife out. You take her as she is. If she is hot-tempered, lazy, deformed, conceited, ugly—whatever defect there is, you learn after the wedding. A horse, a donkey, a cow, a dog . . . are tried out first and then paid for. A wife is the only thing that isn't demonstrated. They're afraid that she'll displease you before she's taken home.

'You have to keep noticing her face all the time and praising her and telling her how pretty she is for fear that, if you look at another woman, she'll think she's unattractive. . . .

'If you entrust the entire house to her to be managed, you have to be her servant. If you reserve anything to your own judgment, she doesn't think you trust her. Then she turns to hatred and quarrels; and if you don't look out at once, she'll get some poison ready.'[14]

Jerome has never been accused of understating his case; and of course, he is merely quoting a pagan author. Still his own conviction is clear.

During the Middle Ages some writers quote him. Others take the side of the wife. But all agree,

That contract is of itself difficult to keep faithfully, because of the many miseries of the contracting parties and the infirmities, physical and moral, of two people who are bound to come to each other's aid until death.[15]

Scotus thinks it is harder to live in a home than in a monastery,

where a hundred people are taking care of one and helping him in his infirmities.[16]

One of the most widely published books of the 1300's, Ludolph of Saxony's *Life of Christ the Lord*, quotes both Chrysostom and Jerome on the trials of having a spouse.[17] A century later Denis the Carthusian observes,

It also turns out on many occasions that they do not get along well together and frequently quarrel and, little by little, conceive a great distaste for each other, until finally an amazing and very deep-rooted hatred arises between them.

Then side by side they lead a bitter life. The more they are together every day, at home, at table, in bed, in conversation, in work that they do, the harder it is to bear.[18]

Writers after the Council of Trent continue the warnings.[19] After quoting Theophrastus on the trials of a husband, Lessius adds those of a wife.

Subject to her husband in everything, she must put up with his moodiness, contrariness, nights of eating too much and drinking too much, jealousy, suspicions, incontinence, adulteries, quarrels, blows. She must follow him, be with him everywhere, obey and serve him like a slave. . . . He uses up the money they have on dice, card games, drink, dinners, lavish gifts, ruinous contracts, ill-advised lawsuits and other ways, and the wife can apply no remedy.[20]

The great French preachers of the late 1600's point to the more subtle conflicts that arise between every husband and wife. Bossuet takes the case of an ideal couple:

Both of them are equally reasonable, if you like—something amazingly rare and not to be hoped for. Even then each has moods, prejudices, habits, associations. Whatever be the things they have in common, people's dispositions are always different enough to cause a frequent chafing in so long a life together. They see each other so near at hand, so often, with so many defects on either side, in the most natural situations and ones so unexpected that it is impossible to be prepared.

They get tired. The thrill is gone. The other's imperfection is irritating. Human nature makes itself felt more and more. . . . They love their cross, I am happy to say, but what they are carrying is the cross.[21]

Fénelon agrees that,

They get tired of each other in this need of being almost always together and acting in unison on every occasion. It requires a great grace and great fidelity to the grace received to bear this yoke patiently. . . . A person must prepare for it in a spirit of penance when he believes he is called to it by God.[22]

Bourdaloue summarizes the problem.

In religious life I do not find myself bound to one person in particular. It is not exclusively and forever to this one or that but now to the one and now to the other, and this tends to make the yoke infinitely easier to bear. In marriage, however, your pledge is perpetual to this man or this woman. . . .

May I add one more difference between our two states of life that is new, my friends, but very notable? For the religious state there is a noviceship and a time of testing. There is none for marriage. . . .

Now that this young man is courting you, he has only words of agreement with you, only tokens of kindness, moderation, virtue. But once the knot is tied, you will soon learn what he is like. . . .

Now while this girl is not yet settled in life and you strike her as an agreeable choice, she knows how to calm herself and hide her feelings. But once she no longer has so many tactics to adopt or so many things to gain by pleasing you, you will soon experience her caprices, her oddities, her fits of stubbornness, her expressions of conceit. . . .

Bear well in mind then, my friends, what such a pledge is, or such a slavery for the rest of your life and without remission. There is no vow so solemn that the Church cannot dispense it; but when it comes to marriage, she has her hands tied. . . . What I say is in no way meant to give you a horror of it. It is to make you realize how much you need God's help in marriage.[23]

Though the rhetoric of authors like Jerome is not the word of God, we cannot ignore this persistent reaction of men who have looked at marriage in the light of faith. Besides the distracting cares and a distaste for things of the spirit, revelation seems to have shown them another problem. To marry is to lose a basic autonomy. Time and work and even prayer will now depend on another, and this can be painful.

A sermon by Ephrem the Deacon during the late 300's points to something still more serious. A husband is deeply sensitive to the wishes of his wife, and this

often leads a man off to punishment.[24]

The Greek Fathers a few years later also see married life not just as a trial but as a danger.

He who has a wife will find it easier to be pure, since he has a great comfort. But in other things the matter is not so clear. And what is more, even in that area we see more married people falling than monks. There are not as many leaving the monasteries for marriage as the marriage bed for impurity.

Now, if they fall so frequently in contests that are easy for them, what are they likely to do in the face of other affections of soul by which they are more tried than monks? . . . If anyone has reason to be afraid, surely it is not those who flee the storms or those who hurry to port but those who are tossed by squall and tempest. In their case there is more reason to fear a shipwreck since there is more disturbance and those who should be resisting are more sluggish . . . This is why we draw them into the desert, not just to put on sackcloth, not just to spread ashes to sleep on, but first of all to flee vices and elect virtue.

What then? Will all married people perish? I certainly do not say that. But I do say that they are faced with greater labors if they wish to achieve salvation, and this because of the 'imminent necessity.' The man who is unhampered runs more easily than the one who is bound with chains.[25]

The mind of the Latin Fathers at this time is summarized by Ambrose.

If a good marriage is slavery, what is a bad one in which they cannot sanctify each other but cause each other to perish?[26]

Two centuries later Pope St. Gregory the Great describes the problem in words which will often be quoted.

Some things are harmful in themselves such as sins and crimes. Others, such as temporal power or marital relations, hurt us because of the things that surround them. For marriage is good, but the things which grow up around it due to concern for this world are evil. . . . Thus, while a person has something which does not hurt him, because of the things nearby he very often does what will hurt him. We are often travelling a straight and clear road, and yet our clothes are caught and we are held back by thorn bushes that have grown beside the roadbed.[27]

Writers around the year 800 agree that,

A wife is a heavy burden, since husbands are not permitted to dismiss them nor may women dismiss their husbands no matter how they may be toward each other. . . . Each then must realize his or her danger.[28]

The most influential voice of the 1100's, St. Bernard of Clairvaux, will brook no talk from Cathars about marriage being a sin, but he admits,

It is clear that the road is dangerous. We find ourselves grieving that so many perish on it and seeing so few travel it in the right way.[29]

The Schoolmen a century later feel that this is why marriage demands special grace from God.[30] Bonaventure asks,

How many annoyances do you think married women who are religious and anxious to give time to God endure when they are forbidden by their husbands, to whom they must be subject? This is a great burden in marriage when wives are joined to such men as disagree with their good habits and devout way of life. How many married women do you think there are who would be willing to buy even at the price of death the ability to pay the Lord free homage, released from the power of evil men?[31]

During the 1400's Denis the Carthusian describes the dangers of married life,[32] and a century later Salmeron calls attention to the self-control that a husband needs to avoid offending God "as Adam did to keep from saddening Eve."[33]

Writing to a Frenchwoman during the early 1600's, St. Francis de Sales is kind but no less forthright.

Ah, my daughter, how pleasing the virtues of a married woman are to God! For they have to be strong and of extremely high quality to survive in that vocation.[34]

Toward the end of the century Claude de la Columbière explains why this is so.

You must join the use of legitimate pleasures with a complete removal from those that are not allowed, a very minute care of temporal goods with a perfect detachment of heart from these same goods, a great readiness to assent to the wishes of the person to whom God has bound you with an inviolable fidelity to the desires of God, not to take any part in his passions.[35]

He goes on to point out "the dangers in which the love of a husband involves you if he is given to sin."[36] Bourdaloue, though aware of this danger,[37] sees a greater one if there is no love.

The one thing really deplorable is that these household trials only serve to remove you farther from God and make you more guilty before God. You look for compensation outside. You turn your inclinations toward others. To what disorders do you not allow yourself to be borne?[38]

This complete oneness of life with another has thus appeared to Christians as a cause of real concern. It involves more than a certain loss of freedom, more than the chafing of two personalities so different and so imperfect. There is also a definite risk.

The restrictions and irritations can lead to sins of anger or impatience or contempt. If the pain grows too serious and constant, escape can be so attractive a thought that moral considerations are put aside. And on the other hand, love has its problems. The terrible choice can present itself between God and this human being.

To run such a risk day in, day out, to fall at times, to see no hope of a change—this wearying existence can lead to more chronic illnesses: discouragement, disillusionment with life. If such dangers are too extreme to be likely for most married couples, there is another that is common: the continual drag of sharing life with someone whose ideals are not as high as your own.

A final difficulty, the most common of all and the one that really underlies these others, is disclosed by Paul to the Corinthians.

12 *"DIVISION"*

I would have you free from concern. He who is unmarried is concerned about the interests of the Lord, how he may please the Lord. But he who is married is concerned about worldly interests, how he may please his wife. Thus his interests are divided.

The unmarried woman or the virgin is concerned with the Lord's interests, is intent on being holy both in body and in mind. But the married woman is concerned with worldly things, how she may please her husband.[1]

Paul's Greek word *merimnâ*, "is concerned," occurs also in Matthew's Gospel when Christ urges his hearers not to be too anxious about what they are going to eat or what they are going to wear.[2] This concern, it now appears, is a problem for a married couple. They are prone to be "divided." Not that they deliberately ignore God. The problem is simply that their absorption in each other makes it harder to think of Him.

St. Zeno, a North African who began a celebrated reign as bishop of Verona in 362, illustrates this as Paul does by comparing the good housewife with the consecrated virgin.

The married woman is thinking of how to please her husband, the virgin of how to please God. The one is set off by lavish adornments, the other is far more attractive for not knowing how to be adorned. The one is fragrant with ointments and scents, the other, more pleasant than any meadow with that flower that is herself, sends the fragrance of joyful service up as high as heaven.[3]

A few years later Chrysostom speaks of "the spirit that is melted and softened by concern for a wife."[4] Gregory Nazianzen explains this.

Just as one who looks at two heads or two faces
Or words written on two pages
Does not really comprehend the whole form, though he wants to,
But grasps one part, while the other
Escapes his imperfect vision
Which must look at once in two directions,
So is weak love divided between the world and Christ. . . .
Either, having Christ as all, a man despises his wife,
Or fostering fleshly love, he forgets about Christ.[5]

Ambrose recalls the man in the Gospel parable who could not come to the banquet because he had married. Married people do come, but "not as promptly as virgins," because their attention is partly turned from God.[6]

There are many chains in this world. The desire to live is a chain. The allurements of pleasure are a chain. There are chains of honor, chains of marriage. . . . He does not sin who takes a wife, but he fastens himself in chains of the mind because he is anxious about how to please his wife. More fortunate would he be if his only desire was to please God.[7]

To married people Augustine applies Paul's words about being saved "but as though by fire."

The fire of tribulation will burn away . . . delights of this kind and worldly loves. By that fire is meant bereavement and any other calamities that snatch these things away. . . . What a man has not possessed without an enticing love he does not lose without burning pain.[8]

His care in another passage not to exaggerate makes his view of the matter all the more evident.

It is not as though the Catholic wife . . . does not think how she may please the Lord. But she thinks of it a good deal less, because she is also thinking about the things of this world, how to please her husband.[9]

Both East and West in their commentaries on Paul continue to point to this "division."[10] During the high tide of Scholasticism, Bonaventure explains that, although there is one kind of anxiety which makes a person forget God completely, "and this is suffocating," the kind that married people have is not so extreme. It is "under God" but "distracting and absorbing."[11]

Thomas describes how strong it is.

Among the many attachments to those around us, the human mind is especially ensnared by the love of wife or husband. Thus for those who are making their way toward perfection, the marriage bond is especially to be avoided. It entangles a person as does nothing else in the concerns of this world.[12]

St. Antoninus tries to prove this with an argument that would always have weight in Florence during the Renaissance: the example of Greece and Rome.

Cato of Utica said, 'If the world could exist without a woman, we would not lack the company of the gods.' And when Cicero was asked why he had divorced his wife, he replied that he could not have time for both a wife and philosophy. Hence Plato, too, who had no intercourse with any woman but also remained celibate, wrote more than other pagan philosophers about the things of God.[13]

If these illustrations do not help the saint's reputation as an historian, they at least show his own deep conviction.

Denis the Carthusian understands Paul's term "divided" to mean

wandering in mind and split in affection, partly seeking to please God, partly his wife, and partly seeking temporal things, partly spirit-

ual. The Apostle says this because the man with a wife has less apti-
tude for serving God than one who is unattached.[14]

He sees this as clear proof that all men and women are not intended by God to marry, since the world always needs a few
contemplatives.[15]

Luis de Granada, one of the most popular spiritual writers for
laymen during the 1500's, feels that a married man bears a
double burden, his own worries and those which he sees afflicting
his wife. The second is the harder one to bear.[16]

Other books during this and the following century present
"division" as an unmistakable feature of marriage as seen in the
light of Christ's revelation.[17] Bossuet, criticizing one author's
notes on the Bible, remarks,

> The other advantages in celibacy which St. Paul cites, such as being
> more in a state of prayer, more occupied with God alone and less
> divided in heart . . . this author, like the Protestants, counts for little.
> He does not deign to call attention to them.[18]

Bourdaloue, whose sermons are regarded by Frenchmen of
these years as second only to Bossuet's, shows them what this
division can mean.

> A married woman is always wondering anxiously how to keep
> herself in her husband's good grace and at the same time in God's.
> She finds herself obliged to content both of them as best she can and
> yet, in a thousand different situations that arise, uncertain how to suc-
> ceed or in what way to harmonize their wishes.
> This can reach the point where by sad necessity she must renounce
> the one for the other, abandon the one to attach herself inviolably to
> the other. And this is what troubles her, divides her heart, fills her
> mind with conflicting thoughts, views, emotions, keeps her in con-
> tinual bewilderment and sometimes in the cruelest uncertainties.[19]

During the last century and now in our own, Catholics are still
alerted to the problem.[20] Pius XII gives them the traditional interpretation of St. Paul.

The Apostle does not rebuke husbands for being anxious about their wives or wives for making every effort to please their husbands. But he does claim that their souls are divided between love of God and love of their spouses.[21]

Being male or female involves something more than the ability to have children. It is part of the most basic feature of a human being, an ability to make a gift of oneself. But making such a gift causes a total change. Worry and fear and joy are now reactions to what happens to someone else. The whole surge of life is toward another. Success is to win that other's love. Happiness is to find oneself able to make that other person happy.

When such a gift is made to God, it is psychologically possible to center life on Him as never before. When it is made to a human being, even the most lovable and deserving human being, it cannot be made as readily to God. There is something exclusive about it. The person who tries to make it twice feels himself divided. God can certainly be loved but not with the same spontaneous energy and absorption. The thoughts that come most readily to mind, the worry and joy that really overwhelm, have to do with this other human being.

Thus the same revelation which makes it clear that marriage is good makes it just as clear that it gives rise to problems. How typical and serious these problems are may be gathered from Paul's conclusion.

13 *THE BETTER WAY*

IN VIEW OF THE TIMES in which Christians live and the obstacles to serving God that face anyone who marries,

He who gives his virgin daughter in marriage does well, yet he who does not give her does better.[1]

By the year 200 it is obvious what Christians have concluded from Paul's words about those among them who have chosen to make their way to God alone.

Married people, even those outstanding in holiness and those whose marriage bed has been unsullied, cannot be compared to them. For the place in which they will dwell is not just the kingdom of heaven common to all the elect. Their lot is with the holy angels, so that the nobler and more excellent kind of life they have elected may have its reward.[2]

Zeno, who from his consecration as bishop of Verona in 362 has found himself acclaimed a champion against heretics as well as pagans, takes up an objection to this tradition.

Someone will say, 'Even the Virgin Mary both married and bore a child.'
Find me her equal and I yield my case. Besides, she was a virgin after her marriage, a virgin after conceiving, a virgin after her son was born. If there was something better than virginity, the Son of

God could have given that to His mother instead, but He arranged that she enjoy the honor of divine virginity.[3]

The conviction of both Eastern and Western bishops of the late 300's is summarized by Ambrose.

With reason do we praise the good wife, but with more reason do we prefer the dedicated virgin.[4]

And yet Ambrose himself is witness that this view is still being challenged even by some of the clergy. The reaction to the challenge is a pronouncement by the bishop of Rome.

We certainly do not despise marriage. We receive the marriage vows and are present at the conferring of the veil. But on the virgins devoted to God whom marriage begets we bestow still greater honor.
. . .
Hence we must follow the command of the apostle. Because they kept teaching notions that were different from what we have received, know that the opinion of all of us, priests and deacons as well as the entire clergy, was unanimous that Jovinian, Auxentius . . . and Ingeniosus, who have been found the fomenters of a new heresy and blasphemy, forever condemned by God's sentence and our judgment, should remain outside the Church.[5]

The movement does not die at once. Three years after this condemnation Jerome assails Jovinian.

The nobles make way for you in the street. The rich fondle you and take you to their hearts. Just think. If you had never been born, the drinkers and gluttons would never find their way to paradise.[6]

But during the troubled times which follow, with Africa under the Vandals and bishops beset by Arians and Pelagian heretics, this discussion is considered as closed. Lesser known writers of the next few centuries agree with the Fathers that marriage is not the higher state of life.[7]

How widespread this conviction has become by the 700's is apparent from an anecdote which Bede the Venerable relates to the young Church in England. According to Bede, the man whose wedding feast Christ attended at Cana was the Apostle John. He had just married, or at least was just about to marry, but was now called away by Christ.[8]

This story will still be in circulation, with occasional remarks that "It is not certain,"[9] when in 1255 a Dominican friar, James of Varazzio, will issue one of the most influential books of the Middle Ages. Despite the already large number of "legends" or lives of the saints designed to be read on their feast day, Caxton will explain in his English edition that "As gold is the most noble of all metals, so is this legend held most noble of all works." And John the Apostle, whom Catholics in every country of Europe will come to know through this *Golden Legend*, is presented as the bridegroom at Cana.[10]

A century later in a book which will have almost as wide a circulation, Ludolph of Saxony's *Life of Christ the Lord*, they will read,

Although there is a doubt as to whose wedding it was, we ourselves are inclined to think that it was John's.[11]

Though other authors will repeat the story, more and more will deny it[12] until Juan Maldonado, whose commentary on the Gospels will be representative of Scripture studies during the 1600's, will pronounce it impossible.[13]

Regardless of whether they know or accept this legend, theologians on the continent a generation after Bede feel as he does. Marriage is good, but virginity better.[14] This theme is echoed, not only by those who content themselves with copying the Fathers but by the more original thinkers of the High Middle Ages and by their followers down to the 1500's.[15]

Luther's violent denial of the whole idea makes it an urgent question once again. John Eck, the Catholic champion, takes issue with him;[16] and the *Spiritual Exercises* of St. Ignatius Loyola, the founder of the Jesuits, propose as one of the "Rules for Thinking with the Church":

To have great praise for religious orders, virginity and continence, and not to praise marriage as much as any of these.[17]

Finally the Council of Trent declares,

If anyone says that the married state is of higher rank than the state of virginity or celibacy and that it is not better and more blessed to remain in virginity or celibacy than to be joined in matrimony, let him be anathema.[18]

In his celebrated catechism St. Peter Canisius, himself a theologian at the Council, voices the sentiment which has been taught and believed by Catholics ever since.

We must be most careful to avoid two errors, that of people who, along with Jovinian, so extol marriage that they make this state either equal or superior to virginity . . . and that of people who imagine that continence and celibacy simply cannot be practiced by Christian men.[19]

In view of the conclusions drawn by some Catholics of the present century from recent trends in psychology, Pius XII feels called upon to discuss this second error.

They certainly wander far from the common sentiment of knowledgeable men—and one which the Church has always held in honor—who consider the natural sex instinct as the strongest and greatest driving force in the makeup of a human being and conclude from this that a person cannot check the thrust of such an appetite for an entire lifetime without grave danger of disturbing the internal functions of the body, especially the nervous system, and thus upsetting the balance of forces in his personality.

As St. Thomas has with good reason observed, the deepest-rooted tendency in our spirit really has to do with self-preservation. The driving force that issues from the sex faculties has second place. And besides, it belongs to the impelling and directive function of human reason, that singular privilege of our nature, to regulate these deep impulses and instincts and make them more noble by its right rule. . . .

More recently we reproved with sad heart the opinion of those who go so far as to assert that marriage is the only thing which can protect the natural development of the human personality and its due perfection. . . .[20]

It cannot be asserted—as some do—that the 'mutual help' which a couple seek in Christian marriage is something more perfect for achieving one's sanctity than the so-called solitude of heart found in virgins and celibates. Granted that all who have embraced the state of perfect chastity have renounced this kind of human love, it still cannot be concluded that, as a result of this privation, they have diminished and despoiled their personalities. For they receive something spiritual from the giver of heavenly gifts Himself which immeasurably surpasses the 'mutual help' which married people give each other.[21]

If a woman commonly expresses the gift of herself by marriage and motherhood, she can also respond in a more direct way to God's design and make the riches of her personality bear fruit by consecrated virginity. Far from being a turning inward on herself or a recoil from the tasks of life, this state responds to the desire for a gift that is more complete, more pure, more generous.

In Christian country as well as mission land the woman who renounces marriage to give herself without hindrance to comforting the sick and unfortunate, educating children and bettering the lot of families shows in this way to minds still unaware of Him the presence and activity of God. In this manner she fulfills her own unique vocation with the highest fidelity and maximum effectiveness.[22]

Virginity has often been said to make human beings like angels. It apparently does something more than that. It makes them men and women in a truer sense. In every cell of the body, every thought that issues from the composite of body and soul, the rational animal is male or female; and foregoing marriage "for the sake of the Kingdom of God" develops the distinctive powers of manhood and womanhood as nothing else in this life can.

Although the more insistent probing of this truth in recent years has drawn more attention to it, those who have studied marriage precisely as a sacrament have always insisted that, although this sacrament will help a man to increase his store of grace, he would have gotten still more in a celibate life.[23] Any doubt about the Church's certainty of this is removed by Pius XII.

Some affirm that God's grace conferred *ex opere operato* by the sacrament of matrimony makes the use of marriage so holy that it becomes a more effective method of joining individual souls with God than virginity itself, since Christian marriage is a sacrament but virginity is not. This opinion we denounce as false and harmful.[24]

The concerns of our own time have turned the attention of Catholics to one final aspect of virginity. Besides being a constant proof to those who are married that the passion which ever tries to turn their love toward selfishness can be overcome, it leaves a person free to devote himself to the good of society.[25] Pius XII denies that the Church has more need of married couples who influence their neighbors than of celibates who withdraw from the world. The latter are still members of the community. In fact, they do more good for more people than they ever could if they had married.[26]

In a word, the full development of a human being does not necessarily demand that he marry. Paul says just the opposite.

He who is unmarried is concerned about the interests of the Lord, how he may please the Lord. . . . The unmarried woman or the virgin is concerned with the Lord's interests, intent on being holy both in body and in mind.[27]

This holiness "in body and in mind" is apparently a type which married people cannot have. But Paul is hardly implying that marriage is sinful. The holiness he is speaking of is something like that of the vessels used in worship. Because of their contact with the divine, they are removed from other uses, reserved for God. In this sense the body and mind of the virgin are holy. As Augustine puts it,

> Even the bodies of married people who keep faith with each other and with the Lord are holy. . . . Therefore this passage is alluding to the greater holiness of the unmarried woman . . . since she has only one thing on her mind, how she may please the Lord.[28]

During the early 500's Fulgentius of Ruspe compares virginity to fasting. Both free a person, not from evil, but from things that encumber his way to God.[29]

Commentators during the Dark Ages take their ideas from the Fathers.

> Virginity deserves such praise, not because it is also found in martyrs but because it itself makes martyrs.[30]

The Schoolmen are more precise. According to Thomas, the soul's good is greater than the body's, contemplation is nobler than action, and God's interests are more important than man's. Marriage looks to the body, action, the concerns of another human being. Virginity favors the soul, contemplation, "the things which have to do with God."[31] It makes the way to heaven easier and quicker. It is also something loftier in itself.[32] Eve's being fashioned separately by God is a symbol that man should have a preference for contemplation, a nobler way to spend his time.[33]

Later theologians show little disagreement.[34] The settled conviction of Christians from Paul's time till the present is summarized by Pius XII.

> We must first of all affirm—as the Church plainly teaches—that holy virginity by its own excellence ranks higher than marriage . . .

This doubtless derives mostly from the fact that it aims at a more excellent goal and is also the most effective help for putting oneself entirely at the service of God. The soul of one who is involved in the chains and cares of marriage is more or less 'divided.'[35]

Thus the new light of the Christian revelation discloses depths and shadows that Old Testament authors had not seen in marriage. To set out with a life-companion is no longer the ideal way of reaching God. Christ has come and invites His followers to be living reminders that the world has reached its final stage.

Working life out with a companion appears to have limitations as well as advantages. The fault lies not in God's arrangement but in man's rebellion against it. As in his own fallen nature, so in a helpmate, he now finds an incentive to live for the present day, for pleasure, for another human being, for anything but God.

The Old Testament view of marriage has been refined and developed, and yet it has not been contradicted. The Christian revelation goes on to show that even now "It is not good that the man be alone."

14 *AS IN THE TIME OF NOE*

IN THE SAME PASSAGE which first suggests the limitations of marriage as a way to God, Our Lord adds,

Not all master this lesson, but only such as have received a special gift.[1]

Marriage, then, is still included in God's designs for the world. But how? As a concession to human weakness or as a positive good which He still desires?

This passage does not say explicitly, but the reference to "such as have received a special gift" recalls Our Lord's reply in the same Gospel when asked to explain the parable of the sower.

You are privileged to know the mysteries of the kingdom of heaven, but these others are not so privileged; for the man of means will be given yet more till he abounds in wealth while the man of no means will have taken away from him even what he has.[2]

In the present case the evangelist seems to be saying that those who have opened their minds to Him are given light to see the advantages of foregoing marriage.

Does this mean that all Christians at some time in life are offered the gift of consecrated virginity? More than one in the early Church appears to have thought so. Chrysostom, for example, explains that the gospel is only talking of a special gift so that you learn that there is a great struggle, not that you imagine a necessitating fate of some kind. It has been given to those who have wanted it.[3]

The same idea appears to be current in Italy during this period. Jerome warns,

Let no one think that fate or fortune is introduced in this verse, that those are virgins to whom it is given by God or whom some accident has led to it. It is given to those who have sought, those who have desired, those who have worked to receive it. For to everyone who asks it will be given, and one who seeks will find, and to one who knocks it will be opened.[4]

Though Augustine's interest is the psychological state of the man with whom God is dealing, he seems to agree with Jerome.

Those to whom it has not been given either have no desire or do not carry out what they desire. On the other hand, those to whom it has been given desire in such a way that they carry out what they desire. It is thus that this word . . . is both a gift of God and a free decision.[5]

A century later Fulgentius of Ruspe declares that God will give virginity to all who pray for it and do good works to reinforce their plea.

Still, if a person is more anxious about his weakness than sure of God's power, let him marry.[6]

Bede the Venerable teaches this point of view to the English,[7] and later writers on the Continent reflect it.[8] Their two main impressions are summarized by Albert the Great.

With the help of grace all are able, but as it is said in 1 Cor. 7, 'It is better to marry than to be on fire with passion.'[9]

Some in the 1300's quote Chrysostom and Jerome.[10] In the course of replying to Luther's attacks against monastic life, Canisius' catechism does the same.[11] Salmeron explains that "The Lord . . . wishes to be asked by some people."[12] Leonard Lessius goes into detail.

Not all are well enough instructed to appreciate so great a good or inspired by God to love it. And yet all are able 'to grasp' with remote power which could be brought to yield results if they wished. For all (I speak of Christians), when they hear sermons on the fruits of virginity can ask God's help to enter that state and be able to live in it.[13]

No one is held by the law of nature to marry unless it is necessary for the propagation of mankind . . . or for him personally, for instance if he is unable to remain continent. But this necessity does not exist either. It is absolutely certain and must be held as an article of faith that man, if he prays, can obtain from God the grace which is needed to remain continent.[14]

This argument is difficult to reconcile with a statement of Paul which discloses an impression of other Christians about this matter during the same centuries.

But in case they lack self-control, they should marry, because it is better to marry than to be on fire with passion.[15]

Whether or not there was a time when he could have elected celibacy, an individual's difficulties can show him that, now at least, marriage is the state that God desires for him.

St. Methodius, the talented bishop of Olympus, who was martyred in 311, compares a person of this type to a sick man who would die if he did not eat on the Easter Vigil, though the rest of the Church is observing the fast.[16] Later in the century some of the Greek Fathers speak in this vein. Even Chrysostom believes, as we have seen, that virginity is at some time possible to all. The unrest a man feels is a sign that he is called to marriage.[17]

Ambrose warns Latin-speaking Christians that each must consider his own strength to see how arduous a life he can embrace.[18] Even Jerome warns,

> In itself chastity is attractive and draws everyone to itself. But individual strength must be considered.[19]

These statements, made as some of them are by men who feel that all Christians are invited to the celibate life, may only refer to those who have not disposed themselves for that vocation. But another and more significant current of thought is evident during these same early years. Christ had spoken about a special gift. The same term reappears in Paul's letter to the Corinthians. To settle any doubts about whether a Christian should marry he tells them,

> I certainly wish you were all in the same state as I, but each one has his own gift from God, one to live in one way, another in another.[20]

His desires for them strike him as hopeless. However preferable virginity may be, it is simply not in God's plan for everyone. Some marry because they have declined the greater gift, but Paul implies that others are entering the state God intended for them from the beginning.

Around the year 300 Methodius of Olympus has one of the participants in his *Banquet of the Ten Maidens* remark,

> To me it seems that we can see clearly in the Scriptures that, after He brought virginity into the world, the Word of God did not wish to abrogate marriage entirely. Just because the moon is greater than the stars, the light of the other heavenly bodies is not at once extinguished.[21]

St. Philastrius, bishop of Brescia, whose book on the heresies current during the late 300's will be cited by Augustine, affirms that virginity, though desirable in itself, demands a grace that is not given to all.[22] Cyril, named bishop of Alexandria in 412 and acclaimed not only as an assailant of the Nestorian heresy but as the most perceptive Greek theologian since Origen, seems to share this opinion.

> He proposed it to those who wished to do well but did not put them under the yoke of any law, beause He knew that all cannot master the cravings of the flesh.[23]

A century later Fulgentius of Ruspe, though affirming, as has been noted, that theoretically everyone may receive the higher gift, also feels that, whatever the reason be, some are not offered any gift but marriage.[24]

Among the Schoolmen, Thomas is convinced that it is good for some to be virgins but not all. No one can follow this way of life without a special grace, and the grace is not given to everyone.[25] As proof, he cites both Paul and the observation in Matthew's Gospel that "Not all master this lesson." To him this whole matter is an application of Christ's parable of the talents. God gives virginity to one Christian, marriage to another.[26]

Even the Protestant attacks on monastic life do not provoke a more sweeping claim by Catholic theologians. Cajetan, the one dispatched by the Holy See to deal with the new situation in Germany, notes that Christ does not say virginity is reserved to

> those who have desired it. 'It depends not on the one who wishes or the one who runs but on the merciful God' who gives the gift of practicing celibacy.[27]

This is the mind of Jesuit spiritual writers during the early 1600's. De la Puente admits that marriage has its burdens but feels that some should bear them for the glory of God.[28] Alvarez de Paz writes,

> Not all understand the preeminence and peace of chastity . . . only those who have received from God the gift of understanding

it. . . . Therefore there need be no fear that the human race will lack the propagation necessary to it and will abruptly cease to exist.[29]

Maldonado, one of the better known Biblical scholars of this period, will not even admit the claim that a special gift from God is needed to live a celibate life but not to understand its advantages.

Even to understand it is a gift from God, as Christ Himself declares in John's gospel. 'No one can come to Me unless my Father, who sent Me, draws him.'[30]

During the 1890's a significant statement occurs in a letter of Leo XIII.

Virginity is indeed in itself more outstanding . . . but this gift of perfect continence is not given to all; and in that case, according to the words of the Apostle, 'It is better to marry than to be on fire with passion.'

In similar fashion the malice or weakness of human nature can sometimes bring it about that . . . sinful dealings between the sexes have become too habitual in the case of certain couples for them to forego marriage without . . . the danger of losing eternal salvation.[31]

Noteworthy here is the distinction he makes between those who have simply not received any other gift and those whose personal defects are what suggest marriage.

Among the better known theologians of the decade after World War I, Billot declares,

It is entirely false that all men should be indiscriminately invited to things which are better in themselves. In the order of God's Providence there is no place for that fantasy which people call equality. On the contrary, from the inequality of ranks, vocations, offices, and other things of this type arises the needed perfection of the social body. 'For if the whole body were eye,' says the Apostle, 'where would the hearing be?'[32]

Pius XII discusses the question in his encyclical on virginity. After repeating that this way of life demands a gift which all do not receive, he warns candidates for religious life, and the superiors who must admit them, to investigate carefully whether they seem to have it.

For in the case of many people, the burden of perpetual continence is undoubtedly too great to be recommended.[33]

It does not seem rash to conclude from these different indications that some are never intended by God for any state but marriage.

St. Luke's Gospel seems to go farther. Elizabeth's joy that she is no longer barren recalls the Old Testament view that marriage is the normal state of God-fearing men,[34] and a saying of Christ includes a significant detail about life in the age of the New Covenant.

People went on eating and drinking, marrying and giving in marriage, up to the day when Noe entered the Ark; then the flood burst and destroyed every living soul. . . . The very same will happen when the Son of Man reveals Himself.[35]

Men will be going about their usual concerns, and among the details chosen to illustrate this are eating, drinking, and marriage. In God's providence most men will be working out their destiny in pairs.

Paul, as has been noted, saw personal disturbances as a sign to a Christian that he should marry. He goes on to apply this norm to actual cases.

Now concerning the matters about which you wrote me: It is well for a man to have no intimate relations with woman. Yet to avoid the danger of fornication every man should have a wife of his own, and every woman should have a husband of her own.[36]

Even among the pagans of this time Corinth is a byword for sexual immorality. Paul feels that the life best suited to the average Corinthian, and therefore the one intended for him by God, is marriage.

Though he does urge widows not to marry again, he speaks in a different vein a few years later.

But refuse to enroll younger widows, because when they wantonly turn away from Christ, they wish to marry; thus they incur condemnation because they have broken their prior pledge . . . I desire, therefore, that the younger widows should marry, bear children, manage their households, and thus give the adversary no occasion to criticize them. For already some have strayed after Satan.[37]

Advice of this kind to whole groups of people seems to imply that the average Christian's gift is marriage.

A passage in the Acts of the Apostles tends to confirm this impression.

This man, therefore, set himself to speak with firm assurance in the synagogue, and, on hearing him, Priscilla and Aquila took him home and expounded the Way of God to him more precisely.[38]

It was this couple who were Paul's hosts at Corinth and who left with him for Syria. Typical Christians are walking this new Way of God in pairs.

Around the year 300 St. Methodius of Olympus sees an allusion to this question in the Apocalypse, where John speaks of the virgins who follow the Lamb.

He wishes also to teach us here that the multitude of virgins has been set from the beginning at so small a number (144,000), while the multitude of the other saints is infinite. For we must notice what he implies when he describes the others. 'Suddenly there appeared a great multitude that no one could number, from all nations and tribes and peoples and tongues, standing before the throne and before the Lamb.'[39]

Working from a different text, Ambrose arrives at the same conclusion.

The Lord, who knew that virginity should be preached to all but put into practice by few, says, 'Not all master this lesson, but only such as have received a special gift.' In other words, virginity is not something for the multitude, something common to many. It is not permitted in view of a person's infirmity but granted in view of his virtue.[40]

The thoughtful guide points out many roads, so that each may travel by the one he thinks is suited to him as long as he comes upon one by which he can press forward to the camp. The road of virginity is good, but high and hard. It calls for more than ordinary strength. Good too is the road of widowhood, not so hard as the higher road, but bumpy and rough and demanding more caution. Good too is the road of marriage. Flat and extending the entire distance, leading to the camp of the saints by a somewhat roundabout way, it receives the largest number.[41]

One of Jerome's arguments against Jovinian, though it does not establish what his opinion really is, at least removes him from the number of those who reflect a constant conviction that all are called to virginity.

You say, 'If all were virgins, how would the human race survive?' . . . Have no fear that all will be virgins. A difficult thing is virginity and therefore rare because difficult. . . . If all could be virgins, would even the Lord say, 'He who can grasp this, let him grasp it.'?[42]

We have seen how both Aquinas in the Middle Ages and Billot in more modern times feel that there are individuals who are never offered the gift of celibacy. Both of them go on to suggest that this is actually true of most people in the Church. Thomas is convinced that "the common virtue of men" is not equal to such a life.[43] Billot adds,

As a matter of fact, there are very few, relatively speaking, whom it is wise to impel to perfect continence.[44]

Pius XII expresses his own conviction on more than one occasion.

Other young people—the vast majority—are called by God to be His co-workers in the production of new life. See that they know the beauty of Christian love and . . . taste the happiness of an untainted purity.[45]

Some of you—not all of you, and not even most of you—will be called by God to consecrated virginity . . . There are others among you—and they are the great majority—whom God has called or will call soon to be flowers which do not remain as they are because they are to bear fruit one day, please God, in a holy Christian home.[46]

Marriage is not the ideal way to God. In fact, some aspects of married life make it more difficult to serve Him. And yet this is the life He provides for the vast majority of Christians, either because they have never disposed themselves for any other calling or, as seems more likely, because when He decides in accord with the providence by which He directs the world that they, with their individual dispositions and individual roles in His universe, shall exist, He never intends any other state for them but marriage. The conclusion from either supposition is the same. Though each human being has his own completeness and autonomy, and his relationship with God retains that privacy which is typical of love, our usual way of regarding religion in terms of the individual and God has an emphasis which is really false. Most human beings born into this world are intended to save their souls in pairs. For most, the words of Genesis are literally true: "It is not good that the man be alone."

Virginity itself, as it is first proposed in the Gospel, reveals a still deeper aspect of this truth. Christ, it should be noted, lists three distinct classes of people who do not marry.

As there are those barred from marrying by a natural defect and those barred by an act of man, so there are those who bar themselves from marrying for the sake of the kingdom of heaven.[47]

He does not say that there is some advantage in merely being unmarried. Everything depends on the reason why. The only ones He singles out for praise are "those who bar themselves from marrying for the sake of the kingdom of heaven."

Paul speaks in the same vein. What he recommends is not so much virginity as the combination of virginity and undivided attention to God.[48]

Catholics in Italy during the late 300's are instructed very clearly on this point. Forsaking marriage is good only if their motive is to be freer for the service of God.[49] A few years later Augustine declares,

What we preach about virgins is not that they are virgin but that they are virgins dedicated to God by pious continence. I would not feel rash in saying that to me a married woman seems better off than a girl who is eventually to be married. She has what the girl is still anxiously seeking, especially if the girl is not yet even spoken for. The wife is eager to please one person to whom she has been given, the girl to please many, because she does not know to whom she is to be given. . . .

Therefore the virgin who deserves to be ranked above a married woman is the one who neither presents herself to many to be loved, because she is seeking the love of one of those many, nor adorns herself for one she has already found, thinking about the things of the world, how to please her husband, but instead has loved the most handsome among the children of men and loved Him so deeply that, since she could not conceive Him in her flesh like Mary, she keeps even her flesh intact for Him. For He has been conceived in her heart.[50]

With heretical groups around the year 500 still looking on marriage as evil, the faithful are warned,

Continence is better but is not of itself enough to win the joys of heaven if it is kept from mere fastidiousness, only if it is chosen with affection for the sake of being occupied with the Lord.[51]

According to one commentator during the 800's,

Many there are who have integrity of the body but are not virgins in mind. If they could, they would already have married.[52]

The Schoolmen are fond of repeating a statement of Augustine's that the virginity of the Apostle John was not superior to Abraham's marriage. If God does not wish virginity and it is not practiced as a means of being more completely at His disposal, there is no advantage in it.[53]

During the 1300's Pierre de la Palu maintains, as had others, that Our Lady must have consecrated her virginity to God by a vow. By way of proof he quotes Augustine's dictum:

Virginity is praised not because it is virginity but because it is dedicated to God.[54]

This theme is repeated during the Counter-Reformation,[55] and in our own day Pius XII makes it the basis of his entire treatment of virginity.

As the holy Fathers and Doctors of the Church have very clearly taught, virginity is not a Christian virtue unless we embrace it 'for the sake of the kingdom of heaven,' that is, unless we make it our way of life because we desire to give our time more easily to the things of God, have a securer means of arriving at last at eternal happiness, and conduct others to the kingdom of heaven more readily by making this our full-time concern.[56]

The Church's constant praise of virginity has disconcerted not a few religious men. They see the single life as a frustration, the tragedy of a personality that will never come to fruition, never use all its latent powers. They have seen crochety bachelors or eccentric old maids, and to praise such a condition seems monstrous.

If those who would like to marry but have never been able to can see their situation as an opportunity to consecrate their years on earth to God and their neighbor, then the Church's praise of virginity applies to them. But if they never really accept what has befallen them, or if they give no special thought to making their inescapable way of life a form of consecration to God, they are among the first two classes named by Christ, "those who are barred from marriage," and neither He nor the Church has claimed that theirs is a higher calling.

Granted then, that those whom God has invited to dedicate their virginity to Him have received a greater gift than married couples, both they and the married couples are better off than the person who has not entered either state. It is only consecrated virginity which has the advantages, and this because of special help from God.

Consecrated virginity is thus the ultimate proof that sex is not a peripheral quality of human nature, designed exclusively for begetting children. It pervades the entire person. It is one of two distinctive ways of tending with all the thrust of life itself toward a total gift to another person. Virginity that is consecrated does not suppress this drive. It turns it in a new direction. The other person, the beloved, the one-and-only, is God Himself. The nun is not simply a woman who does not marry. She is a woman whose spouse is Christ.

"It is not good that the man be alone," because God has not made him psychologically neutral. Men and women are designed by the very nature that makes them human beings for a spiritual life in pairs.

PART III

"I must make him a helpmate . . ."

INTRODUCTION: SECTION I

THE PRESENCE OF YAHWEH

It is God's idea that Adam have a helpmate, and it is He who presents her to him:

Yahweh God fashioned a woman and led her to the man.[1]

This narrative, as we have seen, is intended by its author to do more than recount the past. It is somehow the story of every marriage. Apparently that episode in most men's life on earth, the day on which they marry, involves them in some unusual way with God.

This impression is deepened by the Canticle of Canticles. Of course, the meaning of this book depends on a question: What kind of poetry is it? The answer is suggested by the allusions of other Old Testament authors to traditional songs with alternating verses which engaged couples sang to each other.[2]

The Canticle of Canticles is thus intended to teach only in the way a lyric poem teaches. It reflects a state of soul, an experience of life, the experience of two people about to be married.

This does not mean that it was composed to celebrate human love. The Jews never made such precisions. Like the Psalmist who surveys the world around him and exclaims, "How amazing is your Name over all the earth!"[3] the author of the Canticle is reacting to one of the wonders of life: the way two human beings

begin to live as one. This marvel too suggests the presence of
Yahweh.

In the Book of Tobit, which dates from the third or second
century before Christ, the connection with God emerges more
clearly. Perhaps this charming story of an old couple whose
fidelity to Him is tested and two newlyweds whose marriage is
arranged by Him, has its origin in events which really happened.
No one can say, and it does not seem to matter to the author. He
has taken such obvious liberties with history and geography that
his intent is plain. This is a wisdom book. By presenting the example of these two model couples, he is exhorting the reader to
be like them.

The significant passage for our investigation is the prayer of
the newlyweds, Sara and Tobias, on their first night together:

> It is You who created Adam.
> It is You who created Eve his wife . . .
> It is You who said,
> 'Man must not remain alone.
> Let us make him a helpmate like himself.'[4]

As the Old Testament authors see it, marriage is somehow religious. It evokes a feeling of awe. It has the air of something
pervaded by God.

15 *THE NATURE OF MARRIAGE*

THOUGH THE MOST NOTABLE PERSONNAGE in Jerusalem during the late 300's was Cyril, the bishop, that name is in history chiefly because of an accident. Someone in his congregation decided to copy down the instructions he was giving to recent converts during Lent and Eastertime.

An invaluable picture of the Church in that area, these eighteen discourses show the attitude that a prospective Christian was given toward marriage.

What has the gravity and holiness of the Church to do with the accursed institutions of the Manichaeans? Here marriage is holy.[1]

The mind of the Church in Rome at this time is evident from a letter of Pope St. Siricius,

As for the veiling of a girl for marriage, you have asked if a man may take to himself a girl who has been pledged to another. We absolutely forbid that this be done. In the minds of the faithful it is a sacrilege of some sort if that blessing which the priest has imposed upon a girl to be married is violated by some transgression.[2]

The ordinary Christian of this period takes it for granted that marriage is associated with God.

This conviction is shared by the Latin Fathers[3] and later by medieval theologians.[4] In fact, during the early 1200's Pope Innocent III insists that marriage is due "not to something that man has devised but rather to the authority of God."[5]

This is equally true of marriage "among believers and non-believers."[6]

His successor, Honorius III, concludes,

Since marriage is something sacred not only among Latins and Greeks but also among believers and non-believers, it will not be permitted to recede from the strictness of the Church's laws about it.[7]

Among the more prominent of the Schoolmen who lecture at Paris during this century, Alexander of Hales insists that marriage is more than just a way of life.[8] If it falls within the ambit of the natural law, this is because the natural law prevails

even in regard to things which take place in some extraordinary way.[9]

Bonaventure explains this. Marriage is not so entirely a matter of the natural law that God's will was known to man only through the promptings of conscience. It was founded in a special way. God gave Adam an illumination by which he realized he should take Eve as his wife and that later men and women should likewise marry.[10]

Thomas agrees that marriage did not originate merely in the sense that man's conscience told him what to do. It was established by some more positive act of God.[11] This was necessary, according to Scotus, because,

It is self-evident that the law of nature makes little impression on many.[12]

During the 1300's Pierre de la Palu concludes that as a man who had marital relations exclusively for the pleasure involved would be guilty of sin, so one who would marry for the same motive would be guilty of greater sin because he has abused something sacred. The two of them are like two men who drink immoderately, one from a cup, the other from a chalice used at Mass.[13]

Denis the Carthusian's view of God's role in a marriage leads him to affirm that,

The husband and wife ought to pay each other mutual honor and deserve to be honored in some way by others.[14]

The first Protestants launch an attack not only against the notion of consecrated virginity but also against this view of marriage. To Calvin, marriage is no more religious than "agriculture, architecture, shoemaking and many other things."[15] Luther advises that

ministers interfere not in matrimonial questions. First, because we have enough to do in our own office; secondly, because these affairs concern not the Church but are temporal things, pertaining to temporal rulers. Therefore we must leave them to the lawyers and magistrates.[16]

The Catholic reaction is to look more closely at the role of God in a marriage. The result is evident from the Roman Catechism, issued at the Council of Trent's bequest for the guidance of priests. A prospective bride and groom

. . . should realize that they are approaching something that is not human but divine. The examples of the Fathers of the Old Law make it plain enough that it calls for an unusual purity of intention and religious spirit. Their marriages were not endowed with the dignity of a sacrament, and yet they thought that they should be conducted with the deepest religious feeling and personal holiness.[17]

Bishops like St. Charles Borromeo are soon telling their priests,

The nature and holiness of marriage require a religious preparation of the soul. Since lay people do not understand this very well,
it happens that they sin gravely in something which they should
enter upon in a holy manner. The pastor is to give his people frequent instructions on this point when the opportunity arises, and for
these let him use the words and doctrine of the Roman Catechism.[18]

Walks of Life, by the Jesuit, Peter Buys, who had worked
with Canisius on his celebrated catechism, is still more explicit
about the difference between marriage and other things that
come from God.

There are no grounds for someone to object that the mating of
animals and the creation of farmers, shoemakers and tailors, in fact
of the entire world, are from God and yet no special preeminence
appears in them . . . Christ and the Apostles clearly declare that
marriage is more than a natural and civil union of man and woman.
The union itself is also a symbol of something sacred and represents
to us a reality that is most holy.[19]

Others too in this and the following century see marriage as
something more than a "purely civil society."[20] Toward the end
of the 1800's a definitive expression of the Church's view appears
in an encyclical of Leo XIII.

Marriage has God as its founder and was, even from the beginning, a kind of foreshadowing of the Incarnation of God. Therefore,
there is something in it that is sacred and religious, not adventitious
but inborn, not agreed upon by men but inserted by nature.[21]

In this present century Cardinal Billot feels that

As a way of life in the natural order of things, marriage is not
sacred in its being. And yet it does have an intrinsic relation to those
sacred actions in which worship of God consists, inasmuch as it is
mainly directed toward raising worshippers of God.[22]

But Pius XI's encyclical on marriage not so many years later seems to imply that it has something more.

Even by the light of reason alone, especially if the ancient monuments of history are studied, the constant sentiment of the people examined, the institutions and customs of all races consulted, it will be evident enough that there is something sacred and religious even in natural marriage, 'not added to it but inborn, not agreed to by men but inserted by nature.'[23]

Though he says that the human mind can know this even without the help of faith, he does not deny that, as happens with other religious truths, the actual historical condition of mankind may make it impossible for some to use this native ability. But whatever unaided reason may be able to discern, it is clear at least from revelation that couples who treat their marriage as something no more religious than work or politics are like tourists who stroll through a cathedral in shorts, chatting and taking pictures.

Civil society is a work of God's providence. Its rulers share His authority. Its essential purpose and some of the norms which govern the life of a citizen are presented by the natural law, speaking through conscience, as something given, something we may not tamper with. But that other "natural" society, marriage, is all this and something more. It did not begin in quite the same way as did the state. Somehow God took part in the process more directly. And to say merely that it is good is to fall short of the truth. It is awesome. It involves a person in some unusual way with God. The act by which a man and woman become life-companions must be ranked with prayer and sacrifice among things that are essentially religious.

The Gospel points to another feature when the couple are Christians.

Two days later a wedding took place at Cana. . . .[24]

John presents this episode as one of Jesus' "signs."[25] To under-stand it we have to recall that the Gospels were intended to help Christians appreciate not only the life of Christ but their own new life.[26] This account of the wedding feast at Cana, so crammed with symbols, is, among other things, a reminder that marriage, already holy, has a new holiness when the bride and groom are in the Church.[27]

During the early 400's Augustine concludes that this would make adultery a different and more serious sin for Christians.[28]

The year after his death a new name comes into prominence at the Council of Ephesus: Cyril, bishop of Alexandria, Father of the Church, leader of the attack against the Nestorians. His gen-eral agreement with Augustine's view is apparent in a com-mentary on the events at Cana.

Since the wedding is celebrated chastely and honorably, the mother of the Savior is indeed there; and He himself, invited along with His disciples, comes not so much to dine as to perform a miracle and also to sanctify the source of man's bodily generation.

For it was fitting that He who was to renew the very nature of man and recall the whole of it to a better state, should not only im-part a blessing on those who had already been brought to birth but also prepare grace for those to be born later and make their birth holy.

Honorable marriage is made holy and the curse against women removed. They will no longer bear children in sorrow now that Christ has blessed the very starting point of our generation.[29]

St. Maximus, the noted preacher and bishop of Turin, reflects the mind of the Western Church during the middle years of this century.

The Son of God goes to the wedding so that what He has for-merly instituted by His power He may make holy on this occasion by the blessing of His presence.[30]

During the Middle Ages the Schoolmen repeat that marriage is now doubly holy. God founded it in the beginning, and Christ consecrated it anew by His presence at Cana.[31] Albert the Great explains that,

Nothing prevents marriage from thus having two or even three inaugurations by God: one for nature in itself, another for corrupted nature, and a third in accord with the condition of nature restored by Christ.[32]

This view is shared by later writers.[33] During the time of the Council of Trent Salmeron explains how much that episode at Cana should mean to every married couple.

The wedded state might possibly have seemed to be frowned upon by Christ, especially since it involves amazing annoyances and an almost continual cross which devout married people are supposed to accept as theirs.

Then, too, marriage seems to have nothing great when it comes to outward appearances. In fact, it seems to concern only those who are less perfect. Virginity and celibacy are things which impress everyone; and, what is more, they are commended by Christ and St. Paul.

Add to this the fact that marriage, since olden times, had been hearing little praise from the wise men of the world. Cato . . . Theophrastus . . . Cicero . . . It could thus have seemed that all was over for married people.

This is why by His presence and miracle Jesus had to make marriage honorable and teach that it is a state which God approves of. This alone ought to make all the annoyances of marriage easier to bear.

If Jesus is invited to it, He will be on hand for it, making it holy and providing for the couple's future needs. For by this miracle He seems to oblige Himself and give His word, as it were, that He will be present at marriage and that there will be money and food and clothing enough if they summon the Lord.[34]

The great French preachers of the 1600's speak of this new intervention by Christ;[35] and Matthias Scheeben, whose *Mys-*

teries of the Christian Religion has been acclaimed now for over a century, shows how different it has made Christian marriage.

The matrimonial relationship between Christians is rendered supernaturally holy from every point of view: by reason of the supernatural character of the married couple themselves, the supernatural end, and the sublime intervention of God, to whom husband and wife are so closely linked. And this holiness is greater and more excellent than the holiness of marriage in the Garden of Eden. . . .[36]

A few years later Leo XIII calls attention to one result of this change.

When He had fashioned marriage anew to such a peak of excellence, Christ confided and entrusted the whole regulation of it to the Church. In every time and place she has exercised this power over marriage and in such a way that it appeared to be exclusively her own, not sought from the consent of men but possessed by the will of God its founder.[37]

Pius XI affirms that this view of marriage is a constant element in Christian tradition,[38] and this tradition is summarized by Pius XII.

Jesus and Mary, by their presence, sanctified the wedding of Cana. There the divine Son of the Virgin performed His first miracle as though to announce that He was inaugurating His mission in the world and the Kingdom of God by sanctifying the family and the marriage union, the source of life.[39]

Baptized human beings—soul, body, entire person—are different, and for such a man and woman marriage is also different. As the Old Testament's history of salvation begins with God presenting a woman to a man to be his wife, so the Gospel account of Christ's redemptive "signs" begins with Him making marriage something even holier than it had been before.

But why has all this happened? Why is even a pagan marriage so hallowed by His presence? Why does He enter so directly into this one area of human life?

In the Old Testament we find the beginning at least of an answer.

INTRODUCTION: SECTION II
THE WILL OF YAHWEH

IN HIS TREATMENT of different types of discernment Ben Sira observes,

> A woman accepts any husband at all,
> But there are some girls more beautiful than others.[1]

When it comes to selecting a life-companion, people should do what they can, a woman putting up with her tactical disadvantage, a man making use of the freedom and range of choice that his role in society gives him.

But the book of Genesis suggests that they are not really left on their own.

In the second chapter, after God says, "I must make him a helpmate," He sets about fashioning Eve and then conducts her to Adam. Since the author is presenting this story about the past to explain the present, the impression arises that God not only arranges that there should be such a thing as marriage but presents every wife to every husband. In a later chapter of Genesis this is suggested clearly. Abraham's servant, pledged to find a wife for his master's son, prays,

> Yahweh, God of my master Abraham, be propitious to me today and show your good will toward my master Abraham. Here I am near the spring, and the daughters of the townspeople are coming out

to draw water. Let the girl to whom I shall say, 'Let your pitcher down so that I can drink' and who shall reply, 'Drink, and I shall also water your camels,' be the one You have destined for your servant Isaac, and from this let me see your good will toward my master.[2]

When Rebecca gives the sign he had prayed for and he asks permission to take her away, Laban and Bethuel tell him,

This has all come from Yahweh. It is not for us to tell you yes or no. Rebecca is here before you. Take her and go, and let her become the wife of your master's son as Yahweh has said.[3]

And when they want Rebecca to delay awhile, he protests,

Do not keep me back. It is Yahweh who has led me to what I was seeking.[4]

This is only the account of one particular instance in which God had a certain woman in mind to be a man's wife. But these chapters of Genesis are religious folklore. Even when the events are historical, they embody certain perennial truths. Abraham and Isaac and Jacob are described with traits that the Jews saw in themselves.[5] This account of Isaac's marriage shows what the author is taking for granted as God's role in the marriage of a man who has tried to serve Him.

Later in Psalm 128, which was sung on pilgrimages to Jerusalem and used in the Temple worship, we read,

> Your wife shall be a fruitful vine
> In the inner court of your house,
> Your sons young olive trees
> Around the table.
> See how he shall be blessed,
> The man who fears Yahweh.[6]

It has already been noted how the prophets include weddings among the signs of God's favor. Now a fruitful wife is described as a reward God gives to those who serve Him.

The Book of Proverbs, completed after the Jews returned from exile in 539 B.C., imitates the style of earlier Old Testament books, because its aim is to guide the man who wants to make a success of his life by presenting him with the best of traditional wisdom. In this vein it tells him,

> A house and wealth are inherited from parents,
> But a sensible wife is a gift from Yahweh.[7]

Since every good thing that comes to a man comes from Yahweh, the contrast here seems to imply that there is something special in the providence by which He provides a wife. This is certainly the mind of Ben Sira:

> A capable wife is a choice inheritance
> Awarded to those who fear the Lord.[8]

> A silent wife is a gift from the Lord. . . .[9]

God rewards the man who does His will by seeing that he receives a certain woman as his wife.

The Book of Tobit is still more emphatic about His initiative in a marriage. In this tale of model Jewish life, when young Tobias fears that he will die like the others who had been wedded to Sara, the angel tells him,

Do not be afraid. She has been destined for you from the beginning. You are the one who is to save her.[10]

Sara's father is also convinced of this but, unaware of the angel's identity, he sees the will of Yahweh expressed in a more normal way.

Since she is given to you by the terms of the law of Moses, it is Heaven who decrees that she be given to you. . . . The Lord of Heaven will be favorable to you this night, my child, and will grant you His favor and His peace.[11]

This theme reaches a climax in the prayer of the newlyweds:

> It is You who created Adam.
> It is You who created Eve his wife
> To be his help and support,
> And from those two has been born the human race.
> It is You who said:
> 'Man must not remain alone.
> Let us make him a helpmate like himself.'
> And now it is not my own delight
> That I seek in taking my beloved.
> One thought is in my heart: to do Your will.
> Deign to have pity on her and me
> And lead us together to old age.[12]

Not only has God arranged that these two work out their lives together, but they are aware of His design and enter marriage precisely in order to cooperate with it.

To treat this as an isolated case would be to ignore both the literary form of the book and the mentality of its author. This bride and groom are presented to the Chosen People as an ideal. The implication is that for the young man or woman who has tried to serve Him, God has a particular spouse in mind. When they marry it will be because they realize that this is His will.

16 *THE SACRED PLEDGE*

THE GOSPEL THROWS a new light on this role of God in an individual marriage. When the Pharisees try to learn whether Our Lord favors their stricter or more liberal set of requirements for a divorce, He tells them,

> What God has yoked together man may not separate.[1]

The significant point for our present study is not His prohibition of divorce but the reason He gives. Though all human undertakings are in some sense the work of God, this one is His work in a way so superior that neither the couple themselves nor any human authority may presume to tamper with it.

And Christ is alluding to something more than marriage as an institution. It is an individual marriage that would be ended by a divorce, and the reason He gives why no human authority may grant one is that God was involved in the act by which that particular man became the husband of that particular woman.

Tertullian shows how this is understood by Christians toward the end of the following century. The oath of a Roman recruit, given as was supposed in the presence of the gods, was regarded as making him a sacred person. Tertullian, who has already called baptism a soldier's oath to Christ, now sees marriage too as a *sacramentum*, a pledge-taking which involves a person with God.[2]

Augustine, after explaining that "When symbols have some connection with divine things, they are called 'sacraments,' "[3] uses that term to describe the pact by which a couple take each other for husband and wife.[4] This sacred and symbolic pledge is one of the three good things he finds in marriage.[5]

The liturgy during these years reminds a bride that by this rite she is being designated for the service of God,[6] and as the medieval Church begins to assume its distinctive features, there are different indications of a conviction that God is involved in the marriage pledge. The earliest writers allude to the third asset that Augustine had seen in marriage, the *sacramentum*.[7] Couples are ordered to pledge their troth in the presence of a priest, but a clandestine marriage is held as inviolable. It will not be until the Council of Trent that the presence of a priest as official witness is made essential in ordinary circumstances for the pledge to be valid.[8] The holiness of a wedding is apparently not supplied by the priest or the ceremonies. God is involved in the very act by which the couple pledge themselves to each other as husband and wife.[9]

As St. Victor's in Paris becomes a center of the new progress in theology during the 1100's, Hugh of St. Victor reflects on Augustine's concept of the *sacramentum* and notes that for a true marriage there need not be either children or fidelity, but there must be this sacred pledge.[10] And as the Schoolmen of the following century try to determine what it is that establishes the connection between the couple and God, they agree that it is this very act of taking each other as husband and wife.[11] In confession a priest is the means of establishing contact, but as Aquinas notes,

In marriage our actions are a cause sufficient to induce the immediate effect, which is the obligation; for whoever is capable of acting in his own name is capable of obliging himself to another. And therefore the blessing of the priest is not required in marriage as of the essence of the sacrament.[12]

During the 1300's laymen are told,

Vows differ from one another. Some are never dispensed, for example the marriage vow. Though made in the hands of the priest, it is still as sacred as though vowed to God in His open divine presence.[13]

The agreement of subsequent theologians with this position[14] is strengthened by the Council of Trent's directive,

The bishops must be careful to see that weddings take place with the modesty and uprightness that is fitting. Marriage is a holy thing and should be dealt with in a holy manner.[15]

But a discordant note is struck by one of that century's leading theologians. Melchior Cano insists that it is the priest's blessing which involves God in an individual marriage. As for the pledge itself,

I deny that that matter has any connection with faith and religion.[16]

Though a few in later years will also take this position,[17] Dominic Soto, Cano's fellow-professor at Salamanca, has a refutation published before Cano's idea is even in print and claims he has never encountered such an opinion in the Church before.[18] Salmeron, alluding to Trent's new regulation that from now on a priest will normally be required for a valid marriage, insists,

This does not make the pastor of the couple the minister of the sacrament of matrimony. He is necessary now the way two or three witnesses are required as necessary.[19]

During the late 1600's Segneri, whose missions to country parishes are making him known all over Italy, calls their attention to the dignity of a bride and groom. Since baptism by laymen is an emergency measure, this is the only time when laymen are consecrated precisely for a sacred function. Even a priest is incompetent to perform that function for them.[20]

From this time on, canon law and papal encyclicals begin to give authoritative expression to the conviction that the act by which a couple take each other as husband and wife cannot be a genuine pledge of marriage without involving the presence of God.[21] Pius XII tells a group of newlyweds,

> You gleam in our eyes, not only with the dignity with which you are marked by the mystic chrism common to all the faithful, which has made you a holy nation and a royal priesthood, but also with that of ministers of the sacrament to which you have elevated your mutual consent.[22]

There is more here than on other occasions when men call upon God to witness some promise that they make. Those who make this pledge acquire a special dignity and holiness. They have been dealing with God in a most unusual way.

During the early 500's Fulgentius of Ruspe sees one reason for this in a fact which Christians have taken for granted.

> The Teacher of the Gentiles . . . asserts that, with absolutely equal rights, the wife has power over the body of her husband and the husband over the body of the wife. . . . But in another place he says, 'There is no authority except from God.'[23]

Though his intent is simply to show that sexual intercourse can hardly be intrinsically evil, this proof of his throws new light on the involvement of a bride and groom with God. The authority they will have over each other as husband and wife is something which they themselves cannot give. It can only come from Him.

To medieval theologians this is a case like having God's permission to sell oneself into slavery.[24]

A man and woman are entirely under the dominion of God, and the one would not be allowed to give his body into the power of the other unless the will and authority of the Lord agreed to this.[25]

When Protestant writers begin to deny that marriage is indissoluble, one answer given is that, since God alone has dominion over our person, no two human beings may make so complete a gift of themselves as marriage involves unless He gives them the right. And He does this only if the gift is permanent.[26]

Matthias Scheeben, whose lectures are drawing attention to the Cologne Seminary during the 1860's, sees this matter of authority as a reason why, even outside the Church, a wedding is something holy. The bride and groom are binding themselves, not just to each other, but to God. He is the one who receives their pledge. It is to Him that they are responsible for keeping their word. And if they are Catholics,

they can dispose of their bodies as generative principles only with the approval of Christ and according to the mind of Christ, for their bodies are no longer their own flesh but the flesh of Christ (1 Cor. 6, 15–20). They can unite with each other only on the basis of their oneness with Christ; the union of each with the divine Head is carried over into the union which they contract with each other.[27]

It is not entirely surprising that God should have so direct a part in a marriage pledge. The existence of new human beings will depend on this man and woman. And now it appears that there is a second reason. The effect of this total gift of oneself is so deep and all-pervading that His permission must be had to make it—not just His general approval of marriage but an authorization of this marriage to this particular person.

In fact, when the New Testament speaks of His part in a wedding, it alludes to something more than a mere permission.

17 *THE GIFT OF MARRIAGE*

CHRIST SAYS that not everyone can appreciate virginity,

> but only such as have received a special gift.[1]

The Gospel does not explain this "gift" nor does it ever apply the same term to marriage. But Paul does both.

> I certainly wish you were all in the same state as I, but each one has his own gift from God, one to live in one way, another in another.[2]

Marriage as well as virginity is due to one of these "gifts," and a later chapter of the same letter shows what this word means by connecting it with an Old Testament tradition.

The Hebrew word *Ruah*, wind or breath, had at times a special religious meaning. A *Ruah* that issues from Yahweh gives life and order to the world.[3] It also fills certain men, giving them the ability for some role He desires them to play in the life of His people, some work which will benefit not so much themselves as this community chosen from among all nations and set apart as His own. Not only Moses and prophets and kings but musicians and the artisans who work on the Temple receive this *Ruah* of God.[4]

At Pentecost a sound like the wind is heard by the Apostles, and the mysterious divine person who then transforms them,

fitting them for their role in the lives of the new Chosen People,
is at once called the *Ruah,* the Spirit of God. Through baptism
this Spirit is imparted to other men, and Paul tells the Corinthians,

There is a distribution of gifts, but the same Spirit distributes them.
There is a distribution of ministrations, but it is the same Lord to
whom we minister. There is a distribution of activities, but it is the
same God who activates them all in everyone. The manifestation of
the Spirit is given to each individual for the common good. . . .

For example, just as the body is a unit, although it has many members, and all the members of the body, many though they are, are but
one body, so too is Christ. . . .

Suppose the foot should say, 'Because I am not a hand, I am no
part of the body,' is it for all that no part of the body? And suppose
the ear should say, 'Because I am not an eye, I am no part of the
body,' is it for all that no part of the body? If the whole body were
eye, where would the hearing be? If the whole body were hearing,
where would the sense of smell be? But as it is, there are certainly
many members, but a unified body. The eye cannot say to the hand,
'I have no need of you. . . .'

You are Christ's body and individually its members. And God has
established in his Church some in the first rank, namely apostles,
others in the second rank, namely fervent preachers, and still others
in the third rank, namely teachers. After that come wonder-workers,
then those with gift of healing, then assistants, administrators, and
those that speak a variety of languages.[5]

Each Christian has a "gift" from the Spirit which will make him
the reason for some aspect of the Church's life and growth. If
marriage is one of these gifts, if it is classed with virginity and
the role of the twelve Apostles among the different functions
which the Spirit assigns to members of the Mystical Body of
Christ, one cannot help but recall the words which the Letter
to the Hebrews says of the priesthood:

And no man takes the honor to himself; he takes it who is called by
God. . . .[6]

God is involved in every marriage, and not merely to authorize the pledge. Paul seems to imply that the initiative is with Him. Christian marriage is a commission to a certain rank, a designation to a certain function.

This adds a whole new dimension to the relationship of husband and wife. It is God who has given them to each other—and not just for their own sakes. The welfare of the Mystical Body of Christ is what the Spirit has in mind when He determines what different ways of life there shall be in the Church and who shall be called to each of them. Not only their own lives but the life of the Mystical Body is to depend on how they live together. This will be obvious when they have children, but there is no reason to regard this influence as limited to them. Paul says simply that the Spirit distributes these callings with an eye to the good of the Church. How the Church is to benefit from each individual married couple is a question which only He can answer.

During the early 200's this same awareness of God's initiative appears in Clement of Alexandria's warning about the reason a Christian should have for marrying.

He eats and drinks and takes a wife, not for their own sake and as his chief concern, but led by necessity. And when I say takes a wife, I mean if the Word has said to.[7]

All things are to be subordinated to God. Though a Christian has practical needs and sees marriage, like food and drink, as the answer to one of them, the will of Christ should still be a factor in his decision.

A century later Eusebius, bishop of Caesarea in Palestine and author of a well known history of the early Church, makes a significant comparison between marriage and virginity.

Two kinds of life have been set up in the Church of Christ, one really outstanding and exceeding the common practice of men. . . . The other . . . allows a modest use of marriage and the procreation of children.[8]

Toward the end of that century Gregory Nazianzen empha-
sizes how the two are related to each other in the life of the
Church.

> Marriage is good, but I cannot say that it is superior to virginity.
> . . . Do not take this hard, you who are under the yoke of marriage.
> 'God must be obeyed rather than men.'
> For the rest, see to it that you are bound to each other as by a
> chain, both virgins and wives, that you are one in the Lord, that each
> is the adornment of the other.
> There would not be a celibate unless there was marriage. Where
> would the virgin come from into this world? There would not be an
> honorable marriage and one that demanded respect unless it presented
> a virgin both to God and to this life.
> You the virgin, honor your mother too, for from her you have
> been born. You the wife, also pay honor to her who is from a mother
> and who is a mother. Indeed, she is not the mother but the spouse of
> Christ.[9]

St. Epiphanius, bishop of Salamis on the island of Cyprus and
a noted critic of Origen's views, gives a definite rank to the different callings—virginity, the hermit's life, widowhood, marriage
—[10] but insists that each is really a gift.

> The holy Church of God is like a ship. Now, a ship is fastened
> together, not from a single plank, but from many different ones. It
> has a keel of one kind of wood . . . then the anchors are of another
> kind . . . and the other things are all put together from material of
> different types.[11]

The Latin Fathers have their own way of seeing what Paul has
described in terms of a body. Ambrose finds

> this field of the Church fertile indeed, now bright with the flowers
> of virginity, now rich and ripe with the gravity of widowhood, now
> abounding in the fruits of marriage. For though different, they are
> the produce of one field.[12]

Though Jerome's great care is to defend virginity, he quotes Paul as proof that marriage is just as truly a gift of God.[13] Augustine points with awe to the words of Paul.

'Do you not know,' he says, 'that your bodies are the members of Christ?' So great, therefore, is the good of faithful wedlock that they are the very members of Christ.[14]

Though Roman law at this time still allows a divorce when the wife has proved to be barren, he warns his people that this is not for them. Their pledge to each other was no mere human contract. It was a *sacramentum*.

It is just as if there was an ordination of clerics for the sake of a lay congregation. Even if later there is no lay congregation, the sacred pledge of orders still remains in those who were ordained. And if for some fault a man is removed from office, he will not lack that mark of the Lord's sacred pledge that was once imposed, though it remains now as evidence for Judgment Day.[15]

Marriage does not confer an indelible imprint on the soul which gives it a greater share in the priesthood of Christ. But it does something similar. This pledge to each other makes a couple different. They have acquired something holy, a designation by God which even infidelity to the Church or to each other cannot remove until one of them dies.

In the East some fifty years after Augustine's death, Theodoret and later St. John of Damascus claim that Paul has explained how marriage is a gift in order to console married couples. Husbands and wives can see now that they as well as consecrated virgins have been favored by God.[16]

Fulgentius of Ruspe is more forthright.

The Lord Himself has bound them together with the bond of fidelity, favored them with the gift of His blessing, multiplied them by the addition of children. . . . For we confess that the fidelity of marriage is from God, and the love of the spouses and their fecundity. Since "Each has his own gift from God, etc.," we too recognize the distinctive rank of each gift and do not deny that each has been given to the faithful by God.[17]

Pope Gregory the Great is impressed by the sight of the Church as its members with their different gifts make their way through history.

The three daughters can also symbolize three classes of the faithful . . . shepherds, virgins and married people . . .[18]

Even before the coming of the Savior there were preachers and virgins and good married people who stood ready for His coming and, with the great thirst of desire, yearned to see Him. Also after His coming, as we see, there are preachers and virgins and good married people who no longer yearn for Our Savior to take flesh but long to see Him in the glory of His majesty.[19]

In his effort to impart the viewpoint of the Fathers to the new English Church, Bede the Venerable calls attention to a significant point about the life of Christ.

To lend approval to the choice of every rank and yet show the different merit of each, He deigns to be born of the stainless womb of Mary the Virgin, is blessed soon after His birth by the prophetic voice of Anna the widow, as a young man now is invited by those who are celebrating a wedding and honors them with the presence of His power.[20]

Commentators during the 800's find the New Testament explaining this in more detail.

By a comparison with the body he shows, not the nature of the members but that the functions are different and that no one ought to be anxious about the function he has since all are quickened by the same spirit.[21]

Each one who comes to the faith should remain in the state in which he has been called and realize that this state is a call from God.[22]

'From God,' he says in order to show that the good of marriage, though a lesser good, is still from Him, as the one whom we ask, if we do not have it, and thank if we do.[23]

We have put virginity over all but in such a way that we still recognize the order of marriage.[24]

That last phrase should be noted. By the year 1000 it is not uncommon to speak of the "order" of married people.[25] A century later Rupert of Deutz explains,

The tents of the true Israel and spiritual Jacob going on pilgrimage in this present age are the orders—God-fearing and well arranged in positions assigned by Christ—married people, the continent, widows and virgins. . . . These tents, each in its own way, are truly beautiful.[26]

The better known theologians of the time differ on the number of these "orders" in the Church but agree that one is composed of married people.[27] Popular writers of the 1200's take it for granted.[28] Robert of Sorbon, founder of the University of Paris, calls them a "sacred order,"[29] and the celebrated German preacher, Berthold of Ratisbonne, declares,

God has sanctified marriage more than any order in the world, more than the discalced friars, the friars preacher or the grey monks. In one point they cannot be compared with holy marriage: We cannot do without that order.
Therefore God has commanded it. The others He has only recommended. . . . How would heaven be filled without marriage?[30]

As a recent study has noted, "God as the term of all action and inclination is a favorite theme of Thomas."[31] This is apparent in his treatment of marriage. God, he explains, has a purpose for the universe as such, and every creature by its distinctive activity contributes to the overall process by which that purpose is to be achieved.

This process is governed by His providence, which is expressed to a great extent in the laws of nature. Thus nature inclines creatures to what is needed not just for their own perfection but for the good of the whole. In the case of human beings it inclines different men and women to different ways of life,

and so it happens that some elect marriage and some the contemplative life.[32]

In the order of things natural, the perfection which, as found in God, is simple and uniform could not be found in the universe of creatures except in different forms and in many beings. So too, the fullness of grace, which is unified in Christ as in the head, flows out in different ways to His members so that the body of the Church will be complete. . . .

Then too, there must be a way of assigning different men to different activities so that things will be done more readily and without confusion. . . .

Thirdly, this has a bearing on the Church's dignity and beauty, for these consist in a certain arrangement of things.[33]

During the 1400's there is still mention of different "states" of Christians,[34] and Denis the Carthusian concludes,

All cannot be induced to an equal perfection. One should be advised to remain in chastity, another to observe fidelity in marriage, for each of these is a gift of God.[35]

In his *Third ABC of the Spiritual Life*, so prized by saints and mystics during the 1500's, De Ossuna declares that married people belong to an order, not of Dominic or Francis or Peter, but one founded by the Father in Eden, approved by the Son at

Cana, and confirmed by the Holy Spirit, who gives the couple His grace on their wedding day.[36]

From this time on theologians keep repeating that marriage is as truly a gift of God as consecrated virginity.[37] During the 1800's Matthias Scheeben explains that, since husband and wife may use their marital rights only as God's instruments for producing new life, He does not merely accept their dedication of themselves to this goal. He himself consecrates them to it. They do not unite themselves. He unites them by means of their consent.[38] If there were nothing more than some positive law of His providence stating that married people be given help to reach their goal in life, marriage itself, the sacred pledge, would not be a thing so holy, for this is what gives them a new role in the Mystical Body and calls down grace from the Head.[39]

Cardinal Franzelin, one of the leaders in the planning for the first Vatican Council, observes that, when two Christians give themselves to each other as husband and wife, they are acting in the name and person of Christ.[40] In our own century Cardinal Billot sees this designation by Christ as the reason why marriage involves a sacrament while virginity does not. Other sacraments, especially the Eucharist, provide the help needed to achieve the aims of virginity. But marriage assigns the bride and groom to a special role which requires special help.[41] Pius XI concludes,

The holy enterprise of a real marriage is thus founded by the will of God and man together: the institution, aims, laws and assets of marriage are from God; and, by God's gift and help, each particular marriage comes from man.[42]

The same new insight by which Christianity perceived the darker aspects of married life has also disclosed a splendor in this way of life that Old Testament writers could not have suspected. A Christian bride and groom who pledge themselves to each other are receiving a marvelous gift from God, a function, a power, a designation to a life which is somehow to affect the

Mystical Body. This gift of God, this vocation, is as real as that of any priest or nun. To them as well as to His Apostles does Our Lord say,

You have not chosen Me. I have chosen you.[43]

A document from the earliest days of the Church explains in what sense He has chosen them.

18 *THE* PRONUBUS

Ignatius, who may well have been taught by Peter and Paul themselves and at any rate was bishop of Antioch by 70 A.D., writes in one of his celebrated letters to the churches he passed on his way to martyrdom,

> The proper thing is that an engaged couple enter upon marriage with the approval of the bishop. This way the marriage will be suited to the Lord and not to selfish desire. Let all things be to the honor of God.[1]

We have seen that the bride and groom themselves are the ministers of their marriage. Now the role of the clergy begins to be clear. This sacred event should be due to something more than the desire of a man and woman. Marriage is a gift of God. The approbation of His representative, the bishop, will show everyone concerned that He is willing to give His gift to this couple.

In the pagan marriage ceremony of the time there is a *Pronubus*, or best man, who joins the right hands of the bride and groom. Bas-reliefs also have Eros or Juno hovering overhead as a *Pronubus*, and an early Christian sarcophagus found at the Villa Albani shows Christ presiding at the "Joining of Right Hands." He is holding a crown over the head of each.[2]

The same motif has also been found on the base of cups that were given as wedding presents.[3] Christians of these times ap-

parently take it for granted that God is the one who really conducts their wedding. Tertullian exclaims,

> Where would we find words to describe the happiness of that
> marriage which the Church commends, the sacrifice confirms, the
> blessing seals, the angels proclaim, and the Father recognizes as
> valid?[4]

> Where there are two, there is also Christ; and where He is, there
> is no evil.[5]

Their view of the priest's role at the ceremony is evident from
a letter of St. Gregory Nazianzen in which he apologizes for not
being able to come to the wedding of his niece.

> As far as my will is concerned, I am present and celebrating the
> feast together with you. I join your youthful right hands to each
> other and both to the hand of God.[6]

The priest is also a guest at the wedding banquet, and Chrysostom reminds his flock what this is supposed to mean.

> Let what was done by the citizens of Cana in Galilee be done to-
> day as well by those who now take wives. Let them have Christ sit-
> ting in their midst.
> 'How can this be?', you ask. By having the priests. 'For he who
> receives you receives Me.'[7]

Meanwhile in the Latin-speaking Church Ambrose reflects on
an objection to this idea that it is God Himself who unites a
couple.

> Some think that every marriage is from God, especially because it
> has been written, 'What God has joined, let man not separate.' Thus,
> if every marriage is from God, no marriage may be severed.
> But how could the Apostle say, 'If the unbeliever leaves, let him
> leave'?

In his wonderful way, he did not want the cause of a divorce to lie with Christians; and at the same time he showed that not every marriage is from God. Christian women are not joined to pagans by the judgment of God, since the law forbids it. . . .

Harmony is when the pipes of the organ, blended in a certain combination, keep the beauty of a true melody, or when an apt order preserves the concord of the lute strings. Marriage, therefore, does not have its harmony when a pagan wife, in violation of the law, is joined to a Christian husband.

Thus, where there is marriage, there is harmony. Where there is harmony, God has joined them.[8]

During the 500's the Roman liturgy for the veiling of a bride contains the following petition:

In your kindness be present at this institution of Yours by which You have arranged for the propagation of the human race, so that what is joined at Your initiative may be preserved by Your help.[9]

In the canon of the Mass for this occasion the prayer *Hanc Igitur* has a special form.

As You have granted that she arrive at the age of marriage, complete the work by seeing that she, who by Your gift is joined in the marriage union, may rejoice in the children she desires.[10]

During the early 1100's Anselm of Laon, whose *Sentences* are the first attempt to synopsize the whole of theology, summarizes the answer of the three centuries before him to the problem of divorce:

If weddings are lawful, then God has joined them. But if they are not lawful, then God has not joined them, and man can sever these.[11]

The Schoolmen note that the priest is the minister of marriage in one sense only. His presence guarantees that it is taking place "honorably and in accord with God's will."[12]

Confronted with Luther's attacks, theologians of the 1500's emphasize this role of God. Salmeron says of Mary and Joseph,

Not by man's will but by the known good pleasure of God, they who had been unwilling at first came together with joy.[13]

His colleague at the Council of Trent, James Lainez, makes a pertinent remark about a couple whose marriage had angered some of their relatives.

Since God and the Church first gave it their sanction, it doesn't much matter whether the Marquess gives hers.[14]

A few years later De Leon's *The Ideal Married Woman* describes how God

conducted the first wedding that there was in person, joined the hands of the first bride and groom and blessed them, and was jointly the matchmaker, as we would say, and the priest.[15]

During the 1600's these ideas are commonplace,[16] and St. Francis de Sales continually shows their practical consequences to the married people he is directing.

. . . since God has given each of you to the other, be always content with this arrangement.[17]

Love your husband tenderly as one who has been given to you by the very hand of your Lord.[18]

They write me that nothing is so complete and perfect as your love for each other now that you are husband and wife. Is that not the true and certain mark of God's blessing on a marriage? And what does it matter if man find fault with something that God blesses? . . . They will finally open their eyes and see that the will of God should be adored in everything it does and that He has made this union with His holy hand.[19]

Later in the century Segneri tells the Italian peasants who flock to his parish missions that, just as at Cana, Christ is present at the wedding of two good Christians.[20] A husband and wife who strike each other are striking the God who once united them and is with them still.[21]

One of the outstanding laymen in nineteenth-century France is Frederic Ozanam. His cause has been introduced for canonization. Married himself, he remarks in a letter to a friend,

You are marrying a person you love, and I believe that God blesses Christian love.[22]

Centuries of reflection seem to have made the Church ever more aware of God's part in a wedding. If this couple's pledge is truly making them husband and wife, it is because He is giving them His gift.

But as Catholics paid more attention to this fact, they also saw the problem to which it immediately gives rise. What about the husbands and wives who have found good reason to regret the day they were married?

During the 1500's St. Ignatius Loyola's *Spiritual Exercises*, a book which will eventually give rise to the universal custom of making retreats, offers a significant bit of advice to the retreatant who is deciding what changes to make in his life.

In the case of an unchangeable election which has already been made at one time, there is nothing more to elect, because it cannot be dissolved. This is true of marriage, the priesthood, etc.

There is only one thing to be noted. If a person has not made the election in the proper and ordered way, without disordered affections, he should be sorry for his error and take steps to lead a good life in the state he has chosen.

This election of his does not seem to be a vocation from God, since it is a disordered and biased election.[23]

There are couples truly united, but by a God who did not so much prefer their union as tolerate it. And yet the fact remains that He gave it His sanction. The retreatant is therefore assured that even this ill-advised marriage of his can be a setting for spiritual progress. De la Puente, one of the best-known Jesuit spiritual writers of the following century, feels that the Old Testament's account of the marriage of Ruth to Booz should show other couples how God tolerates certain evils because He knows how to make them end in good.[24]

St. Francis de Sales, though convinced that marriage is a vocation, writes,

There are others who are not called at all. Nevertheless, since they have come, their vocation has been made good and ratified by God . . . His liberality is so great that He gives these means to those to whom He has not promised them and has not obliged Himself, since He did not call them.[25]

French Catholics hear the same from preachers like Massillon.

If it is clear that the Lord has in no way at all presided at your choice, if imprudence, human respect, the passions alone have formed a state in life for you, your lot is to be pitied, I admit, but not despaired of. . . . To the grief of an improper choice God can accord the graces He would have accorded to a legitimate choice. Outwardly you are not in His scheme of things, but your heart always is when it is giving itself to Him.[26]

Even ill-sorted husbands and wives cannot therefore conclude that God has not given them to each other. Whether their marriage was their own fault or came about through mistakes for which they could not really be blamed, if it was valid, it was a gift from God. And whether God fosters an event in a person's life or merely permits it, the reasons for it are always the same: His goodness which desires only our good, and His wisdom which knows how to bring good from evil.

These extreme cases only throw into greater relief what Christians have seen in a typical wedding. The priest is a reminder of someone else who is present, of something truly awesome that is taking place. This man and woman whom everyone is watching are receiving a gift from God.

And by the early 200's even this event appears as part of a process that began long before.

19 *MADE FOR EACH OTHER*

THE MOSAIC LAW about marrying girls who were captured in battle strikes Clement of Alexandria as an incentive to bravery. The wife a man receives in this way is meant to be a reward.[1]

Here God is not only sanctioning a union but arranging it; and a century later, again in Alexandria, this appears as a general truth about marriage. Athanasius, the embattled hero of the struggle against the Arians and one of the first to be declared a saint without martyrdom, gives Psalm 127 an interpretation with which several of the Greek Fathers will agree.

To the man who fears God is given, not any wife at all but one who is adorned with good fruits. For a good wife is good fortune.[2]

The qualities of a certain woman being what they are, God intends her to be the wife of a certain man—in this case, a man devoted to Him.

When Abraham sends his servant to find a wife for Isaac, he assures him that God will give him a sign. Chrysostom exclaims,

Do you see the faith of the man? He did not summon friends or relatives or anyone at all but associated God with himself as an agent and companion. . . . When you yourself are to take a wife, do not have recourse to human beings, to women who make money from the misfortunes of others and seek nothing but to profit from the business themselves. Have recourse to God. He will not take it amiss to be your marriage broker. His is the promise: 'Seek the kingdom of heaven, and all these things will be added to you.'

Do not say, 'How can I see God? How can I enter into conversation with Him and question Him directly?' These are the words of a soul without faith. God can accomplish whatever He wishes in an instant even without a word, as also happened on this occasion.[3]

In another discourse he tells men who have marriageable daughters,

When you are worried and looking about for a husband, pray. Tell God, 'Provide the one You wish.' Give the entire business over in trust to Him. Adorned with this honor by you, He will reward you.

You should certainly do two things: entrust the matter to Him and seek the kind of man He wishes, one who is decent and honorable.[4]

It seems obvious to him that God has the personalities of a man and woman in mind when He presents them to each other. Marriages are arranged by Him. It is not any life-companion who is received, but one whom He regards as suitable. Some writers in the Eastern Church even agree with a further gloss on Psalm 127 by Eusebius of Caesarea:

In the same way, an evil wife is a sign of God's anger.[5]

In the Latin-speaking Church at this time Ambrose remarks,

There is also another motive for chastity if you believe that the marriage which you have drawn as your destiny has been given to you by your God. This is why Solomon says, 'A wife is prepared for a man by God.'[6]

A few years later a similar view seems to inspire a comment by Pope St. Innocent I.

When a wife is taken strictly in accord with the precept of the law, as in Paradise when the parents of the human race were joined, they are blessed by God Himself. And Solomon says, 'A wife shall be prepared for a man by God.'[7]

Amid the early ventures of medieval theology, Rupert of Deutz reflects on the wedding of Isaac.

Well indeed has the providence of God prepared Rebecca. Abraham's servant is not wrong when he says, "She it is whom You have prepared, Lord, for the son of my master."[8]

William of Tournai, one of the better known Dominican professors at Paris during the 1200's, applies the Old Testament narratives to young men of his own time.

If they keep their virginity now until their marriage, they will then receive wives designed for them by God's providence—'A prudent wife is a special gift from the Lord,' says the Book of Proverbs—and many good things will accrue to them, as to Tobias and his sons.[9]

During the 1400's this aspect of marriage begins to receive more attention. St. Antoninus shows his people in Florence what it should mean to them.

The wise man of Proverbs says that a house and wealth are prepared by parents—in other words, they give them to their children —but a good wife is prepared by the Lord. It is a special grace of God that a person have a good wife. And therefore, when a marriage is to take place, each party should say prayers and get them from other good people that the Lord may give them a good life together.[10]

In the Low Countries Denis the Carthusian keeps returning to this subject as he comments on the Old Testament.

As Tobias merited by his virtues to acquire so virtuous a wife, Sara merited so virtuous a husband.[11]

What is more, a person ought to call upon the Lord God, who provides for all His creatures every day, that He deign to grant him such a wife. For most truly does Solomon speak: A house and wealth are given by parents but a prudent wife is a gift from God Himself.[12]

. . . in other words, it is from God's providence that such a woman is granted to a good man because of his virtuous deeds. This is a kind of reward for them.[13]

Cajetan's commentary shows the mind of Scripture scholars during the 1500's. It was God who took the initiative in the marriage of Isaac and Rebecca.[14] And the Book of Proverbs has two lessons for the man in search of a wife:

the one, that he make use of a diligent investigation; the other, that he acknowledge this blessing from God on high, his finding a wife such as has been described.[15]

This gift is attributed to God for the reason that to inherit from parents is common to all, but to have a wife with sense is rare and to be attributed, not to chance but to God.[16]

Luis de Granada, the best known Dominican spiritual writer of the period, and one who shows special concern for laymen, tells them,

This love between married people flows from the very will of God. The happiness they enjoy in that state, the actual benefits it produces, and the inclination of nature clearly display this will.[17]

You who are not yet married and have the intention to be, put the Lord uppermost in your mind and the desire to please Him and save yourself. Then ask Him for the companion who can help you in this.[18]

The same spirit is evident in De Leon's *The Ideal Married Woman:*

Just as this good is indeed precious and rare and a gift given exclusively by God, so none receive it from God except those who, by fearing and serving Him, merit it for themselves by their unusual virtue.[19]

During the early 1600's Bellarmine explains how God is the founder of marriage in two ways: first, as the one who instituted the sacrament; secondly,

If God inspires the two contracting parties to be joined in marriage.

The signs of this will be that their motive is to serve Him, that they have given due consideration to the advice of their parents, and finally that all the usual requirements are fulfilled and the marriage is to take place in fitting circumstances.[20]

Lawrence of Brindisi remarks,

The special blessings of women are that they receive good husbands and good children from God. When girls are to be given in marriage, all who are moved by good will toward them should pray for a happy outcome and desire good men for them.[21]

De la Puente sees the marriage of Tobias as the classic lesson for laymen.

His design was to show His invisible providence toward His own by this visible example, the deeds of His angels. They are their guardians and are wont to exhort and persuade them interiorly to whatever is needed to make a correct choice of this state.

First, they set everything in motion by their inspirations and impulses, making each feel inclined and affected toward that person who is likely to be the most useful to him for achieving salvation. Then they persuade that person's parents to consent, using that efficacious reason, "Your daughter is destined to be the wife of this God-fearing man. That is why no other was able to have her." . . .

From all this we gather that one who desires to make a good elec-

tion in this matter should with prayer and confidence have recourse
to the guardian angels. They are the invisible matchmakers and instruments of God for directing marriages and leading them to a
happy ending.[22]

St. Francis de Sales tells a widow,

It was God, my dear cousin, who gave you this husband. It is He
who has taken him back to Himself. He is obliged to be favorable
to you in the afflictions which the good and proper feelings He be-
stowed on you for your marriage will cause you now in this privation.[23]

French Catholics later in the century are told from the pulpit
that,

A person must prepare himself in a spirit of penance when he believes he is being called to this state by God.[24]

Bourdaloue warns them,

I claim it is not enough that Jesus Christ be invited to it by men,
if they are not first invited to it by Jesus Christ . . . But if it is God
who is calling you, and if you in turn call upon God, that is the
perfect model and true idea of a Christian marriage.[25]

Claude de la Columbière asks,

Indeed, Gentlemen, is it not entirely reasonable that a girl who
has kindness, prudence and virtue be reserved for a man who is himself very wise? . . . A good man surely deserves to meet a woman
who will make him happy, and a woman who can be some man's
happiness should not be destined for a man who would make her
unhappy.[26]

'What God has joined let no man put asunder.' A command. We
can also say a prophecy. . . . It is the same as in the life of religious.

You persevere, you enjoy continual delights in it when you have been called to it by God.[27]

In Italy Segneri affirms that the reason why Joseph was given to Mary, not by chance but by God, is that he was the man most suited to her, because he most resembled her in goodness.[28] A man should look for a woman who is not merely good but good for him. She should fit him like a suit. But only God knows who such a woman is. He is the tailor who takes the material furnished by the world and fits it to an individual's measurements. A man should beg Him to point out the woman who is "tailor-made" for him.[29]

Late in the 1700's Jean Grou concludes,

Beyond all doubt a man's inclination, that indefinable something which touches his heart and determines it in favor of one person rather than another, is something to be taken seriously. This inclination, which has its source in nature, . . . we can regard as produced by God Himself.[30]

God knows the one whom He has destined for you. Ask Him for her and wait for her with confidence from His hand. If, however, you on your side did all that a young man, wise and Christian, ought to do for the success of such a design and yet God permitted you to have to suffer from your wife without having given her any reason, then look at her as a cross offered by Providence and a means of sanctification. Job and Tobit will be your models, and their example will bear you up.[31]

The marriage liturgy has long since been standardized for Churches of the Roman rite. Petitions we have already noted in older forms still appear, and the Introit today echoes the blessing from the Vulgate version of Tobit,

May the God of Israel join you as one, and may He who has fulfilled His merciful design in both of you be always with you. . . .[32]

Though it is the interplay of millions of causes which results in a man's meeting a certain woman, deciding that she would be the kind of wife he is looking for, falling in love and wanting to marry her, it is no less true that God has called him to be her husband. The free decisions of all the people responsible for the fact that a bride and groom arrive at the altar no more rule out God's initiative than the existence of free will rules out the existence of His providence.

Of course, we see the same thing in any vocation to the priesthood. A boy raised in a home where priests are held in honor, hears occasional sermons on that way of life, admires some of the priests he meets, may well feel that he would like to be what they are. But neither these nor the million other "natural" events that lead to his ordination in any way alter the fact that "No man takes the honor to himself; he takes it who is called by God. . . ." They merely show how the call usually comes.

In the case of marriage the man is called, not just to a way of life, but to a person. Since two people are involved in this vocation, it cannot consist in an invitation simply to marry or to marry any one of several good women. Both parties are loved by God. Neither is merely used for the other's sake. Both are led to this particular marriage because it will be good for each of them.

Revelation does not say that this woman is the ideal human being or that no other could help this man to save his soul. It simply says that, if he follows the lead of God's providence, this is the one he will receive as his wife. If he does not, he may still find another who can help him, but we are always better advised to follow God's lead.

Revelation has not disclosed the mechanics by which His designs are to work themselves out in human history. It has simply stated the fact. Everyone in the Church has some vocation from God, some function to perform in the Mystical Body. If it is marriage, God also has a particular wife or husband in mind. A person will find that partner if he follows His lead, and obviously the signs of it cannot be so subtile and vague that most Christians would become nervous wrecks trying to detect them. This would be a defect in God's providence.

A man should pray, since everything ultimately depends on God, but he must also realize that providence acts through our free will and common sense. God cannot be blamed if Catholics in a particular country drift along with customs which make it extremely difficult for a young man or woman to find a suitable mate. If the families arrange all marriages and their only thought is money, or if a young girl may select her own husband but is encouraged to "go steady" before she has met enough different men to know a good husband when she sees one, this can hardly be blamed on God. We do not know all the intricacies of His providence, but we do know that it sometimes allows us to learn by suffering, not only for our sins but for our mistakes.

The man who has done his best to find the right partner and has seen God, in the person of the Church, ratify his choice, has reason to look at his wife with awe. This person is from God. And God's reason for providing her? The one He has for everything He does in the world: He is good and He loves us. This life-companion is one expression of that love. More treasured by Him than the life of His only Son, she has needs and weaknesses; and from now on, the test of love for Him will be an effort to provide for them.

Thus not only as a biological group but even when considered as individuals, human beings are arranged in pairs. More is disclosed by the Christian revelation than the general way in which male and female personalities blend with each other. There is question of each individual couple. When God decides that a certain man shall exist with a certain personality, He usually has a woman in mind who will need that man's strength and will be able to help him overcome his weaknesses. Her own personality is the reason why she is to be offered this particular husband and why he is intended for her.

The mystery of God's providence is that the very freedom

and initiative of the couple are the things that will bring them together. The idea will seem to be their own. But to be "practical" and describe their marriage solely in terms of these two human beings is to ignore providence or assume that free will can block it. It is also to ignore the really distinctive feature of what has been revealed to us about marriage. In most philosophies—and the Christian world is so strongly influenced by them—the individual has counted for nothing. What is important is always the universe or the human race. But Christ has disclosed a fact that we are afraid to believe at times, it is so wonderful. The individual is important. He is loved by God Himself.

And this love that has fashioned two individuals, that knows them in all their uniqueness and watches each of them as though there were no one else in the world who needed such love and help, designed them with each other in mind. The husband and wife who have done what they could to find a suitable partner can be amazed and comforted by the fact that they were made for each other.

But what about the obstacles to their spiritual growth which the same revelation discloses in married life? If virginity is now the ideal way to God, what are the prospects of that vast majority in the Church to whom God has given a lesser gift?

SECTION III: *Their Prospects*

20 *ROADS AND TRAVELLERS*

THE TEACHING OF CHRIST on virginity as it appears in Matthew's Gospel ends with the words,

Let him accept it who can.[1]

This is a challenge, an invitation, but not a command. Apparently those who hear it are still free to marry. This is stated explicitly by Paul.

As regards virgins, I have no precept of the Lord, yet, as a man who, by the mercy received from the Lord, is worthy of trust, I think that it is excellent, in view of the present distress, yes, that it is excellent for a person to remain in this state of virginity.[2]

This clear statement that Paul has no command is made all the more emphatic by the contrast with his words earlier in that chapter about divorce.[3] And not only is he sure of his judgment, but he expects his followers to accept it as coming from one whom God has deemed an authentic teacher of His revelation.[4]

Denis, the bishop of Corinth a century later and so venerated that his letters too were read at Mass on Sundays, warns his fellow bishop at Cnossos not to lay the burden of continence on the necks of all.[5] Christians in Alexandria during the early 200's and in Carthage later in the century are also assured by their eminent bishops, Clement and Cyprian, that God has left them completely free to choose between marriage and virginity.[6]

The mind of both Greek and Latin Fathers is expressed by Ambrose.

> Virginity is something not to be commanded but begged for.[7]

There is usefulness in a counsel but a snare in a command. A counsel invites those who are willing, a command binds the unwilling. Therefore if a woman has followed a counsel and has not regretted it, she has acquired something useful. But if another has regretted it, she has no reason to blame the Apostle. She should have made her choice with an eye to her weakness. She is bringing charges against her own will, in whose snare and knot, harder than she can bear, she has caught herself.[8]

Jerome feels that the reward of virginity will be greater precisely because a person is giving up something he could have enjoyed without sin.[9]

During the early Middle Ages there is little doubt how Paul and the Fathers are understood.

> We should notice here how great a distance there is between a precept and a counsel. For what has been prescribed cannot be corrupted without sin. But if something that is a counsel is violated or corrupted, there is no sin.[10]

During the 1200's the question is asked,

> If a person called to virginity does not follow the call but marries, does he commit a sin?
> Solution: Without prejudice to a better opinion, I say that he does not sin, provided he has not yet made a vow to live in a higher state. Every man owes God more than he can repay, and for this reason God deals mercifully with all, accepting from each one less than he owes and giving rewards beyond the amount of merit.[11]

The common conviction both before and after Trent is voiced by Salmeron.

Let each one's decision be free. Let each examine himself and come forward to receive so lofty a gift only willingly and with joy.[12]

During the last century and in our own as well the faithful are told in papal encyclicals,

It must be noticed that God does not compel all Christians to virginity by a command. . . . We are moved to embrace perfect chastity only by counsel, in other words, because it has the power to guide 'such as have received a special gift' . . . by a way that is safer and easier. Hence, as Ambrose rightly notes, 'It is not imposed but proposed.'[13]

Those called to virginity are still perfectly free. This sheds new light on marriage. If the same revelation which discloses the obstacles facing the man who tries to serve God with a life-companion insists that he is still free to have one, those obstacles, to some extent at least, can be overcome.

But to what extent? Some of the Fathers see an answer in Christ's parable of the sower. During the early 300's Athanasius tells the people of Alexandria,

If someone chooses the worldly way, marriage, he is certainly without fault but will not acquire such numerous and splendid gifts. He will acquire some, though, since he is bearing fruit thirtyfold.[14]

Jerome finds a similar lesson in the Gospel parable,[15] as do other writers as late as Bellarmine.[16] But it would be unwarranted to see anything more in their words than a general impression that a more or less helpful way of life is obviously going to affect a person's prospects for the life to come. Another conviction which is evident during these same centuries, and often in the writings of the same men, must be accounted for before we can draw conclusions.

To settle the quarrels among his Corinthians, Paul tries to

show them that there is no point in a Christian's growing conceited about the role that God has given him in the Church or jealous of the ones given to others. The reason for such a detailed lesson about the gifts of God appears in the application he suggests to them.

> Be eager always to have the gift that is more precious than all the others. I am now going to point out to you the way by far the most excellent.[17]

The gift he goes on to describe is charity. And this gift, he implies, can be confidently asked of God no matter what other gifts a man has in the Church.

This is the letter in which he has pointed out the obstacles to love of God that are an unavoidable part of married life. And yet he tells them in the very same chapter,

> I always promulgate this rule in all the congregations: Everyone is to continue in the condition to which the Lord has assigned him, in which he was at the moment of God's call.[18]

> Are you bound by marriage to a wife: Do not seek to be free from her.[19]

If a man is settled in a legitimate way of life, he is not to change it. Apparently the Christian ideal can be reached by those who marry as well as by those who do not.

Ignatius, the bishop of Antioch, warns some of the Christians to whom he writes on his way to martyrdom in 107,

> If someone can remain in chastity in honor of the Lord's flesh, let him remain in humility. If he prides himself, he has perished, and if he thinks himself greater than the bishop, he is lost.[20]

Bishops at this time are usually married. Holiness is therefore to be judged by the person, not his state. Toward the end of the century Clement of Alexandria shows how this must be kept in mind when reading Paul's statement that the married man is "divided."

> What? Cannot those too who please their wives in accord with the will of God give thanks to God? Is it not permitted to him who has taken a wife to be anxious both about his marriage and the things of God?
>
> Just as 'she who is not married is anxious about the things of the Lord that she be holy in body and spirit,' so also she who has married is anxious in the Lord about the concerns of her husband and the concerns of the Lord. Both women are holy in the Lord, one as a wife, the other as a virgin.[21]

Italian bishops around the year 400 show this same concern not to exaggerate the teaching of Paul.

> If virgins have their minds on God and women with husbands have theirs on the world, what hope in the things of God is left to those who marry? If this is how things are, there is doubt about their salvation.
>
> No; we see virgins with their minds on the world and married people eager for the works of the Lord. To those virgins sainthood will never be granted by God, and for these married people there will be a reward from God, because though they were bound by earthly and fleshly bonds, they took care to merit an imperishable reward of some kind in the hereafter.[22]

It is Augustine who gives this question the most detailed consideration. Reflecting on the parable of the sower, he declares,

> Those who understand this better than I will have to see what that difference in fertility means. . . .
>
> One person is fruitful with fewer but more potent gifts, another with lesser gifts but more of them. And what man dares to judge whether they are equal or different from each other when it comes to receiving heavenly honors?[23]

He does venture to formulate some principles for judging.

> How can it reasonably be asserted that a body is chaste when the
> soul itself is fornicating by yielding itself to another than the true
> God? . . . Therefore the only thing that should be called true
> chastity, either married, widowed or virginal, is what is bound to the
> true faith. Although sacred virginity is with good reason preferred
> to marriage, what Christian with sense does not put even Catholic
> women married to one husband ahead of vestals and even of the
> virgins among the heretics?[24]

> No one wants to be insane, even though he sees that maniacs are
> often stronger than sane men. Sound doctrine is the thing that adorns
> and strengthens the goodness of our intentions.[25]

As for those who are in the Church,

> If I were to consider each of your good qualities separately, you,
> the man who has renounced marriage, are better than your father,
> and you, the woman who has renounced marriage, are better than
> your mother. For virginal holiness is better than married chastity. . . .
> But which is better, pride or humility?. . . If you hold fast to pride
> and your mother to humility, the mother will be better than the
> daughter.[26]

This question of pride leads him back to his basic conviction.

> The gifts of God are secret. Only putting them to the test, even
> within oneself, brings them to light. For, not to mention other cases,
> a virgin may be anxious about the things of the Lord, how to please
> the Lord; and yet for all she knows, it may be that, because of some
> weakness of soul unknown to her, she is not yet ripe for martyrdom,
> while that wife to whom she used to be so happy to prefer herself
> can already drink the chalice of the Lord's humility, which He once
> offered to disciples eager for high places.[27]

> It is one thing not to consent to persuasion and blandishments for
> the sake of truth and a holy ideal, but another not to yield to torture
> and blows. These things lie hidden in the powers and strength of

souls. Temptation spreads them out for display. Experience makes them public knowledge.[28]

Really, there are many twists and turns in questions that touch on these three matters, marriage, widowhood and virginity. There are many perplexities. When we try to penetrate and solve them by discussion, we need unusually great care and really ample consideration so that our views on each of them will be the right ones, or if we do have some other view, that God will bring this to our notice as well.[29]

Writers of the next few centuries echo Augustine.[30]

It does not follow that, if there is greater toil in one case than in another, there will thus be greater glory. Virginity is a greater good in itself than marriage, and yet some married people are not of less merit than some virgins.[31]

If you look at the dignity of the state, the celibacy of John was greater than the marriage of Abraham, although the person of John was not greater in merit than the person of Abraham.[32]

Pierre de la Palu reflects the mind of the High Middle Ages.

Many virgins bring very little good to the world spiritually, just as many married women bring little good bodily, since they turn out to be barren.[33]

Those who serve the king in different ways but with equal readiness to follow the king's good pleasure, as he now desires one thing, now something else, receive an equal recompense.[34]

Another Dominican, John Tauler, whose eloquence is such that notable sermons of later writers will often be attributed to him, shows Catholics of the Rhineland during the early 1300's what this fact should mean to them.

Each should consider interiorly and settle in his mind what his vocation from God is. Otherwise you will try one way of life today and want to change it and try another one tomorrow, as you see and hear things round about you.

Know your own place well. Pay no attention to any other, for it does not concern you. One man's meat is another man's poison. Look to yourself carefully. Let nothing cause you to neglect yourself.

I tell you, there are many men living in the world with wife and children, sitting in the shop and making shoes, who have nothing in mind and heart but God and the decent support of their family. There are many poor peasants who earn their daily bread with hard toil, thinking only of God. And it may well be that these souls, following their humble calling in all simplicity of heart, shall fare better at the last day than many members of orders who are not true to their vocation.[35]

Laymen of the following century are assured by Denis the Carthusian that they can rival monks and hermits, "even if they are married."[36] During the 1500's Salmeron agrees that some of them may be the ones who win the most praise from God,

just as the widow giving her poor alms of two brass coins was pointed out by the Lord as greater than the others who were giving very much, because of her good intentions and her charity.[37]

Preachers and writers of his time, and of later years as well, agree with St. Francis de Sales.

Provided we have the fear of God for a guide, it matters little what road we keep to, although in themselves some are more desirable for those who have the freedom to choose.[38]

When it comes to success in life, the most important consideration is not the vocation but the person. What, then, should a person who marries expect from himself?

Answering this for Catholics of the late 300's, the Greek Fathers propose not just salvation but sanctity.[39] Chrysostom reminds them of Priscilla and Aquila.

Look. Here too were a man and his wife. They ran a workshop and practiced a trade and displayed a much higher perfection of soul than those who live in monasteries.

How do we know? From the words which Paul addresses to them —or rather, not so much from those he spoke to them as from the testimonials by which he later commended them to others. . . .

We can also judge their virtue from the fact that he lived with them, not one or two or three days but two whole years. Men of rank do not deign to take up lodging with lowborn and common people. They seek out the mansions of certain famous men, so that the greatness of their dignity will not be impaired by the low estate of their hosts. The Apostles did the same. They were not the guests of anyone they happened to meet. Just as those others have eyes for the splendor of buildings, they looked for virtue of soul. . . .

These people, then, were worthy of Paul, and if of Paul, they were worthy of angels. Why, I would even dare to call that little home heaven and the Church. For where Paul was, Christ was too. . . . And where Christ was, angels would often come.[40]

No one has described the spiritual hardships of marriage more vividly than Chrysostom, and yet the same view of revelation makes him declare that married people can be as close to God as anyone in the Church.

Scripture scholars in the West around the time of Charlemagne call attention to the policy of Christ.

As His apostles He chose some married men, some continent, some virgins. And yet He placed St. Peter, a married man, over all the orders so that the virgins would not grow proud or married people despair of being able to arrive at that perfection which virgins achieve.[41]

More significant than any document is a movement which begins to sweep through medieval Europe, as the same spirit that is impelling thousands to join the new mendicant friars leads others to beg for rules by which married people can reach the

Franciscan or Dominican ideal. Denis the Carthusian will remark later on of Francis,

> He drew up that third Rule especially and chiefly for people in the world and married couples ånd lay people of either sex.[42]

During the 1500's De Ossuna's *Third ABC of the Spiritual Life* poses the question of whether married people can hope to arrive at the higher stages of prayer. To the author this is the same as asking whether they can reach the pinnacle of sanctity, and he replies emphatically that they can. Those who deny this he compares to the Apostles who tried to keep the children from Christ. Was not Anna the housewife more perfect than Heli the priest? Was not Christ a guest in the homes of people like Matthew and Zaachaeus? And did not the Holy Spirit come, not just to the Apostles but to all who were in the cenacle?[43]

Not many years later in another celebrated book on different vocations in the Church the Spanish Jesuit De la Puente declares,

> The state of perfection and the care of souls give more help to acquiring great sanctity. Still the lack of these is often made up for by the copious grace and favor of God and the great diligence of the man himself, aided by the same grace. The result is that, though living in a less perfect state, he mounts to a more excellent sanctity than those who are in a state of great perfection.[44]

> The state of marriage is the most imperfect of all the states of the gospel law, and yet the highest perfection of those who are in the most perfect states can be obtained in it. For as has been said above, the grace of God is not really bound to the different ways of life . . . Think of Abraham, Job, Joseph, David and other holy patriarchs, prophets and kings.

> The state of continence and the religious life are more preeminent in the New Law, and still, even in the married state, there have been the bravest of martyrs, the holiest of confessors, the most famous of kings, etc., persons of truly heroic virtue. Even now there are many outstanding people who arrive at the highest peak of Christian perfection.[45]

In 1609 an announcement by St. Francis de Sales introduces one of the most influential theological developments of the century.

Almost all of those who have treated of devotion have had in mind the instruction of people completely withdrawn from the business of the world. At least, they have taught a kind of devotion which leads to this complete withdrawal. My intention is to instruct those who live in cities, ordinary homes, at the court, people who by their state are obliged to live a life that is ordinary as far as externals go, who very often, under the pretext of an alleged impossibility, do not even want to think of undertaking the devout life.[46]

Time and again he tells them,

Wherever we are, we can and should aspire to the perfect life.[47]

He bases the program he outlines for them on one principle:

It is a certain fact that when God calls someone to a vocation, He obliges Himself as a consequence, in His divine providence, to furnish him with the helps he needs to make himself perfect in his vocation.[48]

From this he concludes,

It is a mistake, even a heresy, to want to keep the devout life from soldiers' companies, workmen's shops, the courts of princes, the homes of married people.[49]

Whether these are the sentiments of the entire Church may be gathered from the number of Catholics who still read the *Introduction to the Devout Life,* and from an encyclical of Pope Pius XI:

St. Francis de Sales seems to have been given to the Church by the singular plan of God to vanquish both by the action of his life and the power of his teaching that opinion already deep-rooted in his times and still alive even today, that sanctity in its true sense as the Catholic Church proposes it, either cannot be achieved or is certainly so hard to reach that it is beyond the grasp of most of the faithful and suited only to a few great and lofty souls, that it also involves things so repellent and tedious that it is in no way suited to men and women living outside the cloister.[50]

If there is any doubt about the Pope's own views, he removes it a few years later in his encyclical on marriage.

All men, no matter what class they belong to or what honorable way of life they have entered upon, can and should imitate the outstanding model of all holiness set before men by God, Christ Our Lord, and with God's help arrive even at the summit of Christian perfection, as is proved by the example of so many saints.[51]

This is clearly the settled conviction of Catholics during the reign of Pius XII.

Because virginity is to be regarded as something more perfect than marriage, it does not follow that it is necessary for reaching Christian perfection. Holiness of life without chastity dedicated to God can really be achieved, as is borne out by the many holy men and women who are honored by the Church in its public worship, and who were faithful husbands or wives or shone as examples of excellent fathers or mothers of families. In fact, it is not rare that we too see married people who are most earnestly striving for Christian perfection.[52]

It is a road to sanctity that is travelled by a Christian couple, and so the Church, like the faithful themselves, venerates and exalts the heroes of that way of life in its temples and on its altars.[53]

Though we have looked long at the darker hues of married life, it now appears that, when we stand back to survey the entire picture, it is amazingly bright. Despite obstacles which they cannot avoid, two Christians who marry can hope not only to save their souls but to reach the highest sanctity.

And this does not mean that it will be possible, just barely possible, if they are willing to strain with superhuman efforts. The more the Church has turned its attention to married life, the more emphatically it has declared that this hope is not restricted to a handful of heroic souls. Every Catholic bride and groom can become saints together if they want to.

It does not seem rash to say that most couples today would accept this idea with their intellects but not with their emotions. Unfortunately, it cannot be taken for granted yet that the old suspicions of marriage which have come down as a cultural legacy from pagan times have been completely dispelled. And most Catholics, even those who do not have these feelings, hear more sermons on virginity than on marriage. The word "vocation" suggests only *that* vocation.

With all the shock of personal experience, they know the difficulties that revelation has disclosed in married life. Even more profound than this is the feeling that falling in love with someone, marrying, raising a family is a process no more religious than eating when you are hungry. There is no Roman collar or convent silence which make other ways of life so obviously filled with God. Continual reminders are needed to see His role in marriage.

But if they smile wistfully at the thought of themselves as saints, wanting to think it possible but afraid that it seems too good to be true, they have only to look at the precise reason for hope. It is not the fact that their life is like a day in a monastery or that God is the only thought in their minds. It is simply a question of common sense. They want a practical goal in life, one they can actually arrive at. But being practical means facing all the facts, and one great fact about married life is that the same Christ who shows them its problems also makes it clear that the average couple who enter it can be saints. It would be foolish to settle for anything less.

But how is all this supposed to happen? What would they be expected to do?

21 *A WAY TO GOD*

AMONG THE BITS of practical advice to Timothy on directing the Christians in his care, Paul tells him,

Woman's salvation is in childbearing, if she perseveres in faith and love and holiness with modesty.[1]

This is not in contradiction with what he has told the Corinthians. It is a more comprehensive view of married life. The spiritual obstacles are real, but marriage is a gift of God, designed like all His gifts to make a person better off than he was before. The resources of virtue which motherhood will call forth are what will bring a Christian woman to heaven.

As the early Church moves into its most eloquent years with the Fathers of the late 300's, Ephrem the Deacon describes how women, resting at last in heaven from "the annoyances and dangers of married life," will rejoice at the sight of their children.[2] Even Jerome, for whom the virgin is the symbol of the Christian saint, remarks,

The wife will be saved if she begets children who are to remain virgins, if what she herself has lost, she gains in her offspring and the loss and corruption of the root is compensated for by the blossom and fruit.[3]

Addressing his people on the feast of an early martyr, Augustine asks,

What is the hope of good Catholics who, bound by a marriage contract, bear the yoke of marriage chastely and in concord? . . . What hope is there for them, what hope for all of us if the only ones who follow Christ are those who have shed their blood for Him? Is Mother Church to lose her children, for she is all the more abundantly surrounded by them the more secure are the years of peace? Must she pray for persecution, pray for temptation lest she lose them?. . .

You surely see, beloved, that besides the shedding of blood, besides chains and prisons, besides scourges and hooks, there are many things in which we can follow Christ.[4]

In another discourse he draws the practical conclusion for those who are married.

Lot's wife, because she looked back, was stopped where she was. Let everyone be afraid, then, to look back at where he could have gone. Keep to the road, follow Christ, forgetting what is behind, intent on what is ahead. . . . Let married people regard the unmarried as above themselves. Let them admit they are better. Let them love in them what they themselves do not have, and in them let them love Christ.[5]

The writers who try to preserve the teaching of the Fathers during the turbulent 800's affirm that the housewife will achieve her spiritual ideals,

if she has begotten sons and raised them in the belief and service of Almighty God and led them on to the perfection of a good life. If she has been negligent in anything, she shall be saved in view of the work which she constantly strove to do for them.[6]

As medieval theology begins to come of age during the 1100's, Robert Pullen advises laymen,

Whatever your work in life is, busy yourself in it in your own way for the sake of God so as to acquire lawfully the means to live lawfully.[7]

Ramon Lull, saintly, talented, one of the most colorful theologians of the High Middle Ages, portrays the medieval ideal of marriage in his didactic tale, *Blanquerna.* The hero's father, urged to enter a monastery, declares,

Never will I abandon the estate in which God has placed me. Nor shouldst thou, saving thy honor, counsel me to enter another estate to the which I am the less devoted than to that of marriage wherein I now am. For lack of devotion causes many a man and many a woman to despise their state and to forsake it.[8]

A few years later John Tauler warns the people of Strasbourg not to imitate those laymen who

hurry off to church in the early morning, as if God were not to be found in their homes or upon the streets in the duties of their state of life.

Such a hurrying to church in neglect of home duties is an injury to yourself, and you will not find God in it. This is why some do not find peace of heart and do not really find God, now doing a good work, now saying a prayer to God or a saint—hurrying and scurrying in a rush of devotions, one of as little profit to them as the other.[9]

The archbishop of Paris later in the century, Jean Gerson, so acclaimed as a writer and director of souls that his name, like Tauler's, will often be attached to the works of other authors, explains,

As in a true body, so too in the Mystical Body the different members do not have the same activity. Now since contemplation demands leisure and rest from outside concerns, and many are found whose state and the duties to which they are bound cannot be managed without a great deal of racket on their jobs and great activity of the body or senses, what is left but to keep such people from seeking the repose of contemplation? A man will do neither happily when he must remain surrounded by noise.[10]

During the 1400's Denis the Carthusian shows them what they should do instead.

It pertains to married people to do all their external works—trades and crafts, housework, civil functions, and such like—with a good intention and order them to the right goal, namely, to the glory and honor of God. . . . For if the Christian is supposed to serve God, he has to live. And if he is to live, he must have the necessities of life. And if he is to have these, he must perform his duties, those activities without which he cannot have or acquire the necessities of life . . . A devout priest merits eternal life by reading his breviary and saying Mass out of charity. A farmer does the same by plowing, gathering the harvest, and working at other such tasks, provided that he does them out of charity to the glory of God.[11]

Even a husband and wife's absorption in each other is part of the process.

Men are withdrawn by married life from excesses of different kinds. They give up their old-time trivialities and vanities. They become prudent, mature, careful.[12]

Amid the upheavals of Reformation and Counter-Reformation this aspect of married life begins to receive more attention. Commenting on the letter to Timothy, Cajetan remarks,

Paul does not teach that the salvation of a woman depends on begetting children, since the virgin will more easily be saved than the married woman. But he does teach that by making use of the role distinctive of her sex, she has a means of being saved by the very use of her sex.[13]

De Granada warns,

You see quite a few people neglect the duties of their state under the slightest pretext to the detriment of many and the scandal of all.

These persons are certainly not the ones who are only seeking the glory of God. They are the ones who are looking for their own satisfaction, a notoriety of some kind, a distraction or some other similar aim. Let the moment of sacrifice arrive and their piety vanishes on the spot. It is to these people that we must attribute the disrepute into which prayer and virtue have fallen.[14]

In *The Ideal Married Woman* Luis de Leon shows what this should mean to a God-fearing couple.

The unique and special concern which falls to each is to respond to the duties of his state in life. . . . In war the soldier who deserts his post is not really loyal to his captain, though in other things he serves him. At a play the audience whistles at the man who is poor as the person he is playing, even though in his own person he is very good.[15]

Among married women there are others who, as if their homes belonged to their neighbors, put them out of their thoughts. Their whole life is the oratory and prayerbook and warming the church floor morning and evening. And meanwhile the maidservant is lost, and the daughter picks up alarming bad habits, and the house falls into ruin, and the husband turns to the devil.[16]

I do not say, nor do I claim to think that the married man or anyone has to lack prayer. I do say what a difference there has to be between two good women, the nun and the wife.

As for the first, praying is her whole work in life. For her, praying has to be the means by which she best does her duty. She has not sought a husband. She has forsaken the world and deprived herself of everything to stay always and without hindrance close to Christ.

The other woman has to deal with Christ to obtain some grace and favor with which to succeed in having a son, managing her home well, being as useful as she should to her husband.

The one has to live by praying continually, the other has to pray by living as she should. The one pleases God by giving herself entirely to Him, the other has to serve by working at the management of her home for Him.[17]

This view of married life is still more evident during the 1600's.[18] St. Francis de Sales bases all his advice to couples on the assumption that their state, as a gift from God and a true vocation, is a sign of how they are to serve Him.

I ask you, Philothea, would it be appropriate . . . for married men not to want to amass any more material goods than Capuchins . . . ? No, Philethea, devotion does not spoil any type of vocation or activity. On the contrary, it adorns and embellishes them . . . and each individual becomes more suited to his vocation if he joins it to devotion. Devotion makes the management of the household more tranquil, the love of husband and wife more sincere . . . and when it sets itself against someone's legitimate vocation, it is undoubtedly false.[19]

From this he derives a basic rule for married people.

Do not desire to be what you are not. Desire to be very well what you are. Occupy your thoughts with perfecting yourself in that and carrying the crosses small or large that you will meet in it.

Believe me, here is the great adage and the one least understood in the spiritual life: Everyone shows his love according to his taste. Few show it according to their duty and Our Lord's taste. What use is it to build castles in Spain? We have to live in France.[20]

Do not think that Our Lord is farther away from you while you are amid the bustle into which your calling bears you than He would be if you were among the delights of the quiet life. No, my dear daughter, it is not quiet that brings Him near to our hearts, it is the fidelity of our love. It is not the feeling we have of His kindness but the consent we give to His holy will.[21]

My goodness, dear daughter! How holy and pleasing to God we would be if we really knew how to use the opportunities for mortifying ourselves that our calling provides for us. They are undoubtedly greater than among Religious. The trouble is that we do not make use of them as they do.[22]

We must realize that there is no vocation which does not have its annoyances . . . and what is more, except for those who are fully resigned to the will of God, each of us would like to change his state in life to that of other people. . . . Those who are married would like not to be, and those who are not would like to be.

Where does that general restlessness of mind come from if not from a certain displeasure that we feel at constraint and a contrariness of spirit which makes us think that everyone is better off than ourselves . . . ? We must not simply want to do the will of God, we must do it gladly.[23]

God be blessed and glorified for this change of state that you have made for His sake, my dearest daughter. . . . You will see clearly that, if you resign your soul completely to the providence of Our Lord, you will advance in this vocation, have great consolation in it and become really holy in the end.[24]

In Italy toward the end of the century Segneri concludes that mere temporal advantages are an unworthy motive for such a thing as marriage. A man should choose this state because he sees it as a help to serving God.[25]

This is the view constantly in evidence from that time till today.[26] Pius XII feels that a woman's personality is so designed that, as a rule, she finds even her full spiritual growth in being a mother.[27] Time and again he returns to one idea: Not only can married people be saints but married life itself will provide what they need to reach this ideal.

The life of a Christian couple has its own hidden heroism, extraordinary heroism in cruelly tragic situations that the world does not know of, daily heroism in the unfolding succession of sacrifices renewed at every hour.[28]

There must be born in you and grow ever stronger the resolute desire to be saints, to be saints as husbands and wives, in the marriage union itself, in the very expression of your love.[29]

This conviction of Christians ever since Paul, peripheral at first, but continually clearer and more influential as attention is

turned to it, reveals a certain mystery. Most human beings are
called to be saints in pairs, to serve God by praying, working,
living for each other and their children. Marriage itself, the day-
in-day-out scolding and laughing and worrying and loving, is
radioactive with grace.

Conclusions

THIS STUDY BEGAN as an attempt to answer two questions: Does marriage demand a really basic change in a person's life with God? What connection is there between his spiritual growth and that of his partner in marriage?

The questions are not really answered yet, but a few facts seem to have emerged upon which any answer will have to be built.

A husband and wife are not living in a state that is frowned upon by God. Though there has been a tendency for many centuries and in many different lands to be ashamed of manhood and womanhood—and the swings of Western culture during the past hundred years between prudery and a compulsive "frankness" suggest that it is with us still—this feature of human life was designed by God. The person who is insensitive to certain stimuli is not an ideal.

True, there has been an original sin. But the sex instinct is not concupiscence, and what the Church preaches is modesty, not shame. Its very insistence on restraint only underlines one of the basic facts about human sexuality. It is wrong—whether done by voluptuaries or prudes—to see nothing there but a type of pleasure. The activity of a husband and wife is designed by God to express one of the purest, deepest, noblest kinds of love. It must not be desecrated by selfishness.

God does not merely tolerate marriage. It is not an aftermath

of original sin. The Christian is contradicting the revelation he
believes in if his everyday words and conduct imply that marriage is a concession to human weakness. The fact that men and
women are so attracted to it does not make it any less moral.
Granted the unruly aspects of this attraction since original sin,
the tendency itself is part of the nature fashioned by God. The
perennial error of the Cathar is to assume that if you like something, it must be wrong.

Work and worry do keep the eyes of a married couple on
the world around them. So much time must be expended. So
many errands and plans and emergencies clamor for attention.
How shall they manage some time for God? How can they
sustain their interest in Him?

For even when their gaze does turn from the world, it is toward each other. Instincts which, like spoiled children, demand
satisfaction here and now can make spiritual things unreal or
somewhat boring. And this is merely a reflex of a deeper change.
The thrust of a man's personality is deflected by another personality. His whole orientation is toward another. This other
is now the great good at which everything aims and by which
everything is measured.

A romantic view which ignores these problems of being husband and wife will soon leave a couple disillusioned. They must
face them frankly even if they do not see any answers at first.
It is foolish to hope and drift. Marriage is going to affect their
ideals in life. There will be no time for them, no interest. Together they must look for ways to make time and sustain the
interest.

In the present stage of salvation-history there is a better way
to God than marriage. And yet what the Church has praised
is not virginity but consecrated virginity, foregoing the chance
to have a life-companion so that time, talent, life itself can be
put more completely at the disposal of the Total Christ: Our
Lord and His Church. Those whose vocation was marriage are
supposed to be better off than they were before. God has so

designed human beings that as a general rule they reach their full spiritual development in pairs.

The Word of God, disclosed to the eyes of our faith by teachers as varied as Paul, medieval husbands and wives, and Pope John XXIII, seems to have been giving the following picture of the typical Catholic husband and wife.

When God had decided that this man would exist, with certain strengths and certain weaknesses, it was with this woman in mind. Her own distinctive traits were designed with an eye to him. Divine wisdom saw that to have two such people at a certain point in history would be good for them—and for others as well.

For God has so loved us that He sent His only Son to be with us, not only by becoming a man but by founding a strange new reality which we call the Church, the Kingdom of God, the Mystical Body of Christ. This Mystical Body does not cause either Him or ourselves to lose our identity; and yet it is so truly one that, as the soul is a life-giving presence in every part of the body, so the Spirit of Christ animates Head and members. He loves this Church as a part of Himself and concerns Himself constantly with its growth and well-being. As an outpouring of love for the Church and for these two Catholics, He determined to present them the gift that is marriage.

By his design they met. As truly as He calls others to virginity —and perhaps had called one or both of them—He offered them a certain function in the Body. Like the priesthood, their gift was one that no one takes to himself, only those who are called.

Heeding His invitation, they presented themselves at the altar. At His bidding, by His authority, in His Name, each took the other to share the experience that is human life.

This does not mean that they can now drift toward heaven with little effort at all. There are obstacles which they cannot avoid—but which they can certainly overcome. Marriage is not a temptation set in their way. It is a gift from God, given like all His gifts because He wants to give them more of Himself.

It is an improvement over the way they were before, a help to be all they want to be. He has given them an ideal and has put the means to achieve it in their very life together.

What are these means? We hope to explore that question in a second volume. But if any truth has emerged so far, it is this. A bride and groom should look at each other with awe and a breathless hope. They have so much to look forward to. Alone, one of them might have come to regret these years on earth, but God has arranged that they travel them together. By giving themselves to each other now as husband and wife, they can be saints.

ABBREVIATIONS

AAS   *Acta Apostolicae Sedis*
ASS   *Acta Sancta Sedis*
BRC   *Bullarii Romani Continuatio*
CC   *Corpus Christianorum,* Series Latina
CIC   *Codex Juris Canonici*
DAL   *Dictionnaire d'archéologie chrétienne et de liturgie*
DB   Denzinger, Bannwart, *Enchiridion Symbolorum*
DR   *Discorsi e Radiomessaggi di Pio XII,* Milan: 1943
Mansi   *Collectio Conciliorum*
PG   Migne, *Patrologia Graeca*
PL   ———, *Patrologia Latina*
N.B.:   Scriptural abbreviations will follow the system of the
    Catholic Biblical Quarterly, which includes:
        Eccl.   Qoheleth (Ecclesiastes)
        Sir.   The Wisdom of Ben Sira (Ecclesiasticus)

TRANSLATIONS

New Testament citations are from the Kleist-Lilly version.
The translations of all other sources are original unless otherwise
noted.

NOTES

PREFACE

1. Cf. John L. Thomas, S.J., *The American Catholic Family* (Englewood Cliffs, N.J.: Prentice-Hall., Inc., 1956), pp. 16 ff.; 310.
2. Cf. David M. Stanley, S.J., "The New Testament Doctrine on Baptism," *Theological Studies*, vol. 18, n. 2 (June, 1957), p. 173.
3. Mt. 13, 52.
4. Mt. 16, 15.

PART I: INTRODUCTION

1. Gen. 2, 18–24.
2. Ps. 114, 4.
3. Cf. John L. McKenzie, S.J., "The Literary Characteristics of Genesis," *Theological Studies*, vol. 15, n. 4 (Dec., 1954), pp. 541 ff.
4. Cf. John L. McKenzie, S.J., "Myth and the Old Testament," *Catholic Biblical Quarterly*, July 1959, pp. 267 ff.
5. ——, *The Two-Edged Sword* (Milwaukee: Bruce Publishing Co., 1957), pp. 106 ff.
6. Gen. 2, 25.
7. McKenzie, *The Two-Edged Sword*, p. 100.
8. Gen. 3, 7.
9. Gen. 3, 10.
10. Exod. 19, 15.
11. 1 Sam. 21, 4.
12. Exod. 23, 26.
13. Deut. 7, 14.
14. Judges 11, 38.
15. Cf. Deut. 25, 5–10; Gen. 16, 1 ff.; 30, 1; 1 Sam. 1, 5 ff.; Ps. 128.

CHAPTER 1

1. Lk. 14, 20.
2. 1 Cor. 7, 25. Cf. *ibid.*, vv. 28, 36.
3. 1 Tim. 4, 3.

4. Heb. 13, 4.
5. *Contra Haereses*, lib. 1, c. 28, PG 7, 690.
6. Cf. Tertullian, *Adv. Marcionem*, lib. 1, c. 29, PL 2, 280; Clement of Alexandria, *Stromata*, lib. 3, c. 12, PG 8, 1177; *ibid.*, PG 8, 1186; c. 18, PG 8, 1211; c. 10, PG 8, 1170.
7. Mt. 19, 12.
8. *Comm. in Mat.*, tom. 15, n. 4, PG 13, 1263–4.
9. Mansi, 2, 1098–1102.
10. Cf. Joseph De Guibert, S.J., *Documenta Ecclesiastica Christianae Perfectionis Studium Spectantia* (Rome: P.U.G., 1931), p. 17.
11. Cf. Ephrem, *Serm. 19 adv. Haer.*, *Opera Omnia* (Peter Benedict, S.J., ed., Rome: Typographia Vaticana, 1737), vol. 2, p. 476 ff.
12. Cf. *Serm. 28 adv. Haer.*, *op. cit.*, vol. 2, p. 501; *Serm. 19*, p. 476; *Serm. 47*, p. 542.
13. *Serm. 45 adv. Haer.*, *op. cit.*, vol. 2, 540.
14. *De Virginitate*, c. 8, PG 48, 538–40. Cf. *ibid.*, cc. 9–10, PG 48, 539–40; Methodius of Olympus, *Conviv. 10 Virg.*, Orat. 2, c. 7, PG 18, 59; Gregory of Nyssa, *De Virginitate*, c. 8, PG 46, 354; Epiphanius, *Adv. Haer.*, lib. 2, tom. 1, haer. 61, nn. 1–2, PG 41, 1042.
15. *Carmina*, lib. 1, sect. 2, p. 7, PG 37, 647.
16. *Poemata Moralia*, sect. 2, n. 1, vv. 730–2, PG 37, 577. Cf. Epiphanius, *Adv. Haer.*, lib. 2, tom. 2, haer. 67, PG 42, 179; *ibid.* tom. 1, haer. 48, PG 41, 867–870; lib. 1, tom. 2, haer. 23, PG 41, 306.
17. Mansi 1, 29–30; 39–40.
18. *Lib. de Haer.*, c. 84, PL 12, 1196.
19. *De Viduis*, 4, PL 16, 241; Cf. *ibid.*, PL 16, 254–5; *Expos. in Luc.*, lib. 8, n. 37, PL 15, 1866.
20. *Expos. in Luc.*, lib. 4, n. 12, PL 15, 1699.
21. *De Virginitate*, c. 6, PL 16, 288.
22. Cf. Jerome, *Adv. Jov.*, lib. 1, n. 3, PL 23, 213; *ibid.* PL 23, 233; Augustine, *De Virg.*, c. 19, n. 19, PL 40, 405; *De Bono Conj.*, c. 8, PL 40, 379; *De Bono Vid.*, c. 5, PL 40, 434; *Serm. 93*, c. 3, PL 38, 575; *Contra Jul.*, lib. 3, c. 21, PL 44, 724; *Retract.*, lib. 2, c. 2, PL 32, 639.
23. *Epist.*, lib. 4, ep. 112, PG 78, 1179. Cf. Cyril of Alexandria, *Quod Unus Sit Christus*, PG 75, 1271; Theodoret, *Interpr. in Ps.*, in Ps. 50, 7, PG 80, 1243; *In 1 Cor.*, 8, 40, PG 82, 286.
24. Cf. Procopius of Gaza, *Comm. In Isaiam*, c. 56, PG 87, 2567; Gennadius of Marseilles, *De Eccl. Dog.*, cc. 67–8, PL 58, 996; Fulgentius of Ruspe, *De Ver. Praedest.*, lib. 2, c. 23, PL 65, 650; Ps-Isidore of Seville, *De Eccl. Dog.*, c. 64, PL 83, 1241; Gregory the Great, *Moralia*, lib. 16, c. 6, PL 75, 1125.
25. Cf. *Statuta Ecclesiae Antiqua*, PL 56, 880.
26. Cf. 2nd C. of Braga, can. 11, DB 241; C. of Toledo, c. 16, DB 36, Mansi 3, 1004. Cf. also St. John Damascene, *De Fide Orth.*, lib. 4, c. 24, PG 94, 1210.

27. Cf. Sedulius Scotus, *Collect. in 1 Cor.* 7, PL 103, 140, 142; Jonas of Orleans, *De Instit. Laicali,* lib. 2, c. 1, PL 106, 167.

28. *Enarr. in Ep. Pauli,* lib. 23, c. 4, PL 112, 609. Cf. *Comm. In Gen.,* lib. 1, c. 6, PL 107, 461; *Enarr. In Ep. Pauli,* lib. 25, c. 1, PL 112, 662.

29. *Enarr. in Ep. Pauli,* lib. 10, c. 7, PL 112, 64.

30. Cf. Servatus Lupus, *Epist.* 112, PL 119, 587; Haymo of Halberstadt, *Expos. in 1 Cor.* 7, PL 117, 546; Hatto of Vercelli, *Expos. in Ep. Pauli,* 1 Cor., PL 134, 351.

31. Cf. Gerard of Cambrai, *Acta Synod. Atrebat.,* PL 142, 1300. (Mansi 19, 449 ff.)

32. Mansi 21, 583.

33. *Serm. in C. C.,* Serm. 66, PL 183, 1094.

34. *Ibid.,* 1095. Cf. Lanfranc, *Comm. in 1 Cor.,* 7, 34, PL 150, 180; Bruno of Asti, *Expos. in 1 Cor.* 7, PL 153, 155; *Expos. in 1 Tim.,* PL 153, 439; Raoul Ardent, *Homil.,* 21, Dom. 2a post Epiph., PL 155, 1742; Anselm, *De Concept. Virg.,* c. 4, PL 158, 457; Rupert of Deutz, *Comm. in Joan.,* lib. 2, PL 169, 275; Anon., *Quaest. in Ep. Pauli,* In 1 Tim., q. 17, PL 175, 398; Walter of Mortagne, *Summa Sent.,* tract. 7, c. 2, PL 176, 155; Abelard, *Prob. Hel.,* 14, PL 178, 701; *ibid.,* 40, PL 178, 722.

35. 1 Cor. 7, 1.

36. Eckbert of Schaunang, *Serm. Contra Catharos,* Serm. 5, PL 195, 29. Cf. Robert Pullen, *Sent.,* lib. 7, c. 29, PL 186, 947; Peter Lombard, *Sent.,* lib. 4, c. 26; Hugh of Amiens, *Contra Haereticos,* lib. 3, c. 4, PL 192, 1288.

37. DB 424.

38. *De Fide Catholica,* c. 1, DB 430.

39. Bonaventure, *Quaest. Disp. de Perf. Evangel.,* q. 3, a. 1, Quar. 5, 168. Cf. *Comment. in Joan.,* 2, q. 3, Quar. 6, 272; *Quaest. Disp. de Perf. Evan.,* q. 3, a. 3, Quar. 5, 177; Albert the Great, *Summa Theol.,* q. 109, t. 33; Aquinas, *In 4 Sent.,* d. 30, q. 2, a. 1, quaestincula 3; *In Joan.,* c. 2, lect. 1; *In 1 Cor.,* c. 7, lect. 1; *S. T.* III, 29, 1.

40. Hartzheim, *Concilia Germaniae,* vol. 4, pp. 101 ff. Cited by De Guibert, *op. cit.,* p. 154.

41. Cf. Benedict XII, Errors of the Armenians, DB 537; Thomas of Strasbourg, *In 4 Sent.,* d. 26, q. 1, a. 1.

42. Henry Suso, *Horologium Sapientiae,* C. Richstatter, S.J., ed. (Turin; Marietti, 1929), lib. 1, C. 5; *ibid.,* lib. 2, c. 7.

43. St. Vincent Ferrer, *Sermones Aestivales,* Damian Diaz, ed. (Antwerp: John Stelsius, 1572), Serm. 5, p. 443; Manuel Calecas, *De Princip. Fidei Cath.,* c. 6, PG 152, 607; Denis the Carthusian, *De Laudabili Vita Conjugatorum,* a. 5, *Opera Omnia* (Tournai, Cartusia S.M. de Pratis, 1896) vol. 38, p. 62; *Summa Fid. Orth.,* lib. 4, a. 162, Works, vol. 18, p. 209.

44. Cf. De Guibert, *op. cit.,* p. 228.

45. Cf. Cajetan, *In 1 Cor.* 7, 28 (Lyons: J. & P. Prost, 1639); John Eck, *Homiliae super Evang. de Tempore* (1537), Dom. 2 post Epiph., Hom.

1; St. Peter Canisius, *Meditationes,* F. Streicher, ed. (Munich: Officina Salesiana, 1955), vol. 2, p. 385; Alfonso Salmeron, S.J., *Commentarii in Evangelicam Historiam* (Cologne: A. Hierat & J. Gymni, 1612), disp. 10 in 1 Tim.; *ibid.* vol. 6, tr. 6, p. 33; Luis de Granada. *Serm. 1, 2a Domin. post Epiph.,* Oeuvres, M. Beraille, tr. (Paris: L. Vives, 1868), Vol. 1, p. 425; Francisco Toledo, *Comm. in Joan. Evang.* (Lyons: Officina Junctarum, 1589), p. 129; St. Francis de Sales, *Introduction à la Vie Dévote,* p. 3, c. 38, Oeuvres Complètes (Paris: Albanel & Martin, 1839), vol. 1, p. 644; Pius XII, Address to Discalced Carmelite Teachers, 9/23/51, AAS 43 (1951), p. 736.

46. Cf. Martin R. P. McGuire, "The History of the Church from Pentecost to 604—A Survey of Research," *Theological Studies,* vol. 20, n. 1 (March, 1959), p. 91.

CHAPTER 2

1. Cf. *Serm. 45 adv. Haer., Works,* vol. 2, p. 540.
2. *Hymnum II de Oleo et Oliva,* n. 8, *Hymni et Sermones,* Thomas J. Lamy, ed. (Mechlin: H. Dessain, 1886), vol. 2, p. 798.
3. Gregory Nazianzen, *Orat. 37 in Mt. 19,* n. 9, PG 36, 294. Cf. Chrysostom, *De Virginitate,* c. 10, PG 48, 540.
4. *De Virginibus,* lib. 1, c. 7, PL 16, 209.
5. Ambrose, *Expos. Evang. sec. Luc.,* lib. 2, 2, PL 15, 1553.
6. Jerome, *Adv. Jov.,* lib. 1, n. 3, PL 23, 223. Cf. *De Perpetua Virginitate B. Mariae,* PL 23, 213; *Adv. Jov.,* lib. 1, n. 12, PL 23, 237; Augustine, *Retract.,* lib. 2, c. 53, PL 32, 651.
7. Denis the Carthusian, *Enarr. in Gen. 30,* a. 75, *Works,* vol. 1, p. 340. Cf. *De Laudabili Vita Conjugatorum,* a. 2, *Works,* vol. 38, p. 60; 2nd Council of Braga, c. 11, DB 241; Robert Pullen, *Sent.,* lib. 2, c. 27, PL 186, 754; Vincent Contenson, O.P., *Theologia Mentis et Cordis* (Turin: J. J. Avondus, 1768), lib. 11, pars 4, dissert. 4, c. 1.
8. *Contra Haereses,* lib. 1, c. 28, PG 7, 690.
9. *Stromata,* lib. 3, c. 12, PG 8, 1186.
10. *Orat.* 2, c. 2, PG 18, 50.
11. *Serm. 45 adv. Haer., Works,* vol. 2, p. 540.
12. VIII, c. 51, cited by De Guibert, *op. cit.,* p. 5.
13. *Epist.,* 43, n. 3, PL 16, 1124.
14. *Tract. in Matt.,* tract. 10, PL 20, 351.
15. 1 Cor. 7, 25.
16. Ambrosiaster, *In 1 Cor.* 7, 25, PL 17, 233.
17. Cf. Augustine, *De Bono Vid.,* c. 8, PL 40, 437.
18. *Leonine Sacramentary,* Muratori, vol. 1, p. 724.
19. *In 7 Ps. Paenit.,* ps. 4, 7, PL 79, 586.
20. *Hom. in Evang.* lib. 2, 36, 5, PL 76, 1269.
21. Cf. Haymo of Halberstadt, *Homil. de Tempore,* 18, PL 118, 126, 127; Paschasius Radbert, *Expos. in Mt.,* lib. 9, c. 19, PL 120, 647-8.

22. *Expos. in Ep. Pauli*, 1 Cor., PL 134, 350.
23. Cf. Werner, *Deflorationes Ss. Pp.*, lib. 2, Dom. 20, PL 157, 1195; Walter of Mortagne, *Summa Sent.*, tr. 7, c. 2, PL 176, 155.
24. Cf. Abelard, *Expos. in Hex.*, 6a die, PL 178, 764; Robert Pullen, *Sent.*, lib. 7, c. 28, PL 186, 945; Peter Lombard, *Sent.*, lib. 4, d. 26; Pierre Le-Mangeur, *Hist. Scholastica*, lib. Gen., c. 9, PL 198, 1064; Bonacursus, *Lib. contra Catharos*, c. 5, PL 204, 780; Alain de Lille, *Summa de. A. P.*, c. 45, PL 210, 193; *Contra Haer.*, lib. 1, c. 65, PL 210, 368.
25. Aquinas, *In 4 Sent.*, d. 26, q. 1, a. 3. Cf. *ibid.*, d. 30, q. 2, a. 1, quaest. 3; d. 26, q. 2, a. 2, ad 4; William of Auxerre, *Summa Aurea* (Paris: Philippe Pigouchet), lib. 4 de matrim., c. 1; Alexander of Hales, *Summa*, II II, Inq. 3, tr. 4, sec. 2, q. 1, tit. 7, c. 2, Quar. 2, 598; Albert the Great, *In 4 Sent.*, d. 26, a. 5; Bonaventure, *Q. D. de Perf. Evangel.*, q. 3, a. 1, Quar. 5, 168; *In 4 Sent.*, d. 28, dub. 3.
26. *Report.*, lib. 4, d. 31, q. 1.
27. Thomas of Strasbourg, *In 4 Sent.*, d. 26, q. 1, a. 2 (Geneva: Antonius Orerius, 1585); St. Antoninus, *Summa Sac. Theol.* (Venice: Juntas, 1582), III, tit. 1, c. 1, n. 1; Denis the Carthusian, *Summa Fid. Orth.*, lib. 4, a. 163, *Works*, vol. 18, p. 210.
28. *De Summa Doctrinae Christianae* (Cologne: Calenius, 1577), II, p. 1, c. 4, n. 7, q. 129. Cf. *Vita Sancti Iddae*, Epist. et Actus, Otto Braunsberger, ed. (Fribourg: Herder, 1905), vol. 8, p. 808.
29. *La Perfecta Casada*, E. Wallace, ed. (Chicago: U. of Chicago Press, 1903), p. 12.
30. II Quadrages., Dies S. Josephi, Hom. 3, *Opera Omnia* (Padua: Officina Typogr. Seminarii, 1928), vol. 5, p. 466. Cf. St. Francis de Sales, Letter 1738, *Works*, vol. 3, p. 614; DeLugo, *Tract. de 7 Sac.* (Venice: Baba, 1652), Theorema 9, n. 37; Contenson, *op. cit.*, lit. 11, p. 4, dis. 1, c. 1, IV, 418; Leo XIII, *Arcanum*, ASS 12 (1879–80), p. 392; Pius XI, *Casti Connubii*, AAS 22 (1930), p. 541.
31. Jn. 2, 1–2.
32. Jn. 2, 11.
33. *Serm. 47 adv. Haer.*, *Works*, vol. 2, p. 542.
34. Chrysostom, *In Illud, Propter Forn.*, 1, PG 51, 210. Cf. Gregory Nazianzen, *Orat. 40 in Bapt.*, c. 18, PG 36, 382; Epiphanius, *Adv. Haer.*, lib. 2, tom. 2, heeres. 47, PG 42, 179.
35. Augustine, *In Joann.*, tr. 9, c. 2, PL 35, 1458. Cf. Gaudentius of Brescia, *Sermo* 8, PL 20, 388; Theodoret, *De Incarnatione Salvatoris*, c. 25, PG 75, 1463.
36. Cf. Bede, *Hom.*, I, 14, PL 94, 68 (CC 122, 95); Smaragdus, *Collectiones*, Dom. 2a post Theophaniam, PL 102, 85; Haymo of Halberstadt, *Hom. de Tempore*, 18, PL 118, 126–7; Bruno of Asti, *Comm. in Joann.*, pars 1, c. 2, PL 165, 461.
37. Philip of Harveng, *De Continentia Clericorum*, c. 61, PL 203, 745;

Ermengaudus, *Contra Waldenses*, c. 5, PL 204, 1339–42; Walter of Mortagne, *Summa Sent.*, tr. 7, c. 2, PL 176, 155.
38. Cf. Alain de Lille, *Summa de A. P.*, c. 45, PL 210, 193; Bonaventure, *De Perf. Evang.*, q. 3, a. 1, Quar. 5, 168; Aquinas, *In Joann.*, c. 2, lect. 1; Ludolph of Saxony, *Vita Christi Domini* (Venice: V. Bonnello, 1587), pars 1, c. 25, p. 189; St. Antoninus, *Summa Sac. Theol.*, III, tit. 1, c. 1, n. 1; Denis the Carthusian, *Enarr. in Joan.*, 2, a. 7; Works, vol. 12, p. 313; Cajetan, *In Joann.* 2, 2; Salmeron, *op. cit.*, 5, tr. 9, 49–50.

CHAPTER 3

1. Jerome, *Epist.*, 100, n. 12, PL 22, 823.
2. *De Opif. Hom.*, c. 17, PG 44, 187, 190.
3. *De Virginitate*, c. 17, PG 48, 546. Cf. *Hom. in Gen.*, n. 18, PG 53, 153.
4. *Quaest. in Genesim*, c. 3, q. 37, PG 80, 135. Cf. *Graec. Aff. Cur.*, lib. 3, PG 83, 891.
5. *Interp. de Lib. Creat. Hom.*, c. 18, PL 67, 376–7.
6. Cf. Procopius of Gaza, *Comm. in Gen.*, c. 4, v. 1, PG 87, 234; Anon., *Consultationes Zacchaei Christiani*, lib. 3, c. 5, PL 20, 1156; Isidore of Seville, *De Eccl. Off.*, lib. 2, c. 20, PL 83, 809.
7. *De Fide Orth.*, lib. 4, c. 24, PG 94, 1208.
8. *De Fide Orth.*, lib. 2, c. 30, PG 94, 975.
9. *In Gen.*, *Works*, vol. 1, p. 36.
10. *Op. Imperf. Contra Jul.*, lib. 6, c. 30, PL 45, 1582.
11. *De Gen. ad Lit.*, lib. 9, cc. 3–5, PL 34, 394–5.
12. *Op. Imperf. Contra Jul.*, *loc. cit.*
13. *De Gen. ad Lit.*, lib. 9, c. 8, PL 34, 398.
14. *Gregorian Sacramentary*, Muratori, vol. 2, p. 885.
15. Cf. Bede, *Hexam.*, lib. 1, PL 91, 49; Rabanus Maurus, *Comm. in Gen.*, lib. 1, c. 14, PL 107, 482.
16. Angelomus Luxoviensis, *Comm. in Gen.*, 1, 27, PL 115, 123; Remigius of Auxerre, *Comm. in Gen.*, 2, 18, PL 131, 62.
17. Angelomus Luxoviensis, *loc. cit.*
18. Bruno of Asti, *Expos. in Gen.*, c. 2, PL 164, 165; Otto of Lucca, *Summa Sent.*, c. 26, PL 171, 1122; Hugh of St. Victor, *De Sac.*, lib. 2, p. 11, c. 2, PL 176, 481.
19. *Sent.*, lib. 2, d. 20.
20. *Sent.*, cited by Claude Schall, O.F.M., *La doctrine des fins du mariage dans la théologie scholastique* (Paris: Editions Franciscaines, 1948), p. 82.
21. Cf. Dominic Soto, *In 4 Sent.*, d. 26, q. 1, a. 3 (Douai: P. Borremaus, 1613).
22. Cf. Ramon Lull, *Blanquerna*, E. Allison Peers, tr. (London: Jarrolds, 1925), p. 517; Alexander of Hales, *Summa*, Inq. 3, tr. 2, q. 3, tit. 3, a. 1, Quar. 2, 364; Albert the Great, *In 4 Sent.*, d. 26, a. 6.
23. *S.T.* I, q. 99, a. 2 ad 3.
24. *In 2 Sent.*, d. 20, q. 1, a. 1.

25. Cf. Dominic Soto, *In 4 Sent.*, d. 26, q. 1, a. 3.
26. *Explan. in Gen.* 1, 28, *Works*, vol. 3, p. 201.
27. *Arcanum Divinae Sapientiae*, ASS 12, p. 386.

CHAPTER 4

1. *Apolog.*, 1, n. 29, PG 6, 374.
2. *Legatio Pro Christianis*, PG 6, 966.
3. *Stromata*, lib. 3, c. 7, PG 8, 1162.
4. *Hom. 5 in Gen.*, PG 12, 192.
5. Denis the Carthusian, *Serm. 3 in Dom. 3 post Nat.*, Works, vol. 29, p. 192. Cf. *De Laud. Vita Conj.*, a. 5, Works, vol. 38, p. 63. Ambrose, *Expos. in Luc.*, lib. 1, n. 44, PL 15, 1631–2.
6. *Comm. in Ep. ad Gal.*, lib. 3, c. 5, 21, PL 26, 443.
7. *Adv. Jov.*, lib. 1, n. 32, PL 26, 443.
8. Tob. 6, 16–22 (Vulgate).
9. PL 29, 23–6.
10. *Contra Jul.*, lib. 5, c. 9, PL 44, 806. Cf. *De Bono Conjug.*, c. 9, PL 40, 380.
11. *Op. Imperf. Contra Jul.*, lib. 4, c. 29, PL 45, 1353. Cf. *Contra 2 Ep. Pelag.*, lib. 1, c. 16, PL 44, 565; *De Doct. Christ.*, lib. 3, c. 18, PL 34, 76; *Serm.*, 51, c. 13, PL 38, 345–6; *ibid.*, 278, c. 9, PL 38, 1272.
12. *De Bono Vid.*, c. 6, PL 40, 435–6. Cf. *De Bono Conj.*, cc. 17–19, PL 40, 386–9.
13. *De Bono Conj.*, c. 15, PL 40, 385.
14. *Quaest. in Levit.*, c. 15, interr. 20, PG 80, 326.
15. Cf. Procopius of Gaza, *In Gen.* 16, 1, PG 87, 350–1.
16. Cf. Fulgentius of Ruspe, *Epist.*, 1, c. 3, PL 65, 305.
17. Cf. Gregory the Great, *Reg. Past.*, pars 3, c. 27, PL 77, 101–3; Isidore of Seville, *De Eccl. Off.*, lib. 2, c. 20, n. 11, PL 83, 812; Jonas of Orleans, *De Inst. Laic.*, lib. 2, c. 1, PL 106, 167–70; Rabanus Maurus, *Enarr. in Ep. Pauli*, lib. 10, c. 7, PL 112, 64. Hatto of Vercelli, *Expos. in Ep. Pauli*, 1 Cor., PL 134, 350; *Dict. Gratiani*, c. 32, q. 2, c. 2, col. 1120; Hugh of St. Victor, *De Sac.*, lib. 2, pars 11, c. 3, PL 176, 482; *ibid.*, c. 9, PL 176, 496; Walter of Mortagne, *Summa Sent.*, tract. 7, c. 3, PL 176, 156; Abelard, *Ethica*, c. 6, PL 178, 638; *Prob. Hel.*, 42, PL 178, 723–6; *Sic et Non*, c. 130, PL 178, 1560–3; Harvey of Bourg-Dieu, *Comm. in 1 Cor.* 7, PL 181, 875; Robert Pullen, *Sent.*, lib. 7, c. 30, PL 186, 948; Peter Lombard, *Sent.*, lib. 4, d. 31, cc. 6–8, PL 192, 920–1; Bandinus, *4 Sent.*, 29, PL 192, 1108; Richard of St. Victor, *Explic. in C.C.*, c. 38, PL 196, 514; Pierre LeChantre, *Summa Abel.*, cited by Schall, *op. cit.*, p. 85; Peter of Poitiers, *Sent.*, lib. 5, c. 15, PL 211, 1258; Alexander of Hales, *In 4 Sent.*, d. 31, n. 18; *Summa* II II, Inq. 3, tr. 4, sec. 2, q. 1, a. 4, Quar. 3, 597; *ibid.*, tr. 5, sec. 2, q. 1, tit. 3, cc. 1–2, Quar. 3, 631 ff.; William of Auvergne, *De Virtutibus* (Paris: Pierre Aubouin, 1674), c. 13: Albert the Great, *In 4 Sent.*, d. 26, a. 1; Bonaventure, *In 4 Sent.*, d. 31,

a. 2, q. 1; Aquinas, *In 4 Sent.* d. 31, q. 2., a. 2; *In 1 Cor.* 7, lect. 1; Scotus, *In 4 Sent.*, d. 26, q. 1, Schol, 1, 7; Thomas of Strasbourg, *In 4 Sent.*, d. 31, q. 1, a. 4. Cf. also Josef Fuchs, *Die Sexualethik des Heiligen Thomas von Aquin* (Cologne: Verlag J. B. Bachem, 1949), p. 88.

18. Cf. Denis the Carthusian, *Enarr. in Prov.*, 5, a. 5, *Works*, vol. 7, p. 42; *Enarr. in Sap.* 3, a. 3, *Works*, vol. 7, p. 472; *Enarr. in 1 Cor.* 7, a. 7, *Works*, vol. 13, p. 152; *Summa Fid. Orth.*, lib. 4, a. 162, *Works*, vol. 18, p. 210; *Serm. 3 in Dom. 3 post Nat.*, *Works*, vol. 29, p. 191; *Laud. Vita Conj.* a. 5, *Works*, vol. 38, p. 63.

19. Cf. Soto, *In 4 Sent.*, d. 26, q. 1, a. 3; d. 31, q. 1, a. 3; Salmeron, *op. cit.*, 15, disp. 13, p. 263; P. Buys, S.J., *De Statibus Hominum* (Mainz: J. Albinus, 1613), p. 206.

20. *Catechismus ex Decreto Conc. Trid.* (Padua: 1758), pars II, c. 8, par. 13.

21. Cf. Contenson, *op. cit.*, IV, lib. 11, pars 4, dissert. 4, c. 1, spec. 1.

22. DB 1159.

23. *Apol.*, 1, 29, PG 6, 373.

24. *Strom.*, lib. 3, c. 7, PG 8, 1162.

25. *De Nupt. et Concup.*, c. 9, PL 44, 419.

26. *Contra Jul.*, II, c. 7, n. 20, PL 44, 687.

27. Cf. Bede, *In 1 Pet.*, 3, PL 93, 55; Master Bandinus, *Sent.*, lib. 4, d. 29, PL 192, 1108; Denis the Carthusian, *Enarr. in Ecclus.* 23, a. 23, *Works*, vol. 8, p. 132.

28. DB 1159.

29. Address to Italian Midwives, 10/20/51, AAS 43 (1951), pp. 851-3.

30. *De Oratione*, 31, PG 11, 554.

31. Tertullian, *Ad Uxorem*, lib. 1, 1, CC 1, 374.

32. Zeno of Verona, lib. 1, tr. 5, n. 2, PL 11, 302.

33. *Exhort. Virgin.*, c. 6, PL 16, 362. Cf. *De Virg.*, lib. 1, c. 6, PL 16, 206.

34. *De Nupt. et Concup.*, lib. 2, c. 21, PL 44, 457. Cf. *Contra 2 Ep. Pel.*, lib. 1, c. 16, PL 44, 565.

35. Cyril of Alexandria, *Explan. in Ps.* 50, 7, PG 69, 1091. Cf. Gregory the Great, *Reg. Past.*, pars 3, c. 27, PL 77, 101-3.

36. *Lib. Dec.*, lib. 9, c. 8, PL 140, 816.

37. *Expos. in 1 Cor.* 7, PL 153, 156.

38. *Cur Deus Homo*, lib. 2, c. 8, PL 158, 406.

39. *De Nupt. Consang.*, c. 6, PL 158, 560.

40. William of Auvergne, *De Sac. Mat.*, c. 3; cf. *ibid.*, c. 7; Rupert of Deutz, *De Trin. et Op. Eius*, In Gen. lib. 2, c. 40, PL 167, 286; Pierre Le Mangeur, *Hist. Schol.*, Lib. Gen., 20, PL 198, 1072.

41. Cf. Pierre de la Palu, *In 4 Sent.*, d. 31, q. 2, a. 1 (Venice: 1493).

42. *Summa Sac. Theol.*, pars. 3, tit. 1, c. 20.

43. Cf. Cajetan, *In Gen.*, 3, 7.

44. *Op. cit.*, 3, tr. 29, p. 225.

45. *Ibid.*, 5, tr. 8, p. 45. Cf. Lawrence of Brindisi, *Explan. in Gen.* 2, 25, *Works*, vol. 3, p. 248.

46. Gen. 3, 7.

47. *De Gen. ad Lit.*, lib. 3, c. 21. Cf. *Contra 2 Ep. Pel.*, lib. 1, c. 5, PL 44, 555; *ibid.*, PL 44, 565–6.

48. *Contra Jul.*, lib. 4, c. 11, PL 44, 765. Cf. *Contra 2 Ep. Pel.*, lib. 1, c. 17, PL 44, 566.

49. *De Civ. Dei*, lib. 14, c. 24, PL 41, 433 (CC 48, 448).

50. *Ibid.*, c. 26, PL 41, 434 (CC 48, 449).

51. *Ibid.*, c. 20, PL 41, 428 (CC 48, 443). Cf. *ibid.*, cc. 17, 18, 23, PL 41, 425–31.

52. *De Nupt. et Concup.*, lib. 1, c. 5, PL 44, 417.

53. *Contra Jul.*, lib. 4, c. 10, PL 44, 765. Cf. *Op. Imperf. Contr. Jul.*, lib. 5, c. 24, PL 45, 1461.

54. *De Nupt. et Concup.*, lib. 1, c. 14, PL 44, 423.

55. *Serm.* 51, c. 15, PL 38, 348.

56. Fulgentius of Ruspe, *De Fide ad Petr.*, c. 2, n. 16, PL 65, 608.

57. Gregory the Great, *In 7 Pen. Ps.*, Ps. 4, 7, PL 79, 586.

58. *Liber Poenit.*, c. 11, PL 105, 668.

59. Ps.-Greg. M., *Epist.*, lib. 11, indict. 4, epist. 64, PL 77, 1196–7.

60. Angelomus Loxov., *Comm. in Gen.*, 2, 25, PL 115, 135.

61. Remigius of Auxerre, *Comm. in Gen.*, 2, 25, PL 131, 63.

62. *De Trin. et Op.*, In Gen., lib. 2, c. 9, PL 167, 254–5. Cf. *Comm. in Joann.*, lib. 2, PL 169, 275.

63. Otto of Lucca, *Summa Sent.*, c. 33, PL 171, 1136. Cf. Honorius of Autun, *Elucidarium*, lib. 1, n. 14, PL 172, 1118.

64. *Adnot. in Gen.* 3, PL 175, 42. Cf. *De Sac.*, lib. 1, pars 8, PL 176, 317–18; Robert Pullen, *Sent.*, lib. 2, c. 25, PL 186, 753; Peter Lombard, *Sent.*, lib. 2, d. 20; Pierre LeMangeur, *Hist. Schol.*, lib. Gen., c. 22, PL 198, 1073.

65. *Summa*, Inq. 4, tr. 3, q. 2, c. 2 ad 2 & 3, Quar. 2, 703.

66. *Ibid.*, Quar. 2, 702.

67. *In 4 Sent.*, d. 31, n. 19, Quar. 1, 503. Cf. *Summa*, II II, Inq. 3, tr. 5, sec. 2, q. 1, tit. 3, c. 2 ad 3, Quar. 3, 635.

68. *In 4 Sent.*, d. 31, n. 17, Quar. 1, 502.

69. *In 4 Sent.*, d. 26, q. 1, a. 3 ad 3.

70. S.T. I, q. 98, a. 2. Cf. Albert the Great, *In 4 Sent.*, d. 26, a. 11.

71. *S.T.* II II, q. 153, a. 1 ad 3.

72. *In 4 Sent.*, d. 31, q. 1, a. 1 ad 1.

73. *In 2 Sent.*, d. 20, a. 1, q. 2.

74. *In 4 Sent.*, d. 26, a. 2, q. 1.

75. Cf. Bonaventure, *Q. D. de Perf. Evang.*, q. 3, a. 1, ad 7, 9, 15, Quar. 5, p. 109; Scotus, *Report.*, lib. 4, d. 26, q. 1, schol. 7; *ibid.*, d. 32, q. 1, schol. 2.

76. Cf. Thomas of Strasbourg, *In 4 Sent.*, d. 31, q. 1, a. 2.

77. Cf. St. Antoninus, *Summa Moralis* (Florence: P. Viviani, 1741), I, tit. 11, c. 1. n. 4; Denis the Carthusian, *Summa Fide Orth.*, lib. 4, a. 162, *Works*, vol. 18, p. 209; *Enarr. in Gen.* 3, a. 24, *Works*, vol. 1, p. 99; *Enarr. in Luc.* 1, a. 2, *Works*, vol. 11, p. 382; Salmeron, *op. cit.*, 5, tr. 9, 50; Soto, *In 4 Sent.*, d. 31, q. 1, a. 2 ad 3; *ibid.*, d. 26, q. 1, a. 3.

78. *Retract.*, lib. 2, c. 53, PL 32, 651.

79. *De Gen. ad Lit.* lib. 9, c. 7, PL 34, 397. Cf. *De Pecc. Mer. et Rem.*, lib. 1, c. 29, PL 44, 141; *Contra Jul.*, lib. 3, c. 21, PL 44, 725; *Op. Imperf. Contra Jul.*, lib. 2, c. 45, PL 45, 1161.

80. Walter of Mortagne, *Summa Sent.*, tract. 7, c. 2, PL 176, 155. Cf. Thos. of Citeaux, *Comm. in C.C.*, lib. 3, PL 106, 158.

81. Unknown Author, *Allegoriae in N.T.*, lib. 7, PL 175, 910, Cf. Hugh of St. Victor, *De Sac.*, lib. 2, pars 11, c. 7, PL 176, 494.

82. *Contra Haereticos*, lib. 1, c. 64, PL 210, 366.

83. *Summa de Arte Praed.*, c. 45, PL 210, 193. Cf. *Contra. Haer.*, lib. 1, c. 65, PL 210, 369.

84. Cf. Pierre de Poitiers, *Sent.*, lib. 5, c. 15, PL 211, 1258.

85. *Op. cit.*, tom. 1, p. 519, cited by G. Le Bras, DTC 9, 2198.

86. *Summa*, II II, Inq. 3, tr. 4, sect. 2, q. 1, tit. 7, art. 1, Quar. 3, p. 594.

87. *In 4 Sent.*, d. 31, a. 2, q. 1.

88. *Ibid.*, q. 3 ad 5; Cf. d. 31, a. 1, q. 2; *Comm. in Luc.*, 17, 27, Quar. 7, p. 441.

89. *In 4 Sent.*, d. 31, q. 1, a. 1 ad 4.

90. *Ibid.*, a. 3.

91. Cf. Albert the Great, *In 4 Sent.*, d. 26, a. 11; Scotus, *Ox.*, d. 31, q. 1; d. 26, q. 1; *Report.*, lib. 4, d. 31, q. 1, schol. 1; Pierre de la Palu, *In 4 Sent.*, d. 26, q. 2, a. 1; d. 31, q. 1, a. 1–2; Thos. of Strasbourg, *In 4 Sent.*, d. 31, q. 1, a. 2; Capreolus, *Defensiones Theologicae D. T. Aquini* (Tours: Alfred Cattier, 1906), *In 4 Sent.*, dd. 30–2, q. 1, a. 1, a. 3 ad 1, 2.

92. *Summa Sac. Theol.*, III, tit. 1, c. 20, n. 12–13. Cf. Denis the Carthusian, *Enarr. in Ps. 50*, a. 93, *Works*, 6, 43; *Enarr. in 1 Cor.* 7, a. 7, *Works*, 13, 152; *Summa Fid. Orth.*, lib. 4, a. 162, *Works*, 18, 209; a. 171, *Works*, 18, 215.

93. *Ibid.*

94. *Explan. in Gen.* 2, 25, *Works*, vol. 3, p. 248. Cf. Soto, *In 4 Sent.*, d. 31, q. 1, a. 1, 3; Salmeron, *op cit.*, 5, tr. 9, 50; 6, tr. 6, 33; Buys, *op. cit.*, p. 210; *Catechismus Concil. Trid.*, II, 8, 23; Sanchez, *De Sac. Mat.* (Venice: B. Milochus, 1672), lib. 2, disp. 29, q. 1.; Leonard Lessius, *Praelectiones Theol. Posthumae* (Louvain: C. Coenestenius, 1645), Prael. de Sac. Mat., c. 5, nota; Christian Pesch, S.J., *Praelectiones Dogmaticae* (Friburg: Herder, 1900), ed. 2a, tom. 7, p. 313.

CHAPTER 5

1. *De Bono Conjug.*, n. 15, PL 40, 384.

2. *Epist.*, 1, c. 4, PL 65, 306.

3. *Reg. Past.*, III, 27, PL 77, 102.
4. Ps. Greg. M., *Epist*, lib. 11, indict. 4, ep. 64, PL 77, 1196-7. Cf. Isidore of Seville, *De Eccl. Off.*, lib. 2, c. 20, n. 10, PL 83, 812.
5. *Lib. Paenit.*, lib. 1, c. 17, PL 105, 668-9.
6. Erlangen, cited by G. Le Bras, DTC 9, 2177. Cf. Rupert of Deutz, *De Trin. et Op.*, lib. 3, c. 11, PL 167, 297; Walter of Mortagne, *Summa Sent.*, tract. 7, c. 3, PL 176, 157; Hugh of St. Victor, *De Sac. Mat.*, PL 176, 316.
7. *Sent.*, lib. 7, c. 31, PL 186, 949.
8. *Sent.*, lib. 4, d. 31, c. 8.
9. Cf. Pierre de Poitiers, *Sent.*, lib. 5, PL 211, 1258, 1263; Innocent III, *De Contemptu Mundi*, lib. 1, c. 1, PL 217, 703; Eckebert of Schaunang, *Serm. Contra Catharos*, serm. 5, PL 195, 30; Pierre LeMangeur, *Hist. Schol.*, lib. Gen., c. 20, PL 198, 1072.
10. *In 4 Sent.*, d. 31, n. 20, Quar. 1, 504.
11. *In 4 Sent.*, d. 31, a. 2, q. 1. Cf. *ibid.*, a. 3, q. 1; d. 37, a. 1, q. 3.
12. Thomas of Strasbourg, *In 4 Sent.*, d. 33, q. 1, a. 1.
13. *Enarr. in Ps.* 50, a. 93, *Works*, vol. 6, p. 43. Cf. *Enarr. in Tob.* 3, a. 3, *Works*, vol. 5, p. 97.
14. DB 792.
15. Denis Peteau, *Dogmata Theologica* (Paris: L. Vives, 1867), De Incarn., lib. 14, c. 1, n. 2.
16. *Reflections Chrétiennes*, du Mariage, Oeuvres Complètes (Grenoble: Patronage Catholique, 1900), vol. 5, p. 181.
17. *Lib. Paenit.*, PL 105, 668 ff.
18. *De Bono Conjug.*, c. 10, PL 40, 381.
19. Cf. Walter of Mortagne, *Summa Sent.*, tract. 7, c. 3, PL 176, 156; Hugh of St. Victor, *De Sac. Mat.*, lib. 2, pars 11, c. 11, PL 176, 496; Huguccio, fol. 12, cited by Schall, *op. cit.*, p. 75; *Summa Rufini*, Schulte, ed., p. 394, cited by Schall, p. 76.
20. *Sent.*, lib. 4, d. 26, cc. 4, 32; d. 31, cc. 5, 8; d. 32. Cf. Albert the Great, *In 4 Sent.*, d. 31, a. 27; Bonaventure, *In 4 Sent.*, d. 31, a. 2, q. 2; Aquinas, *In 4 Sent.*, d. 31, q. 2, a. 2.
21. *Report.* d. 32.
22. *Op. Ox.*, d. 32, q. 1.
23. *De Sac. Mat.*, lib. 9, disp. 8, n. 1. Cf. St. Antoninus, *Summa Sac. Theol.*, III, tit. 1, c. 20, n. 11; Denis the Carthusian, *Serm. 3 in Dom. 3 post Nat.*, *Works*, vol. 29, p. 191; *De Laud. Vita Conj.*, a. 6, *Works*, vol. 38, p. 64; Soto, *In 4 Sent.*, d. 31, q. 1, a. 3.
24. Abelard, *Prob. Hel.*, 14, PL 178, 701. Cf. *ibid.* 42, PL 178, 723.
25. Robert Pullen, *Sent.*, lib. 7, c. 30, PL 186, 948. Cf. *ibid.*, c. 39, PL 186, 958.
26. *Sent.*, lib. 4, d. 26, c. 4.
27. Lib. 5, c. 17, PL 211, 1260.
28. *Summa Aurea*, lib. 4, de mat., c. 4.
29. *In 4 Sent.*, d. 30, n. 11, Quar. 1, p. 487. Cf. *ibid.*, d. 31, n. 10, Quar. 1, p.

496; Bonaventure, *Q.D. de Perf. Evang.*, q. 3, a. 1, Quar. 5, p. 169; *In 4 Sent.*, d. 31, a. 2, q. 2; Aquinas, *In 4 Sent.*, q. 2, a. 2.

30. *In 4 Sent.*, d. 30, q. 1, a. 3.
31. *In 4 Sent.*, d. 31, q. 1, a. 4.
32. *Ibid.*, a. 3.
33. *Summa Sac. Theol*, III, tit. 1, c. 20, n. 11.
34. *De Laud. Vita Conj.*, a. 5, Works, vol. 38, p. 63.
35. *In 4 Sent.*, d. 31, q. 1, a. 4.
36. *Ibid.*
37. *Ibid.*
38. Cf. De Granada, *Traité de la Doct. Chrét.*, lib. 3, c. 16, Works 17, 219; Lessius, *Prael.*, *De Sac. Mat.*, c. 1, dub. 2; Luis De la Puente, *De Christiani Hominis Perfectione* (Cologne: 1615), vol. 2, pp. 470–1; De Lugo, *Trac. de 7 Sac.*, Theor., 9, n. 39, p. 149.
39. Soto, *In 4 Sent.*, d. 31, q. 1, a. 3.
40. *Ibid.*, d. 26, q. 1, a. 3.
41. *Op. cit.*, 8, tr. 51, 475.
42. *De Sac. Mat.*, lib. 2, disp. 29, nn. 24–5.
43. *Ibid.*, lib. 9, disp. 8, nn. 3–4. Cf. *ibid.*, n. 11.
44. *Introd. Vie Dév.*, p. 3, c. 39, *Works* 1, 618.
45. Cf. Walter of Mortagne, *Summa Sent.*, tr. 7, c. 3, PL 175, 156.
46. *Ethica*, c. 3, PL 178, 640.
47. Robert of Melun, *Sent.*, cited by Schahl, *op. cit.*, p. 85.
48. *Sent.*, lib. 4, d. 31, c. 8.
49. *Summa Aurea*, lib. 4, de mat., c. 1.
50. *Ibid.*
51. *In 4 Sent.*, d. 26, a. 6.
52. *Ibid.*, a. 7.
53. *Ibid.*, d. 31, a. 27. Cf. *ibid.*, a. 21.
54. *S.T.* I, q. 98, a. 2 ad 3. Cf. *In 2 Sent.*, d. 30, q. 1, a. 2 ad 2.
55. *Report.*, d. 31, q. 1.
56. *In 4 Sent.*, d. 31, q. 1, a. 2.
57. *De Cond. Morte.*, c. 6, PG 154, 1179–82.
58. *Enarr. in Ecclus.*, 18, a. 18, *Works* 8, 108.
59. *De Laud. Vita Conj.*, a. 8, *Works* 38, 66.
60. *Ibid.*
61. *In 4 Sent.*, d. 31, q. 1, a. 3.
62. *Op. cit.*, 5, tr. 9, p. 50. Cf. 8, tr. 51, 475.
63. *Ibid.*, 5, tr. 9, p. 50.
64. *De Sac. Mat.*, lib. 9, disp. 19, n. 6.
65. *Introd. Vie Dév.*, p. 3, c. 39, *Works* 1, 648.
66. *Le Livre du Jeune Homme* (Paris: V. Palme, 1874), p. 69.
67. *Ibid.*
68. *Sacra Virginitas*, AAS 46 (1954), p. 169.
69. Address to Italian Midwives, 10/29/51, AAS 43 (1951), p. 851.
70. *De Sac. Mat.*, c. 6, *Works* 1, 521.

71. *De Retributionibus Sanctorum, Works* 1, 323.
72. *In 4 Sent.,* d. 30, dub. 6.
73. *De Laud. Vita Conj.,* a. 5, *Works* 38, 63. Cf. *Serm. 3 in dom. 3 post Nat., Works* 29, 191.
74. *Cat. Conc. Trid.,* II, 8, 14.
75. *De Sac. Mat.,* lib. 2, d. 29.
76. *Introd. Vie Dév.,* p. 3, c. 39, *Works* 1, 648.
77. *Op. cit.,* p. 67.
78. Dominic Palmieri, S.J., *Tractatus De Matrimonio Christiano* (Rome: S.C. de Propag. Fide, 1880), tr. 10, c. 2, p. 289. Cf. Pesch., *op. cit.,* p. 313.
79. Arthur Vermeersch, S.J., *De Castitate* (Rome: P.U.G., 1921), ed. 2a., p. 224.
80. *Casti Connubii,* AAS 22 (1930), p. 561.

PART II: INTRODUCTION

1. Cf. McKenzie, *The Two-Edged Sword,* p. 46.
2. Cf. McKenzie, "The Literary Characteristics of Genesis," *loc. cit.; The Two-Edged Sword,* pp. 52 ff.
3. *Ibid.*
4. Gen. 1, 26–7.
5. Qoh. 9, 9.
6. Sir. 36, 27. Cf. Prov. 18, 22.
7. Cf. Judges 7, 30; 12, 8, 14; 2 Sam. 2, 2; 3, 2–5, 15 ff.; 5, 13–16; 11, 27; 1 Kings 1, I ff.; 11, 1–8; 2 Par. 11, 18–23; 2 Kings 10, 12–14.
8. Cf. Is. 4, 1.
9. Cf. Gen. 2, 24; 4, 19; Deut. 17, 17. Cf. also Roland De Vaux, *Ancient Israel* (New York: McGraw-Hill, 1961), pp. 24–6.

CHAPTER 7

1. Mt. 19, 11.
2. Mt. 13, 11.
3. 1 Cor. 7, 26.
4. Cf. Jer. 16, 1–4. Cf. also L. Legand, "The Prophetical Meaning of Celibacy," *Scripture,* 12 (1960), pp. 97–105.
5. 1 Cor. 7, 29–31.
6. Cf. Legrand, *op. cit.*
7. *Ad Uxorem,* lib. 1, c. 5, PL 1, 1281.
8. *De Virginitate,* c. 58, PG 48, 580.
9. Ambrosiaster, *In 1 Cor.* 7, 29, PL 17, 234–5.
10. *De Perpet. Virg. B.V.M.,* c. 21, PL 23, 215.
11. *Adv. Jov.,* lib. 1, n. 26, PL 23, 239. Cf. Unknown Author, *Consultationes Zacchaei,* lib. 3, c. 5, PL 20, 1157; Isidore of Seville, *De Eccl. Off.,* lib. 2, c. 20, PL 83, 809.
12. *De Bono Conj.,* c. 10, PL 40, 381.
13. *Hex.,* lib. 1, PL 91, 31. Cf. Rabanus Maurus, *Comm. in Gen.,* lib. 1, c. 7, PL 107, 462.

14. Harvey of Bourg-Dieu, *Comm. in 1 Cor.* 7, PL 181, 883. Cf. Rabanus Maurus, *Enarr. in Ep. Pauli*, lib. 10, c. 7, PL 112, 71; *Expos. Super Jer.*, lib. 11, c. 29, PL 111, 1017; Hatto of Vercelli, *Expos. in Ep. Pauli*, 1 or., PL 134, 357; Bruno of Asti, *Expos. in 1 Cor.* 7, PL 153, 156.

15. *In 4 Sent.*, d. 26, a. 1, q. 3.

16. *In 4 Sent.*, d. 26, a. 8.

17. *In 4 Sent.*, d. 26, q. 1, a. 2. Cf. *S. T.* II II, q. 52, a. 12 ad 2.

18. *In 4 Sent.*, d. 26, q. 2, a. 2 ad 1.

19. *In 4 Sent.*, d. 33, q. 1, a. 4. Cf. *ibid.*, d. 26, q. 1, a. 3.

20. Cf. Cajetan, *In 1 Cor.* 7, 26.

21. *In 4 Sent.*, d. 26, q. 1, a. 2.

22. *Op. cit.*, vol. 3, tr. p. 30.

23. *Ibid.*, vol. 5, tr. 9, p. 50; vol. 8, tr. 50, pp. 393, 397.

24. Cf. Buys, *op. cit.*, p. 210.

25. *Med. de Dominic.*, Dom. 2 post Trin., Streicher, II, p. 106.

26. *Explan. in Gen.*, 1, 29, *Works* 3, 202.

27. *Prael., De Sac. Mat.*, c. 1, dub. 3. Cf. *De Justitia et Jure*, (Antwerp: B. Moreti, 1632), ed. 7a, lib. 4, c. 2, dub. 15 ad 1.

CHAPTER 8

1. 1 Cor. 7, 28.

2. Gregory Nazianzen, *Carm.*, lib. 1, sect. 2, 6, 1. 7, PG 37, 643.

3. Gregory Nazianzen, *De Virginitate*, c. 3, PG 46, 327–35. Cf. Basil the Great, *De Vera Virg. Integ.*, n. 23, PG 30, 715; *Epist.*, 1 ad Greg., PG 32, 226. Cf. *Consult. Zacchaei*, lib. 3, c. 5, PL 20, 1156–7; Isidore of Seville, *De Eccl. Off.*, lib. 2, c. 20.

4. *Ad Theod. Lap.*, lib. 2, n. 5, PG 47, 314.

5. Ambrosiaster, *In 1 Cor.* 7, 28, PL 17, 234. Cf. *ibid.*, 7, 26, PL 17, 233.

6. *Exhort. Virg.*, 34, PL 16, 346.

7. *De Virg.*, c. 6, PL 16, 287. Cf. *Lib. de Vid.*, c. 13, PL 16, 273.

8. *Adv. Jov.*, lib. 1, n. 13, PL 23, 241.

9. *Epist.*, 117, n. 10, PL 22, 959.

10. *De Sancta Virg.*, c. 16, PL 40, 403–4. Cf. *Confessiones*, lib. 9, c. 9, PL 32, 772.

11. Cf. Gregory the Great, *Reg. Past.*, pars 3, c. 27, PL 77, 103; Ps-Chrysostom, *De Sancta Thecla*, PG 50, 547; Damascene, *Sac. Paral.*, tit. 6, PG 95, 1282; Theodoret, *Graec. Aff. Cur.*, serm. 9, PG 83, 1055; Theodore of Studium, *Epist.*, lib. 2, n. 128, PG 99, 1414; Tajon, *Sent.*, lib. 3, c. 7, PL 80, 857–8; Isidore of Seville, *De Eccl. Off.*, lib. 2, c. 20, PL 83, 809.

12. Cf. Sedulius Scotus, *Coll. in 1 Cor.* 7, PL 102, 142–3; Rabanus Maurus, *Enarr. in Ep. Pauli*, lib. 10, c. 7, PL 112, 70; Haymo of Halberstadt, *Expos. in 1 Cor.* 7, PL 117, 547; Hatto of Vercelli, *Expos. in Ep. Pauli*, 1 Cor., PL 134, 357.

13. *Comm. in 1 Cor.* 7, 22, PL 150, 178.

14. Cf. Bruno of Asti, *In 1 Cor.* 7, PL 153, 160; Alain de Lille, *Summa de Arte Pr.*, c. 46, PL 210, 194.

15. *Opusc. 10 Vitis Myst.*, Add. 4, c. 30, n. 105, Quar. 8, 209–10.

16. Cf. Denis the Carthusian, *In 1 Cor.* 7, a. 7, Works 13, 156–7; *De Laud. Vita Conj.*, a. 3, *Works* 38, 61.

17. Cf. Cajetan, *In 1 Cor.* 7, 28; Soto, *In 4 Sent.*, d. 31, q. 1, a. 1.

18. *Op. cit.*, vol. 6, p. 33. Cf. *ibid.*, vol. 5, tr. 9, p. 49.

19. *Forêt de lieux communs*, 2e cl., Marriage, *Works* 21, 436. Cf. *ibid.*, Virginité, *Works* 21, 201.

20. Buys, *op cit.*, p. 225.

21. *Lettres*, 1861, *Works*, 3, 718.

22. *Ibid.*, 808, *Works* 3, 673.

23. *Ad Uxorem*, lib. 1, c. 10, PL 1, 1390.

24. *Demonstrationes Evang.*, lib. 1, c. 9, PG 22, 78–9. Cf. *Comm. in Luc.*, PG 24, 574.

25. Ambrosiaster, *In 1 Cor.* 7, 32, PL 17, 236.

26. *De Paradiso*, c. 11, PL 14, 316.

27. *De Perp. Virg. B.M.V.*, n. 20, PL 23, 214.

28. Cf. *De Sancta Virg.*, c. 16, PL 40, 403; Fulgentius, *Epist.* 2, c. 5, PL 65, 314; *ibid.*, PL 65, 321.

29. *Scala Paradisi*, Gradus 1, PG 88, 639–42.

30. Unknown Author, *Alleg. in N. T.*, lib. 7, PL 175, 912. Cf. Haymo of Halberstadt, *In 1 Cor.* 7, PL 117, 548; Lanfranc, *In 1 Cor.* 7, 24, PL 150, 178; Anon., *In 1 Cor.* 7, PL 153, 161.

31. *Prob. Hel.*, 40, PL 178, 722.

32. Cf. Alain de Lille, *Contra Haer.*, lib. 1, c. 14, PL 210, 366; Harvey of Bourg-Dieu, *In 1 Cor.* 7, PL 181, 883–6; Vincent of Beauvais, *De Eruditione Filiorum Nobilium*, Arpad Steiner, ed., (Cambridge, Mass.: Medieval Academy of America, 1938), c. 38, p. 153.

33. *Q.D. de Perf. Evang.*, q. 3, a. 2, Quar. 5, 172.

34. *In Luc.* 10, 41, Quar. 7, 274.

35. *In 4 Sent.*, d. 31, a. 1 ad 4.

36. *Ibid.*, d. 26, a. 14, q. 2 ad 1.

37. *In 4 Sent.*, d. 30, q. 1, a. 1.

38. *In 1 Cor.* 7, a. 7, *Works* 13, 156.

39. *In 1 Cor.* 7, 26.

40. *Ibid.*, 7, 1.

41. Cf. Buys, *op. cit.*, p. 225; Alvarez de Paz, *De Exterminatione Mali*, lib. 5, pars 2, c. 5, *Works* (Paris: L. Vives, 1875) 4, 579; c. 2, *Works* 4, 558.

42. Bellarmine, *De Sac. Mat.*, c. 5 (*Opera Omnia*, Naples: J. Giuliano, 1856).

43. Lessius, *Opusc.* 885, *De Bono Status Castitatis*, c. 5, Opuscula (Antwerp: B. Moretus, 1626), p. 885.

44. ———, *Disp. de Statu Vitae Eligendo*, q. 12, *Opusc.*, p. 864.

45. Pius XII, *Sacra Virginitas*, AAS 46 (1954), p. 168.

46. *De Virginitate*, c. 45, PG 48, 567.
47. Rabanus Maurus, *Enarr. in Ep. Pauli*, lib. 10, c. 7, PL 112, 74.
48. Unknown Author, *Alleg. in N. T.*, lib. 7, PL 175, 911.
49. ———, *Quaest. in Ep. Pauli*, In 1 Cor., q. 69, PL 175, 527.
50. *Op. cit.*, vol. 5, tr. 9, p. 50.

CHAPTER 9

1. Cf. Ex. 19, 15; 1 Sam. 21, 4.
2. 1 Cor. 7, 5.
3. Cf. Cyril of Jerusalem, *Catech.* 4, de 10 dogmat., 25, PG 33, 487; Augustine, *De Bono Vid.*, c. 3, PL 40, 433.; *Contra Jul.*, lib. 2, c. 7, PL 44, 687.
4. Gregory Nazianzen, *Orat.* 40, n. 18, PG 36, 382.
5. Cf. St. Isidore of Pelusium, *Epist.* 119, PG 78, 1194; Sedulius Scotus, *In 1 Cor.* 7, PL 103, 140; Thomas of Citeaux, *Comm. in C.C.*, lib. 3, PL 106, 159; Rabanus Maurus, *Hom.* 47, PL 110, 88; Unknown Author, *Alleg. in N.T.*, lib. 7, PL 175, 912; Peter Lombard, *Sent.* d. 32, n. 3, PL 192, 923; St. Martin of Leon, *In 1 Pet.*, PL 207, 232; William of Auvergne, *De Sac. Mat.*, c. 10, Works 1, 528; Cajetan, *In 1 Cor.* 5; Francisco de Ossuna, *Tercer Abecedario Espiritual*, Escritores Misticos Espanoles, Mira, ed., (Madrid: Bailly Bailliere, 1911), tract. 8, c. 1, p. 402; *Cat. Conc. Trid.*, II, 8, 34; Lawrence of Brindisi, *2 Quadr.*, Dies S. Josephi, Hom 3, *Works* 5, 467; St. Alphonsus de Ligouri, *Theol. Moral.* (Turin: Marietti, 1846), c. 627; Pius XII, *Sacra Virginitas*, AAS 46 (1954), p. 169.
6. *Hom 3 in Gen.*, PG 12, 180.
7. *In 1 Cor.* 7, 5, PG 82, 274.
8. *Serm.* 25 attributed to Ambrose, PL 17, 678.
9. *Ibid.*, Serm. 1 Dom. 1 Adventis, PL 17, 625.
10. Cf. Egbert of York, *Lib. Paen.*, lib. 2, c. 21, PL 89, 419; Anon., *Poenitentiale*, c. 32. PL 99, 946; Halitgar, *De Poen.*, lib. 4, c. 24, PL 105, 685.
11. Cf. Rabanus Maurus, *Hom.* 9, PL 110, 22; Haymo of Halberstadt, *In 1 Cor.* 7, PL 117, 544; Reginon, *De Eccl. Disc.*, lib. 1, cc. 28–30, PL 132, 256; Ratherius of Verona, *Praeloquia*, lib. 2, tit. 3, PL 136, 195; Honorius of Autun, *Speculum Eccl.*, sermo generalis, PL 172, 867; Peter Lombard, *Sent.*, lib. 4, d. 32, c. 3; Alain de Lille, *Summa de Arte Pr.*, c. 45, PL 210, 193; Albert the Great, *In 4 Sent.*, d. 32, a. 10.
12. *In Eccl.* 3, a. 3, *Works* 7, 227.
13. Cf. *Catech. Conc. Trid.*, II, 8, 34; St. Charles Borromeo, *Acta Eccl. Mediolan.* (Paris: J. Jost, 1643), edicta selecta, p. 513; De La Puente, *op. cit.*, p. 535.
14. Cf. *Canones Apostol.*, c. 60, n. 52, PL 56, 720; St. Antoninus, *Summa Sac. Theol.*, III, tit. 1, c. 24; Council of Trent, Decr. *Tametsi*, c. 10, Mansi 33, 156.
15. Tob. 6, 17 (Vulgate). Cf. Ps. 32, 9; Rom. 1, 21–6.

16. *Statuta Eccl. Antiqua*, c. 101.
17. Ps-Pope Evaristus, *Epist.* 1, PG 5, 1048.
18. Cf. Egbert of York, *Lib. Poenit.*, lib. 2, c. 21, PL 89, 419.
19. Cf. Reginon, *De Eccl. Disc.*, lib. 2, c. 153, PL 132, 312; Hatto of Vercelli, *Capitulare*, c. 94, PL 134, 46; Burchard of Worms, *Lib. Dec.*, lib. 9, c. 5, PL 140, 816.
20. *Hom.* 21, PL 155, 1744.
21. *In Tob.* 6, a. 6, *Works* 5, 107.
22. *Op. cit.* vol. 13, disp. 13, p. 262.
23. Op. cit., Constit. de Dec. Synod., lib. 5, c. 15, p. 287.
24. Cf. *Serm.* 25 attrib. to Ambrose, PL 17, 678; *Serm.* 116 attrib. to Augustine, PL 39, 1976; Egbert of York, *Lib. Poen.*, lib. 2; c. 21, PL 89, 419; Anon., *Poenitentiale*, c. 32, PL 99, 946; Halitgar, *De Poen.*, lib. 4, c. 24, PL 105, 685; Haymo of Halberstadt, *In 1 Cor.* 7, PL 117, 544; Reginon, *De Eccl. Disc.*, lib. 1, cc. 328-30, PL 132, 256; Burchard of Worms, *Decreta*, lib. 19, PL 140, 959; Ivo of Chartres, *Panormia*, lib. 6, c. 21, PL 161, 1247-8.
25. *Sent.*, lib. 4, d. 32, c. 3.
26. Cf. Alexander of Hales, *In 4 Sent.*, d. 32, n. 9, Quar. 1, 510; Bonaventure, *In 4 Sent.*, d. 32, a. 3, q. 2; Albert the Great, *In 4 Sent.*, d. 32, a. 10.; d. 21, a. 23; Aquinas, *In 4 Sent.*, d. 32.
27. Cf. Pierre de la Palu, *In 4 Sent.*, d. 26, q. 2, a. 1.
28. *Serm. 3 in Dom. 3 post Nat.*, Works 29, 192. Cf. *De Laud. Vita Conj.*, a. 5, *Works* 38, 63.
29. Cf. De la Puente, *op. cit.*, p. 535.
30. Cf. Sanchez, *De Sac. Mat.*, lib. 9, disp. 12, n. 5; De Lugo, *Tr. de 7 Sac.*, Theor, 9, n. 39, p. 149; De Ligouri, *Theol. Mor.*, lib. 6, tract. 6, c. 2, dub. 2, *Works* 6, 676; Grou, *op. cit.*, p. 67.
31. *Adv. Jov.*, lib. 1, n. 20, PL 23, 249. Cf. *Epist.* 48, n. 15, PL 22, 506.
32. Jonas of Orleans, *De Instit. Laic.*, lib. 2, c. 11, PL 106, 188; Cf. Ps-Augustine, *Serm. in Pervig. Pasch.*, PL 40, 1204; Ps-Gregory, *Epist.*, lib. 11, ep. 64, PL 77, 1197-8; Reginon, *De Eccl. Disc.*, lib. 1, c. 331, PL 132, 256; Gregory VII, *Council. Roman.* I, c. 13, PL 148, 766.
33. Cf. Ivo of Chartres, *Dec.*, p. 8, c. 88, PL 161, 602; Alexander of Hales, *In 4 Sent.*, d. 32, n. 10, Quar. 1, 511; Albert the Great, *In 4 Sent.*, d. 32, a. 13; Scotus, *Report.*, lib. 4, d. 32, q. 1, schol. 2.
34. *In 4 Sent.*, d. 33, q. 1, a. 1.
35. *C. Sanct. Off.*, 1/24/1587, cited by DeGuibert, *op. cit.*, p. 249. Cf. De Granada, *Forêt de Lieux Communs*, 3e cl., 11, *Works* 21, 382; *Cat. Conc. Trid.*, II, 8, 34; Sanchez, *De Sac. Mat.*, lib. 9, disp. 13, nn. 5-6.
36. *C. Sanct. Off.*, 2/12/1679, DB 1147.
37. *Lettre* 740, *Works* 3, 616.
38. Cf. Ligouri, *Theol. Moral.*, lib. 6, tr. 3, c. 2, dub. 2, art. 2, Works 6, 220.
39. Cf. De Guibert, *op. cit.*, p. 379.
40. *C. Sanct. Off.*, 12/20/1905, DB 1942.

41. *Conc. Elv.*, Mansi 2, 10–11.
42. Cf. Eusebius of Caesarea, *Demonstrationes Evang.*, lib. 1, c. 9, PG 22, 82; Ambrosiaster, *In 1 Tim.* 3, 12, PL 17, 497; Pope Siricius, *Epist.* 1, c. 6, PL 13, 1138–9; 5, PL 13, 1160; Council of Toledo, Mansi 3, 633; C. of Turin, Mansi 3, 860; Innocent I, *Epist.* 2, c. 9, PL 20, 475.
43. Cf. Halitgar, *Lib. Poen.*, PL 105, 698; Salmeron, *op. cit.*, vol. 1, p. 247.

CHAPTER 10

1. *Adv. Jov.*, lib. 1, n. 12, PL 23, 238.
2. Pierre Le Chantre and Robert de Courson, cited by G. Le Bras, DTC 9, 2177.
3. *Summa*, II II, Inq. 3, tr. 5 sec. 2, q. 1, tit. 3, c. 2 ad. 3, Quar. 3, 635. Cf. Haymo of Halberstadt, *In 1 Thes.* 4, PL 117, 769; Albert the Great, *In 4 Sent.*, d. 32, a. 10.
4. *Hom. 19 in 1 Cor.*, n. 2, PG 61, 153.
5. *De Bono Conj.*, c. 10, PL 40, 382.
6. Ambrosiaster, *In 1 Cor.* 7, 5, PL 17, 228.
7. Unknown Author, *Consultationes Zacchaei*, lib. 3, c. 5, PL 20, 1157.
8. Haymo of Halberstadt, *In 1 Cor.* 7, PL 117, 544; Hatto of Vercelli, *Expos. in Ep. Pauli*, 1 Cor., PL 134, 349; Harvey of Bourg-Dieu, *In 1 Cor.* 7, PL 181, 875.
9. De la Puente, *op. cit.*, p. 535. Cf. Alvarez de Paz, *op. cit.*, lib. 5, pars 2, c. 2, *Works* 4, 558.
10. *Serm. de Virg.*, 6, 75.
11. Cf. Gregory of Nyssa, *De Virg.*, c. 8, PG 46, 355; Augustine, *De Bono Conj.*, c. 13, PL 40, 384.
12. Cf. Cassian, *Collationes*, c. 33, col. 21, PL 49, 1212; Rabanus Maurus, *In Eph.* 5, PL 112, 456, Alain de Lille, *Summa De Arte Pr.*, c. 46, PL 210, 194.
13. *De Sac. in Gen.*, c. 3, *Works* 1, 415.
14. *Contra Gent.*, lib. 3, c. 136.
15. Cf. Denis the Carthusian, *De Laud. Vita Conj.*, a. 3, Works 38, 61; Salmeron, *op. cit.*, vol. 5, tr. 9, p. 49; Buys, *op. cit.*, p. 224.
16. Bourdaloue, *Sermons*, 2e D. Epiph., *Works* (Paris: Gaume, 1896) 2, 381–3; Claude de la Columbière, *Réflections Chrétiennes du Mariage*, *Works* 5, 181.
17. *Sacra Virginitas*, AAS 46 (1954), p. 169.
18. *Hom. 6 in Num.*, PG 12, 610.
19. *Dict. Grat.*, c. 32, q. 2, c. 4.
20. *Sent.*, lib. 4, d. 32, c. 3.
21. Alexander of Hales, *In 4 Sent.*, d. 31, n. 10, Quar 1, 495.
22. *Ibid.*, d. 32, n. 13, Quar. 1, 513.
23. *In 4 Sent.*, d. 26, q. 1, a. 3 ad 2.
24. *In 4 Sent.*, d. 31, q. 1, a. 3.

25. Cf. St. Antoninus, *Summa Theol.*, III, d. 26, tit. 1. c. 20; Denis the Carthusian, *Summa Fide Orth.*, lib. 4, a. 162, *Works* 18, 209.

26. *Op. cit.*, p. 401.

27. *De Sac. Mat.*, c. 5.

28. *Prael.*, De Sac. Mat., c. 1, dub. 2.

29. *Nicomachean Ethics*, lib. 7, c. 11.

30. *De Civ. Dei*, lib. 14, c. 16, PL 41, 425 (CC 48, 439).

31. *Contra Jul.*, lib. 5, c. 10, n. 42, PL 44, 808.

32. Cf. Josef Fuchs, *op. cit.*, p. 14.

33. *In Joann.*, lib. 2, PL 169, 275. Cf. Paschasius Radbert, *In Matt.*, lib. 9, c. 19, PL 120, 648.

34. *Collectanea in 1 Cor.*, 6, 13, PL 191, 1583. Cf. Alexander of Hales, *Summa*, II II, Inq., 3, tr. 4, sec. 2, q. 1, tit. 7, c. 2; Quar. 2, 598; *ibid.*, Inq. 4, tr. 2, sec. 2, q. 2, c. 1, Quar 2, 615.

35. *In 4 Sent.*, d. 31, n. 11, Quar. 1, 496.

36. *Q.D. de Perf. Evang.*, q. 3, a. 1, ad 11.

37. *In 4 Sent.*, d. 31, a. 2, q. 1.

38. *In 2 Sent.*, d. 31, a. 2, q. 1. Cf. *Q.D. de Perf. Evang.*, q. 3, a. 1, ad 12.

39. *In 4 Sent.*, d. 31, a. 20, ad 4; Cf. *ibid.*, a. 28.

40. *Ibid.*, a. 19.

41. Cf. Aquinas, *In 4 Sent.*, d. 30, q. 1, a. 1; d. 31, q. 2, a. 1, ad 3; Scotus, *Report.*, lib. 4, d. 32, q. 1, schol. 2; Pierre de la Palu, *In 4 Sent.*, d. 26, q. 2, a. 1; d. 31, q. 1, a. 1; Denis the Carthusian, *In Sap.* 7, a. 7, *Works* 7, 491; Soto, *In 4 Sent.*, d. 31, q. 1, a. 2 ad 3; Salmeron, *op. cit.*, vol. 8, tr. 51, p. 475; Sanchez, *De Sac Mat.*, lib. 2, disp. 29, q. 1; Lessius, *De Jure et Justitia*, lib. 4, c. 2, dub. 15; Contenson, *op. cit.*, lib. 11, Pars 4, dis. 4, c. 1, spec. 1, *Works* 4, 419; John of St. Thomas, *Cursus Theologicus*, I, q. 72, n. 19, *Works* (Cologne: W. Metternick, 1711) 4, 898; Palmieri, *op. cit.* p. 15.

42. Palmieri, *op. cit.*, p. 15.

43. *Adv. Jov.*, lib. 1, n. 7, PL 23, 230.

44. *Ibid.*, n. 28, PL 23, 261. Cf. *Epist.* 58, n. 15, PL 22, 505.

45. *Soliloq.*, lib. 1, c. 10, PL 32, 878.

46. *Epist.*, n. 3, c. 10, PL 65, 330.

47. *De Eccl. Off.*, lib. 1, c. 20, PL 83, 813; Bede, *In 1 Pet.* 3, PL 93, 55; Raoul Ardent, *Hom. in Ep. & Ev. Dom.*, hom. 21, PL 155, 1745; Harvey of Bourg-Dieu, *In 1 Cor.* 7, PL 181, 834; William of Auvergne, *De Sac. Mat.*, c. 3, Works 1, 515.

48. *In 4 Sent.*, d. 32, dub. 5; Cf. *ibid.*, a. 4, q. 1, ad 4; a. 1, q. 1.

49. *In 4 Sent.*, d. 26, a. 2. Cf. *ibid.*, q. 1, a. 3 ad 2.

50. *Contra Gent.*, lib. 3, c. 136. Cf. *In 1 Cor.* 7, 1; *S.T.* I, q. 98, a. 2; II II, q. 153, a. 1; q. 151, a. 3 ad 2; q. 186, a. 4.

51. *Report.*, lib. 4, d. 28, q. 1, schol. 2. Cf *ibid.* d. 32, q. 1, schol. 2.

52. *Summa Sac. Theol.*, III, tit. 2, c. 2.

53. *In Tob.* 6, a. 6, *Works* 5, 106. Cf. *Summa Fide Orth.*, lib. 4, a. 190, *Works* 18, 229.
54. *In 1 Cor.* 7, a. 7, *Works* 13, 152; Cf. *In 1 Pet.* 3, a. 6, *Works* 13, 649; *Laud. Vita Conj.*, a. 4, *Works* 38, 62.
55. *In Luc.* 14, a. 37, *Works* 12, 96.
56. Cajetan, *In Gen.* 2, 21.
57. Soto, *In 4 Sent.*, d. 31, q. 1, a. 2.
58. Cf. De Granada, *op. cit.*, 2e classe, mariage, *Works* 21, 437.
59. *Noctes Vaticanae,* Serm. Contra Lux., *Orationes* (Augsburg: I. Vieth, 1758), col. 603.
60. Cf. Alvarez de Paz, *op. cit.*, lib. 5, pars 2, c. 2, Works 4, 557. Cf. *De Vita Spir.*, lib. 3, pars 1, c. 5, Works 1, 480; Lessius, *De Jure et Justitia*, lib. 4, c. 2, dub. 15; Peteau, *Theol. Dogm.*, De op. 6 Dierum, lib. 2, c. 8, n. 3.
61. *Lutheranismi Hypotyposis*, p. 2, sect. 4, dis. 5, *Works* 22, 407.
62. *Sacra Virginitas*, AAS 46 (1954), pp. 174 ff. Cf. Alloc. to Italian clergy, 9/14/56, AAS 48 (1956), p. 710.

CHAPTER 11

1. Mt. 19, 10.
2. *De Virginitate*, c. 27, PG 48, 552–3. Cf. Gregory of Nyssa, *De Virg.*, c. 3, PG 46, 331–5.
3. *De Virg.*, c. 6, PL 16, 287.
4. *Exhort. Virg.*, c. 4, PL 16, 358. Cf. *De Vid.*, c. 11, PL 16, 268.
5. Cf. Jerome, *Epist.* 123, n. 5, PL 22, 1048–9; Augustine, *Serm.* 37, c. 6, PL 38, 225.
6. Abelard, *Prob. Hel.*, 14, PL 178, 701. Cf. Fulgentius, *Epist.* 2, c. 6, PL 65, 314; Sedulius Scotus, *In 1 Cor.* 7, PL 102, 142; Hatto of Vercelli, *Expos. in Ep. Pauli*, 1 Cor., PL 134, 357; Peter Damian, *Epist.* 14, PL 144, 452.
7. *Summa De Arte Pr.*, c. 46, PL 210, 194.
8. *In Tob.* 3, a. 3, *Works* 5, 97. Cf. *In Matt.* 19, a. 33, *Works* 11, 213; *De Laud. Vita Conj.*, a. 3, *Works* 38, 61.
9. *Summa S. Th.*, III, tit. 1, c. 25.
10. Cajetan, *In Gen.* 2, 23; cf. Soto *In 4 Sent.*, d. 31, q. 1, a. 1; Buys, *op. cit.*, p. 224; Canisius, *Summa Doct. Christ.*, I, P. 1, c. 4, n. 7, q. 207; II, *ibid.*, q. 213; Sanchez, *De Sac. Mat.*, lib. 2, disp. 29, q. 1.
11. *Serm.*, 2e dim. Epiph., *Works* 2, 375–7.
12. *Hom. 62 in Matt.*, PG 58, 599.
13. *Adv. Jov.*, lib. 1, n. 28, PL 23, 261.
14. *Ibid.*, n. 47, PL 23, 289–90.
15. *Report.*, lib. 4, d. 28, q. 1, schol. 2. Cf. Hildebert of Mans, *Epist.*, lib. 1, ep. 21, PL 171, 193–4; Lothair Segni (Innocent III), *De Contemptu Mundi*, lib. 1, c. 18, PL 217, 710; Vincent of Beauvais, *op. cit.*, cc. 37–8, 47.

16. *Report.*, lib. 4, d. 28, q. 1, schol. 2.
17. *Pars* 2, c. 10.
18. *Laud. Vita Conj.*, a. 3, *Works* 28, 61. Cf. *In Matt.* 19, a. 33, *Works* II, 214; St. Antoninus, *Summa S. T.*, III, tit. 1, c. 1.
19. Cf. Soto, *In 4 Sent.*, d. 31, q. 1, a. 1; Alvarez de Paz, *De Exterm. Mali*, lib. 5, pars 2, c. 5, *Works* 4, 577–8.
20. *De Bono Status Cast.*, c. 5, *Opusc.*, p. 884–5. Cf. *De Jure et Jus.*, lib. 4, c. 2, dub. 15.
21. *Serm. sur les oblig. de l'état rel.*, *Works* (Besançon: Outhenim-Chalandre Fils, 1840), 6, 537.
22. *Divers Sentiments*, c. 50.
23. *Serm.*, 2e dim. Epiph., *Works* 2, 375. Cf. De la Columbère, *Réfl. Chrét.*, du mariage, *Works* 5, 180.
24. *Serm. de Virg.*, Works 6, 24.
25. *Adv. Oppugnatores Vitae Monast.*, lib. 3, n. 15, PG 47, 375–6. Cf. Gregory Nazianzen, *Carm.*, lib. 1, sect. 2, n. 6. 1. 6, PG 37, 643; Gregory of Nyssa, *De Virg.*, c. 3, PG 46, 331–5.
26. *De Vid.*, c. 11, PL 16, 268. Cf. Jerome *Adv. Jov.*, lib 1, n. 28, PL 23, 261.
27. *Moralia*, lib. 26, PL 76, 374. Cf. Isidore cf Seville, *De Eccl. Off.*, lib. 2, c. 20, PL 83, 810; Tajon, *Lib. Sent.*, lib. 3, c. 7, PL 80, 857.
28. St. Paschasius Radbert, *In Matt.*, lib. 10, c. 19, PL 120, 651. Cf. Sedulius Scotus, *In 1 Cor.* 7, PL 102, 142.
29. *Sermones de Diversis*, Serm. 35, PL 183, 634.
30. Cf. Scotus, *Report.*, lib. 4, d. 28, q. 1, schol. 2.
31. *Opusc.* 10, Vitis Myst., Add. 4, c. 30, n. 106, Quar. 8, 210. Cf. Aquinas, *In 4 Sent.*, d. 39, a. 4 ad 1; *S.T.* I II, q. 108, a. 4; II II, q. 184, a. 3; *Contra Gent.*, lib. 3, cc. 131–9.
32. *Laud. Vita Conj.*, a. 3, *Works* 38, 61.
33. *Op. cit.*, vol. 5, tr. 9, p. 49.
34. *Lett.* 664, *Works* 3, 550.
35. *Réfl. Chrét.*, mariage, *Works* 5, 179–80.
36. *Ibid.*
37. *Serm.*, 2e dim. Epiph., *Works* 2, 382.
38. *Ibid.*, p. 378.

CHAPTER 12

1. 1 Cor. 7, 32–4.
2. Cf. Mt. 6, 25.
3. Lib. 1, tr. 5, n. 2, PL 11, 302.
4. *De Virg.*, n. 31, PG 48, 554.
5. *Carm.*, lib. 1, sect. 2, 11. 543–563, PG 37, 563. Cf. *ibid.*, poema 2, 469–80, PG 37, 615.
6. *In Luc.*, lib. 7, n. 196, PL 15, 1842.
7. *Expos. in Ps.* 118, 20, PL 15, 1300.

8. *De Civ. Dei*, lib. 21, c. 26, PL 41, 743-4. Cf. *De 8 Dulcitii Quaest.*, PL 40, 155; Jerome, *Adv. Jov.*, lib. 1, n. 20, PL 23, 249.

9. *De Bono Conj.*, c. 11, PL 40, 382-3.

10. Cf. Theodoret, *In 1 Cor.* 7, 32, PG 82, 283; Rabanus Maurus, *Enarr. in Ep. Pauli*, lib. 10, c. 7, PL 112, 763; Haymo of Halberstadt, *In 1 Cor.* 7, PL 117, 548; Servatus Lupus, *Epist.*, 4, PL 119, 443; Hatto of Vercelli, *In 1 Cor.*, PL 134, 358; Bruno of Asti, *In 1 Cor.* 7, PL 153, 161; Harvey of Bourg-Dieu, *In 1 Cor.* 7, PL 181, 886; Philip of Herveng, *De Continentia Clericorum*, c. 60, PL 203, 744.

11. *Q.D. de Perf. Evang.*, q. 3, a. 1, ad 4.

12. *Opusc. de Perf. Vitae Spir.*, *passim*.

13. *Summa S. T.*, III, tit. 1, c. 25.

14. *In 1 Cor.* 7, a. 7, *Works* 13, 158.

15. *Summa Fidei Orth.*, lib. 4, a. 162, *Works* 18, 209.

16. *Introd. au Symbol*, p. 3, tr. 1, c. 9, *Works* 15, 55.

17. Cf. Cajetan, *In 1 Cor.* 7, 33; *In Matt.* 19, 12; *In 1 Cor.* 7, 35; Soto, *In 4 Sent.*, d. 31, q. 1, a. 1; Salmeron, *op. cit.*, vol. 8, tr. 50, p. 395; De Leon, *op. cit.*, p. 15; Sanchez, *De Sac. Mat.*, disp. 29, q. 1; Bellarmine, *De Sac Mat.*, c. 5; Lessius, *De Jure et Jus.*, lib. 4, c. 2, dub. 15.

18. *Instructions sur la version du NT de Trevours*, 2e instr., 1 Cor., *Works* 2, 679.

19. *Serm.*, 2e Dim. Epiph., *Works* 2, 384.

20. Cf. Pesch. *op. cit.*, p. 313; Billot, *De Eccl. Sacramentis* (Rome: P.U.G., 1929), ed. 7a, vol. 2, p. 385.

21. *Sacra Virginitas*, AAS 46 (1954), p. 168.

CHAPTER 13

1. 1 Cor. 7, 38. Cf. *ibid.*, vv. 1, 7-8, 40.

2. Ps. Clement of Rome, *Epist. ad Virgines*, c. 4, PG 1, 388.

3. *Tractatus*, lib. 1, tr. 5, PL 11, 304.

4. *Epist.* 42, n. 3, PL 16, 1172. Cf. *De Vid.*, c. 13, PL 16, 272; Chrysostom, *Hom. 19 in 1 Cor.*, PG 61, 153.

5. Pope Siricius, *Epist. et Decreta*, Ep. 7, PL 13, 1168. For the reply of the Synod of Milan under Ambrose praising this letter, cf. Ambrose, *Epist.* 42, PL 16, 1172-7

6. *Adv. Jov.*

7. Jerome, *De Perpet. Virg. B.M.V.*, n. 21, PL 23, 214; *Adv. Jov.*, lib. 1, n. 13, PL 23, 243; Cyril of Alexandria, *De Ador. in Spir.*, lib. 15, PG 68, 950; *Codex Can. Eccl.*, c. 31, PL 56, 567; Fulgentius, *Epist.* 3, c. 10, PL 65, 330; Cassiodorus, *In 1 Cor.* 7, PL 70, 1333; St. Paterius, *Concordia*, 14, PL 79, 667; Tajon, *Sent.*, lib. 3, c. 7, PL 80, 857.

8. *Hom.*, I, 13, PL 94, 226 ff. Cf. Peter Damian, *Opusc.* 41, c. 2, PL 145, 662.

9. Pierre Le Mangeur, *Hist. Schol.*, In Evang., c. 38, PL 198, 1559.

10. *The Golden Legend*, Granger Ryan and Helmut Ripperger, tr. (London: Longmans, Green, & Co., 1941), Part 2, p. 363, Feast of St. Mary Magdalen.
11. Pars 1, c. 25.
12. Cf. Denis the Carthusian, *In Joann.* 2, a. 7, Works 12, 312; J. Eck, *op. cit.*, Dom. 2 post Epiph., hom. 1, p. 119; Cajetan, *In Joann.* 2 1; Canisius, *Serm.* 12/27/1564, Braunsberger, 4, 838; Salmeron, *op. cit.*, vol. 6, tr. 6, p. 32; Baronius, *Annales Ecclesiastici*, in a. 31, n. 30.
13. *In 4 Evang.*, In Joann. 1, 1226.
14. Cf. Sedulius Scotus, *In 1 Cor.* 7, PL 103, 140; Jonas of Orleans, *De Instit. Laic.*, lib. 2, c. 1, PL 106, 169.
15. Cf. R. Maurus, *In Gen.*, lib. 1, c. 7, PL 107, 462; Haymo of Halberstadt, *In 2 Cor.*, 11, PL 117, 651; Hatto of Vercelli, *Expos. in Ep. Pauli*, 1 Cor., PL 134, 360; Bruno of Asti, *Comm. in Joann.*, pars 1, c. 2, PL 165, 461; Rupert of Deutz, *In Joann.*, lib. 2, PL 169, 275; Harvey of Bourg-Dieu, *In 1 Cor.* 7, PL 181, 880 ff.; Bonaventure, *De Annunciatione*, serm. 1, Quar. 9, 679; Aquinas, *In 4 Sent.*, d. 30, q. 2, a. 1, quaest. 3; *S. T.* I II, q. 152, a. 4; Scotus, *In 4 Sent.*, d. 31, q. 1, schol. 2; Thomas of Strasbourg, *In 4 Sent.*, d. 26, q. 1, a. 1 ad 2; Ludolph of Saxony, *Vita Christi Domini*, Pars 1, c. 25; St. Antoninus, *Summa S. T.*, III, tit. 1, c. 1, n. 1; Denis the Carthusian, *In 1 Cor.* 7, a. 7, *Works* 13, 151.
16. *Op. cit.*, *Dom. post XII. Nat.*, p. 101.
17. N. 356. Cf. 15th Annotation, n. 15.
18. Can. 10 de Mat., DB 980.
19. *Summa Doct. Christ.*, editio 2a, p. 1, c. 4, n. 7, q. 133. Cf. *ibid.*, qq. 213; Serm., 12/22/1563, Braunsberger 4, 827; Salmeron, *op. cit.*, vol. 3, tr. 5, p. 32; *ibid.*, vol. 5, tr. 9, p. 49; vol. 8, tr. 50, p. 395; De Blois, *Collyrium Haereticorum*, lib. 2, cc. 15, 17; Lawrence of Brindisi, *Lutheranismi Hypotyposis*, p. 2, sect. 4, dis. 5, Works 2, 2, p. 406; Alvarez de Paz, *De Exterm. Mali*, lib. 5, pars 2, c. 1, Works 4, 552; Bellarmine, *De Sac. Mat.*, c. 5; Lessius, *De Jure et Jus.*, lib. 4, c. 2, dub. 15; *De Bono Stat. Cast.*, c. 3, Opusc. 882; De la Puente, *op. cit.*, p. 437; Billot, *De Eccl. Sac.*, pp. 382 ff.; Pius XII, *Sacra Virginitas*, AAS 46 (1954), *passim*.
20. Address to Religious Superiors, 9/15/52, AAS 44 (1952), p. 824. Cf. Address to Italian Sodalists, 7/13/58, AAS 50 (1958), p. 533.
21. *Sacra Virginitas*, AAS 46 (1954), pp. 174 ff.
22. Address to Catholic Women, 9/29/57, AAS 49 (1957), pp. 909–10. Cf. John XXIII, Address to Catholic Young Women, 4/23/60, AAS 52 (1960), p. 393.
23. Cf. Bonaventure, *In 4 Sent.*, d. 26, a. 2, q. 2 ad 2; Aquinas, *In 4 Sent.*, d. 26, q. 2, a. 3; Pierre de la Palu, *In 4 Sent.*, d. 33, q. 2, a. 6; Capreolus, *Def, in 4 Sent.*, dd. 26–9, q. 1, a. 3 ad 3; Bellarmine, *De Sac. Mat.*, c. 5; Salmeron, *op. cit.*, vol. 5, tr. 9, p. 51.

24. *Sacra Virginitas, loc. cit.*
25. Cf. Billot, *De Eccl. Sac.*, p. 387.
26. *Sacra Virginitas, loc. cit.*, p. 77.
27. 1 Cor. 7, 34.
28. *De Bono Conj.*, c. 11, PL 40, 382–3. Cf. Isidore of Pelusium, *Epist.*, lib. 3, ep. 151, PG 78, 1007–1010; *ibid.*, lib. 4, ep. 192, PG 78, 1279.
29. *De Fide*, c. 3, n. 43, PL 65, 693.
30. Rabanus Maurus, *Hom.* 38, PL 110, 72; Cf. Harvey of Bourg-Dieu, *In 1 Cor.* 7, PL 181, 887.
31. *S.T.* II II, q. 152, a. 4. Cf. Bonaventure, *Q.D. de Perf. Evang.*, q. 3, a. 3, Quar. 5, 176–7.
32. *S.T.* II II, q. 88, a. 6. Cf. *ibid.*, q. 186, aa. 1, 3–5, 8.
33. *Ibid.* I, q. 92, a. 1.
34. Cf. St. Antoninus, *Summa S. T.*, III, tit. 2, c. 2; Bellarmine, *Doctrina Christiana*, c. 9, *Works* 6, 195; Lessius, *De Bono Status Cast.*, c. 6, *Opusc.*, 887.
35. *Sacra Virginitas, loc. cit.*, p. 170.

CHAPTER 14

1. Mt. 19, 11.
2. Mt. 13, 11.
3. *Hom. 62 in Matt.*, PG 58, 600.
4. *In Matt.*, lib. 3, c. 19, v. 11, PL 26, 135. Cf. Ambrosiaster, *In 1 Cor.* 7, 6–9, PL 17, 217.
5. *De Grat. et Lib. Arbit.*, c. 4, n. 7, PL 44, 886. Cf. *Confess.*, lib. 6, c. 11, PL 32, 729.
6. *Epist.* 1, c. 10, PL 65, 309.
7. *In Matt.* 19, PL 92, 86.
8. Cf. Rabanus Maurus, *Enarr. In Ep. Pauli*, lib. 10, c. 7, PL 112, 64; Paschasius Radbert, *In Matt.*, lib. 10, c. 19, PL 120, 654; Harvey of Bourg-Dieu, *In 1 Cor.* 7, PL 181, 876; Anselm of Laon, *In Matt.* c. 19, PL 163, 1412; Unknown, *Quaest. in Ep. Pauli*, In 1 Cor., q. 58, PL 175, 525.
9. *In Matt.*, 19, 12.
10. Cf. Ludolph of Saxony, *op. cit.*, p. 2, c. 10.
11. Ia edit., c. 4, n. 7, q. 207. Cf. II, *ibid.*, q. 213.
12. *Op. cit.*, vol. 5, tr. 9, p. 51. Cf. *ibid.*, vol. 8, tr. 50, pp. 389, 394.
13. *De Jure et Jus.*, lib. 4, c. 2, dub. 15. Cf. *Disp. de Statu Vitae Delinq.*, q. 12, *Opusc.*, p. 864.
14. *Prael, De Sac. Mat.*, c. 1, dub. 3.
15. 1 Cor. 7, 9.
16. *Conviv. 10 Virg.*, orat. 3, c. 12, PG 18, 59.
17. Chrysostom, *Hom. 19 in 1 Cor.*, PG 61, 153. Cf. Epiphaius, *Adv. Haeres*, lib. 2, tom. 1, haer. 48, n. 9, PG 41, 867–70.

18. *De Vid.*, c. 11, PL 16, 268–9. Cf. *De Abraham*, lib. 1, c. 3, PL 14, 449.
19. *In Matt.* 19, 12, PL 26, 141. Cf. *Epist.* 22, PL 22, 397–8; Ambrosiaster, *In 1 Cor.* 7, 36, PL 17, 237.
20. 1 Cor. 7, 7.
21. *Orat.* 2, c. 1, PG 18, 47.
22. *Lib. de Haer.*, c. 84, PL 12, 1196–7.
23. *In 1 Cor.* 7, 8, PG 74, 874.
24. *De Fide*, c. 3, n. 43, PL 65, 693. Cf. St. John Damascene, *De Fide Orth.*, lib. 4, c. 24, PG 94, 1210.
25. *In Matt.* 19. Cf. *Opusc. de Perf. Vitae Spir.*, c. 8.
26. *In 1 Cor.* 7, lect. 1.
27. *In Matt.*, 19, 11–12.
28. *Op. cit.*, p. 441.
29. *De Exterm. Mali*, lib. 5, pars 2, c. 5, *Works* 4, 579.
30. *In Matt.*, 19, 403.
31. Letter, *Il divisamento*, 2/8/1893, ASS 25, p. 464.
32. *De Eccl. Sac.*, II, p. 385.
33. *Sacra Virginitas*, *loc. cit.* pp. 179 ff.
34. Luke 1, 25.
35. Luke 17, 26–7. Cf. Mt. 24, 37–9.
36. 1 Cor. 7, 2.
37. 1 Tim. 5, 12.
38. Acts 18, 26.
39. *Op. cit.*, orat. 1, c. 5, PG 18, 46.
40. *De Virg.*, c. 7, PL 16, 287.
41. *Epist.*, 63, n. 40, PL 16, 1251.
42. *Adv. Jov.*, lib. 1, c. 36, PL 23, 271.
43. *Opusc. de Perf. Vitae Spir.*, c. 8.
44. *Op. cit.*, II, p. 385.
45. Address to Moderators of Italian Catholic Action, 9/9/53, AAS 45 (1953), p. 611.
46. Address to Italian Sodalists, 7/13/58, AAS 50 (1958), p. 532.
47. Mt. 19, 12.
48. 1 Cor. 7, 33 ff.
49. Cf. Ambrosiaster, *In 1 Cor.* 7, 32, PL 17, 235.
50. *De Sancta Virg.*, c. 11, PL 40, 401. Cf. *De Conj. Adult.*, lib. 1, c. 19, PL 40, 464; *De Bono Conj.*, cc. 21–2, PL 40, 391–2.
51. Unknown Author, *De Eccl. Dogm.*, c. 64, PL 83, 1240–1.
52. Haymo of Halberstadt, *In 1 Cor.* 7, PL 117, 548.
53. Cf. Bonaventure, *In 4 Sent.*, d. 26, a. 1, q. 3; Alexander of Hales, *Summa*, Inq. 4, tr. 3, q. 2, c. 4, Quar. 2, 708; Scotus, *Report.*, lib. 4, d. 31, q. 1, schol. 2.
54. *In 4 Sent.*, d. 30, q. 2, a. 2.
55. Cf. Cajetan, *In Matt.* 19, 12, 29.
56. *Sacra Virginitas*, *loc. cit.*, p. 164.

PART III
INTRODUCTION: SECTION 1

1. Gen. 2, 22.
2. Cf. Jean-Paul Audet, O.P., "Le sense du Cantique des Cantiques," *Revue Biblique,* vol. 62, n. 2 (Apr. 1955), pp. 197 ff.
3. Ps. 8, 1.
4. Tob. 8, 12.

CHAPTER *15*

1. *Catech.,* 6, 35, PG 33, 602.
2. *Ep. ad Himerium,* PL 13, 1136 ff., DB 88a.
3. Cf. Ambrose, *Epist.* 63, n. 63, PL 16, 1257; Augustine, *De Bono Vid.,* c. 8, PL 40, 437.
4. Cf. Peter Damian, *Serm.* 59, PL 144, 902; Peter Lombard, *Sent.,* lib. 4, d. 26; Pierre de Poitiers, *Sent.,* lib. 5, 1. 4, c. 14, PL 211, 1257.
5. *Regesta,* n. 4, PL 214, 3-4.
6. To Bishop of Tiberias, cited by G. Le Bras, DTC 9, 2201.
7. Cited by G. Le Bras, DTC, 9, 2201.
8. *Summa,* IV, q. 2, membrum 2, a. 1.
9. *Ibid.,* II II, Inq. 3, tr. 4, sec. 2, q. 1, tit. 7, a. 2, Quar. 3, 595.
10. *In 4 Sent.,* d. 26, a. 1, q. 2. Cf. *ibid.,* d. 27, dub. 2; *Coll. in Joann.,* c. 2, col. 8, Quar. 6, 545.
11. *In 4 Sent.,* d. 26, q. 2, a. 2 ad 1. Cf. ibid., d. 1, q. 1, a. 2; quaest. 2 ad 2.
12. *Report.,* lib. 4, d. 28, q. 1, schol. 1. Cf. *ibid.,* d. 26, q. 1 passim; d. 28, q. 1.
13. *In 4 Sent.,* d. 30, q. 2, a. 3. Cf. *ibid.,* d. 1, q. 2, a. 3.
14. *De Laudabili Vita Conjugatorum,* a. 1, *Works,* 38, 60.
15. *Instit.,* book 4, c. 19, n. 34.
16. *Table Talk* (London, 1883), n. 748.
17. *Cat. Conc. Trid.,* II, 8, 31, Cf. II, 8, 13; Cajetan, *Jentaculum,* IX, q. 1; *In Gen.* 1, 27; *In Matt.* 19, 4-5; Eck. *op. cit.,* Dom. 2 post Eph., hom. 1, p. 134; Soto, *In 4 Sent.,* d. 26, q. 1, aa. 1-2; Salmeron, *op cit.,* vol. 8, tr. 46, p. 360.
18. *Const. et Decret.,* lib, 5, c. 8 sess. 24, c. 2, p. 287. Cf. *Orationes* (Augsburg: I. Vieth, 1758), orat. in 6a Ponc. Prov., p. 42.
19. *Op. cit.,* pp. 202-3.
20. Bourdaloue, *Serm.* 2e dim. Epiph., Works 2, 368-9; Lawrence of Brindisi, *In Gen.* 2, 23-4, Works 3, 245; Scheeben, *The Mysteries of Christianity,* C. Vollert, tr. (St. Louis: Herder, 1946), p. 600.
21. *Arcanum,* ASS 12 (1879-80), p. 392.
22. *Op. cit.,* p. 454.
23. *Casti Connubii, loc. cit.,* p. 570.
24. Jn. 2, 1.
25. Jn. 2, 11.
26. Cf. David Stanley, S.J., *op. cit.,* p. 174.

27. *Ibid.* Cf. also Raymond Brown, S.S., "The Johannine Sacramentary Reconsidered," *Theological Studies,* vol. 23, n. 2 (June, 1962), pp. 183–206.
28. *De Fide et Op.,* PL 40, 205.
29. *In Joann.* 2, 11, PG 73, 227.
30. *Hom.* 23, PL 57, 274. Cf. Gaudentius of Brescia, *Serm.* 8, PL 20, 888.
31. Cf. Alexander of Hales, *In 4 Sent.,* d. 26, n. 6, Quar. 1, 456–7; Bonaventure, *In Joann.,* c. 2, col. 8, Quar. 6, 545.
32. *In 4 Sent.,* d. 26, a. 5, sol.
33. Cf. Denis the Carthusian, *Summa Fidei Orth.,* lib. 4, a. 163, *Works* 18, 210.
34. *Op. cit.,* vol. 6, tr. 6, p. 33.
35. Cf. Bourdaloue, *Serm.,* 2e dim. Epiph., *Works* 2, 367.
36. *Op. cit.,* p. 600. Cf. Palmieri, *op. cit.,* p. 15.
37. *Arcanum, loc. cit.,* pp. 388–90.
38. *Casti Connubii,* DB 2225.
39. Audience, 4/22/42, DR 4, 45.

INTRODUCTION: SECTION II

1. Sir. 36, 23.
2. Gen. 24, 14 ff.
3. *Ibid.,* 50–4.
4. *Ibid.,* 56.
5. Cf. McKenzie, *The Two-Edged Sword,* p. 113.
6. Ps. 128, 3 ff.
7. Prov. 19, 14.
8. Sir. 26, 3.
9. Sir. 26, 14.
10. Tob. 6, 17.
11. Tob. 7, 12 ff.
12. Tob. 8, 6 ff.

CHAPTER 16

1. Mt. 19, 6. Cf. Mk. 10, 1–9.
2. Cf. *Adv. Marc.,* 5, 18, PL 2, 518; *Exhort. Cast.,* 5, PL 2, 920; *De Monogamia,* 5, *ibid.,* 936; *De Jejunio,* 3, *ibid.,* 958; *De Anima,* 11, 21, *ibid.,* 665, 684.
3. *Epist.,* 138, n. 7, PL 33, 827. Cf. *De Civ. Dei,* lib. 10, c. 5, PL 41, 282.
4. *In Joann.,* tr. 9, 2, PL 35, 1459.
5. *De Pecc. Orig.,* 39, PL 44, 404. Cf. *ibid.,* 42, PL 44, 406; *Contra Jul.,* c. 57, 732; *De Nupt. et Concup.,* lib. 1, c. 10, PL 44, 420.
6. *Leonine Sacramentary,* Muratori 1, 724.
7. Cf. Ratherius of Verona, *Praeloquia,* lib. 2, tit. 3, PL 136, 191–4.
8. Decr. *Tametsi,* Mansi 33, 152.
9. Cf. Nicholas I, *Resp. ad Bulg.,* c. 3, PL 119, 980; Adrian II, *Epist.* 40,

PL 122, 1318; Burchard of Worms, *Lib. Dec.*, lib. 9, c. 3, PL 140, 810; Clement III, *Decreta*, n. 14, PL 204, 1483; St. Antoninus, *Summa S.T.*, III, tit. 1, c. 24.

10. *De Sac.*, lib. 2, pars 11, c. 8, PL 176, 495. Cf. P. Lombard, *Sent.*, lib. 4, d. 31.

11. Cf. Bonaventure, *In 4 Sent.*, d. 27, a. 2, q. 1, sol.; Albert the Great, *In 4 Sent.*, d. 27, a. 6; *ibid.*, d. 31, a. 3, 6; Scotus, *Report.*, lib. 4, d. 28, q. 2, schol. 2, d. 42, nn. 22–4.

12. *In 4 Sent.*, d. 28, q. 1, a. 3 ad 2.

13. John Tauler, *Sermons and Conferences*, W. Elliott, tr. (Washington, D.C.: Apostolic Mission House, 1910), p. 95.

14. Cf. St. Antoninus, *Summa S.T.*, III, tit. 1, c. 2; Denis the Carthusian, *Summa F. Orth.*, lib. 4, aa. 163–4, *Works* 18, 210–11.

15. Decr. *Tametsi*, c. 10, Mansi 33, 156.

16. *De Locis Theologicis*, lib. 8, c. 5, n. 6. Cf. *De Sac. in Genere*, I, n. 23.

17. Cf. Granada, *Tr. de la Doct. Chr.*, lib. 3, c. 16, *Works* 17, 217; Contenson, *op. cit.*, lib. 11, pars 4, diss. 4, c. 1, spec. 3.

18. *In 4 Sent.*, d. 26, q. 2, a. 3. Cf. *ibid.*, d. 31, q. 1, a. 2.

19. *Op. cit.*, vol. 9, tr. 13, p. 87.

20. *Il Crist. Instr.*, p. 3, reason 25, n. 17, *Works* (Turin: Marietti, 1885) 2, 849.

21. Cf. Pius IX, *Syll.*, 67, DB 1766; Scheeben, *op. cit.*, p. 607; Leo XIII, *Arcanum, loc. cit.*, pp. 388 ff.; *C.I.C.*, cc. 1012–16, 1038; Pius XI, *Casti Connubii, loc. cit.*, p. 554.

22. Address, 4/29/42, DR 4, 53. Cf. Address, 3/5/41, DR 3, 6.

23. *Epist.* 1, c. 2, PL 65, 305.

24. Cf. Scotus, *Op. Oxon.*, In 4 Sent., d. 26, q. 1, n. 10.

25. Peter of Tarant., *In 4 Sent.*, d. 27, q. 2, cited by G. Le Bras, DTC, 9, 2190.

26. Cf. De Lugo, *Tr. de 7 Sac*, th. 9, n. 3, p. 143.

27. *Op. cit.*, p. 600.

CHAPTER 17

1. Mt. 19, 11.

2. 1 Cor. 7, 7.

3. Cf. Gen. 1, 2.

4. Cf. Exod. 35, 21–2; Num. 4, 3 ff.; Exod. 31, 2–11; 1 K. 7, 13–14; Exod. 28, 3; Sir. 38, 1ff.

5. 1 Cor. 12, 4–30.

6. Heb. 5, 4.

7. *Strom.*, lib. 7, c. 12, PG 9, 498.

8. *Ad Marinum*, PG 22, 1007.

9. *Orat.* 37, c. 10, PG 36, 294–5.

10. *Adv. Haer.*, lib. 3, tom. 2, 21, PG 42, 825.

11. *Ibid.*, lib. 2, tom. 1, haer. 61, n. 3, PG 41, 1042.

12. *De Vid.*, c. 14, PL 16, 273.
13. *Adv. Jov.*, lib. 1, c. 8, PL 23, 232.
14. *De Bono Vid.*, c. 14, PL 40, 432–3.
15. *De Bono Conj.*, c. 29, PL 40, 394.
16. *In 1 Cor.* 7, 6, PG 82, 274. Cf. Damascene, *In 1 Cor.* 7, PG 95, 622.
17. *Epist.* 3, c. 9, PL 65, 329. Cf. *ibid.*, 2, c. 6, PL 65, 314–7.
18. *Moralia*, lib. 1, c. 14, PL 75, 535–6.
19. *Hom. in Ezech.*, 2, 4, PL 76, 976.
20. *Hom.* I, 14, PL 94, 68 (CC 122, 95).
21. Sedulius Scotus, *In 1 Cor.* 12, PL 102, 153.
22. Bruno of Asti, *In 1 Cor.* 3, PL 111, 159.
23. Hatto of Vercelli, *Expos. in Ep. Pauli*, 1 Cor., PL 134, 351. Cf. Paschasius Radbert, *In Matt.*, lib. 10, c. 19, PL 120, 654.
24. Sedulius Scotus, *In 1 Cor.* 7, PL 102, 142.
25. Cf. Abbo of Fleury, *Apologeticus*, PL 139, 463.
26. *De Trin. et Op.*, In Num., lib. 2, c. 21, PL 167, 901. Cf. *ibid.*, In Lev. lib. 1, c. 3, PL 167, 746.
27. Cf. Honorius of Autun, *Liber 12 Quaestionum*, c. 8, PL 172, 1182; Abelard, *Prob. Hel.*, 14, PL 178, 696–7; Unknown, *Quaest. in Ep. Pauli*, In 1 Cor., q. 67, PL 175, 526; Harvey of Bourg-Dieu, *In 1 Cor.* 7, PL 181, 876; St. Bernard, *Serm. de Diversis*, Serm. 35, PL 183, 634.
28. Cf. Jacques de Vitry, *Hist.*, cited by G. Le Bras, DTC 9, 2180; Ramon Lull, *op. cit.*, p. 517.
29. Cited by G. Le Bras, DTC, 9, 2181.
30. *Bertholds Predigten*, Gobel, 1905, pp. 282 ff. Cited by G. Le Bras, DTC 9, 2181.
31. Cf. John H. Wright, S.J., *The Order of the Universe in the Theology of St. Thomas* (Rome: P.U.G., 1957), p. 166.
32. *In 4 Sent.*, d. 26, q. 1, a. ad 4. Cf. *In 1 Cor.* 7, 17.
33. *S.T.* II II, 183, a. 2.
34. Cf. St. Vincent Ferrer, *Serm.*, Dom. 7a post Trin., p. 475.
35. *In 1 Cor.* 7, a. 7, *Works* 13, 152. Cf. *Enarr. in C.C.* 7, a. 21, *Works* 7, 417.
36. *Op. cit.*, p. 401.
37. Cf. Cajetan, *In 1 Cor.* 7, 7; Salmeron, *op. cit.*, vol. 5, tr. 9, p. 49; Canisius, *Serm.* 3/7/1586, Braunsberger 8, 703; Maldonado, *In Mt.* 19; Bellarmine, *De Sac. Mat.*, c. 2, 5; Lessius, *De Jure et Just.*, lib. 4, c. 2, dub. 15.
38. *Op. cit.*, p. 596.
39. *Ibid.*, p. 593.
40. *Tract. de Sac.* (Rome: S. C. de Propaganda Fide, 1888) ed. 4a, p. 123.
41. *Op. cit.*, p. 389.
42. *Casti Connubii*, *loc. cit.*, pp. 542–3. Cf. Pius XII, Ap. Const., *Sedes Sapientiae*, AAS 46 (1954), p. 357.
43. Jn. 15, 16.

CHAPTER *18*

1. *Epist. ad Polycarpum,* c. 5, PG 5, 723.
2. DAL, vol. 20, c. 1889.
3. Cf. *ibid.*
4. *Ad Uxorem,* lib. 2, c. 9, PL 1, 1415.
5. *Ibid.* Cf. Origen, *In Matt.* 14, 16, PG 13, 1230.
6. *Epist.* 113, PG 37, 1315–6.
7. *In Illud Propt. Forn.,* 1, PG 51, 210.
8. *In Luc.,* lib. 8, 16, 18, PL 15, 1855–6, 8; Cf. Ambrosiaster, *In 1 Cor.,* 11, 11, PL 17, 254.
9. *Leonine Sac.,* Muratori, I, 723.
10. *Ibid.* Cf. *Gregorian Sac.,* Muratori II, 884.
11. *In Matt.* 19, PL 162, 1412. Cf. Procopius of Gaza, *In Gen.* 2, 18; Paschasius Radbert, *In Matt.* lib. 9, c. 19, PL 120, 650; Adrian II, *Epist.* 1, PL 122, 1260; Walter of Mortagne, *Summa Sent.,* tr. 7, c. 8, PL 176, 161.
12. Albert the Great, *In 4 Sent.,* d. 27, a. 4 ad 3. Cf. Bonaventure, *Serm., 3a Dom. In Quadr.,* Quar. 9, 223; *In 4 Sent.,* d. 27, a. 2, q. 1 ad 3; Denis the Carthusian, *Laud. Vita Conj.,* a. 1, *Works* 38, 60.
13. *Op. cit.,* vol. 3, tr. 29, p. 226.
14. *Epist.* 1272, *Monumenta Historica Societatis Jesu* (Madrid: G. Lopez de Horno, 1912), Mon. Laini, IV, 572–3.
15. P. 3.
16. Cf. Lawrence of Brindisi, *In Gen.* 2, 22, *Works* 3, 243; 2 *Quad.* dies S. Jos., *Works* 5, 3, 460; Peteau, *De Op. 6 Dierum,* lib. 2, c. 8, n. 8; de Horno, 1912), Mon. Laini, IV, 572–3.
17. *Lettre* 825, *Works* 3, 687.
18. *Lettre* 1774, *Works* 3, 647. Cf. *Introd. Vie Dev.,* p. 3, c. 38.
19. *Lettre* 807, *Works* 3, 672.
20. *Crist Instr.,* p. 3, r. 25, n. 16, *Works* 2, 849.
21. *Le Felicità Introdotta nelle Famiglie* (Rome: Pagliarini, 1755), p. 9.
22. *Lettre* 103, 7/17/1853, *Works* (Paris: Lecoffre, 1862), 2nd ed., 11, 555.
23. *De Electione,* nn. 171–2.
24. *Op. cit.,* p. 453.
25. *Entr.* 17, Des Voix, *Works* 6, 311, 321–2.
26. *Serm.,* mercr. 2e sem. Carême, *Works* (Paris: Pourrat Frères, 1842) 1, 467. Cf. Segneri, *Felicità,* p. 11.

CHAPTER *19*

1. *Strom.,* lib. 2, c. 18, PG 8, 1022.
2. *Expos. in Ps.* 127, PG 27, 518. Cf. Eusebius, *In Ps.* 127, PG 24, 22; Didymus of Alex., *In Ps.* 127, PG 39, 1583; Basil, *Epist.* 301, PG 32, 1047; Theodoret, *In Ps.* 127, PG 80, 1895.
3. *Quales Ducendae Sint Uxores,* 3, PG 51, 233.
4. *In Ep. ad Col.,* PG 62, 390.

5. *Comm. In Ps.* 127, PG 24, 22, Cf. Maximus the Confessor (citing Chrysostom), *Loci Communes*, PG 91, 911.
6. *De Abraham*, lib. 1, c. 9, PL 14, 473.
7. *Epist.* 2, c. 6, PL 20, 175.
8. *De Trin. et Op.*, In Gen. lib. 7, c. 3, PL 167, 447.
9. *De Instructione Puerorum*, James A. Corbett, ed. (South Bend: Notre Dame Medieval Institute, 1955) c. 10, p. 23.
10. *Summa S.T.*, III, tit. 1, c. 1.
11. *In Tob.* 7, a. 7, Works 5, 109. Cf. *In Gen.* 24, a. 64, Works 1, 300.
12. *Laud. Vita Conj.*, a. 14, *Works* 38, 73. Cf. *In Prov.* 19, a. 19, *Works* 7, 128.
13. *In Ecclus.* 26, a. 27, *Works* 8, 162.
14. *In Gen.* 24, 56.
15. *In Prov.* 18, 22.
16. *Ibid.* 19, 14.
17. *Tr. de Doct.*, lib. 2, c. 7, *Works* 17, 25.
18. *Ibid.*, lib. 3, c. 16, *Works* 17, 223.
19. P. 89.
20. *De Sac. Mat.*, c. 27.
21. *Serm. 8 in Sal. Angel, Works* 1, 221.
22. *Op. cit.*, p. 447–9.
23. *Lettre* 250, *Works* 3, 254.
24. Fénelon, *Divers Sentiments*, c. 50, *Works* 9, 405.
25. Bourdaloue, *Serm. 2e dim. Eph.*, *Works* 2, 367.
26. *Serm.* 36, *Works* 2, 410.
27. *Réfl. Chrét.*, du mariage, *Works* 5, 182.
28. *Pred.* 39, *Works* 1, 423.
29. *II Crist. Instr.*, p. 3, r. 25, n. 12, *Works* 2, 846.
30. *Liv. J. Homme*, p. 62.
31. *Ibid.*, p. 65.
32. *Missale Romanum.*

CHAPTER 20

1. Mt. 19, 11.
2. 1 Cor. 7, 25–6.
3. Cf. 1 Cor. 7, 10.
4. Cf. 1 Cor. 7, 40.
5. Cf. Eusebius, *Hist. Eccl.* IV, 32, PG 20, 387–8.
6. Clement, *Stromata*, lib. 3, c. 9, PG 8, 1169–70; Cyprian, *De Habitu Virg.*, 33, PL 4, 463.
7. *De Virg.*, lib. 1, c. 5, PL 16, 206. Cf. Chrysostom, *De Lib. Rep.*, 2, 4, PG 51, 223; Ambrosiaster, *In 1 Cor.* 7, PL 17, 229–233.
8. *Epist.* 63, n. 38, PL 16, 1251. Cf. *De Vid.*, 12, 72, PL 16, 256.
9. *De Perp. Virg. B.M.V.*, n. 21, PL 23, 215. Cf. Gaudentius of Brescia, *De*

Evang. Lect. lib. 1, serm. 8, PL 20, 889; Augustine, *De Bono Vid.*, c. 5, PL 40, 434.

10. Hatto of Vercelli, *Expos. in Ep. Pauli*, 1 Cor., PL 134, 356. Sedulius Scotus, *In 1 Cor.* 7, PL 102, 142; Haymo of Halberstadt, *In 1 Cor.* 7, PL 117, 546.

11. Unknown Author, *Allegoriae in N.T.*, lib. 7, PL 175, 911. Cf. Harvey of Bourg-Dieu, *In 1 Cor.* 7, PL 181, 883.

12. *Op. cit.*, vol. 8, tr. 50, p. 391. Cf. Denis the Carthusian, *In Matt.* 19, a. 33, *Works* 11, 215; Canisius, *Summa D. C.* I, p. 3, c. 6, q. 207. Cf. II, *ibid.*, q. 210.

13. Puis XII, *Sacra Virginitas*, *loc. cit.*, p. 129. Cf. Leo XIII, *Rerum Novarum* 5/15/1891; Pius XI, *Casti Connubii*, *loc. cit.*, p. 542.

14. *Epist. ad Ammunem*, PG 26, 1173-4.

15. *Adv. Jov.*, lib. 1, n. 3, PL 23, 223.

16. Cf. Fulgentius, *De Ver. Praed.*, lib. 2, c. 23, PL 65, 650; Gregory, *Hom. In Ezech.*, lib. 2, hom. 4, PL 76, 976-7; Bonaventure, *In 4 Sent.*, d. 26, a. 2, q. 3, dub. 3; d. 38, a. 2, q. 3, ad 2; Scotus, *Report.*, In 4 Sent., d. 31, q. 1, schol. 2; Denis the Carthusian, *In Sap.* 3 Works 7, 472; Salmeron, *op. cit.*, vol. 8, tr. 50, p. 395; Bellarmine, *Dott. Crist.*, c. 9, *Works* 6, 195.

17. 1 Cor. 12, 31.

18. 1 Cor. 7, 17.

19. 1 Cor. 7, 27.

20. *Epist. ad Polycarpum*, 5, Kirsch 27. Cf. Cyril of Jer., *Cat.*, 4, 25, PG 33, 487; Procopius of Gaza, *In Gen.* 29, 15, PG 87, 434.

21. *Strom.* lib. 3, c. 12, PG 8, 1190.

22. Ambrosiaster, *In 1 Cor.* 7, 35, PL 17, 236.

23. *De Sancta Virg.*, cc. 45-6, PL 40, 423.

24. *De Nupt. et Concup.*, lib. 1, c. 5, PL 44, 416.

25. *De Bono Vid.*, c. 15, PL 40, 442. Cf. *Contra Jul*, lib. 4, n. 50, PL 44, 763; *De Civ. Dei*, lib. 16, c. 36, PL 41, 514.

26. *Serm.* 354, c. 9, PL 1567-8. Cf. *De Bono Conj.*, c. 23, PL 40, 393; Enarr. *in Ps.* 99, 2, PL 37, 1280.

27. *De Sancta Virg.*, c. 44, PL 40, 422.

28. *Ibid.*, PL 40, 424. Cf. *Enarr. in Ps.* 121, n. 10, PL 37, 1627.

29. *De Bono Vid.*, c. 15, PL 40, 442.

30. Cf. Fulgentius, *Epist.* 3, 15, PL 65, 333; Ps-Gregory, *Concordia*, c. 14, PL 79, 668; Sedulius Scotus, *In 1 Cor.* 7, PL 103, 140; R. Maurus, *In Ep. Pauli*, lib. 10, c. 7, PL 112, 73; Hatto of Vercelli, *In 1 Cor.*, PL 134, 358; Anselm of Laon, *In Matt.*, c. 25, PL 163, 1457-8; Rupert of Deutz, *In Apoc.*, lib. 2, c. 3, PL 169, 899.

31. Unknown Author, *Quaest. in Ep. Pauli*, In 1 Cor., q. 64, PL 175, 526.

32. ———, *Alleg. in NT*, lib. 7, PL 175, 911.

33. *In 4 Sent.*, d. 33, q. 2, a. 6.

34. *Ibid.* Cf. Harvey of Bourg-Dieu, *In 1 Cor.* 7, PL 181, 887; Richard of

St. Victor, *In C.C.* c. 38, PL 196, 514; Alexander of Hales, *In 4 Sent.*, d. 33, IV, Quar. 1, 531; *ibid.*, II, Quar. 1, 528–30; Vincent of Beauvais, *op. cit.*, c. 38, Steiner, p. 156; Aquinas, *S. T.* II II, q. 152, a. 4 ad 2; II II, q. 184, a. 4.

35. *1st Serm. 16th S. post Trin.*, *op. cit.*, p. 537.
36. *Serm. 3 in Dom. 1 Adv.*, *Works* 29, 22. Cf. *In 1 Cor.* 7, a. 7, *Works* 13, 158.
37. *Op. cit.*, vol. 8, tr. 50, p. 395. Cf. *ibid.*, vol. 6, tr. 6, p. 33.
38. *Lettre* 1768, *Works* 3, 642. Cf. Bossuet, *Lettre* 83, *Works* 17, 651; Canisius, *Med. de Domin.*, 2 post Trin., Streicher 2, 105; Lawrence of Brindisi, *Serm. 11 in Conc. Immac.*, *Works* 1, 501; Cardinal Bona, *Principia Vitae Christ.*, 6.
39. Cf. Methodius, *op. cit.*, orat. 3, c. 10, PG 18, 75; Basil, *Serm. de Renunc. Saec.*, PG 31, 630.
40. *Hom. in Illud Salutate A. et P.*, PG 51, 190. Cf. *Hom. in Oziam*, PG 56, 136. Cf. Paulinus of Nola, *Epist.* 39, n. 1, PL 61, 364.
41. Christian Druthmar of Corby, *In Matt.* 19, PL 106, 1414.
42. *Enarr. in 3a Reg.*, a. 1, *Works* 38, 441.
43. *Op. cit.*, p. 401.
44. *Op. cit.*, p. 63.
45. *Ibid.*, p. 530.
46. *Introd. Vie Dév.*, Pref., *Works* 3, 6.
47. *Ibid.*, p. 21.
48. *Entr.* 17, Des Voix, *Works* 6, 320.
49. *Introd. Vie Dév.*, p. 1, c. 3, *Works* 1, 554.
50. *Rerum omnium*, AAS 15 (1923) p. 51.
51. *Casti Connubii*, *loc. cit.*, p. 548, DB 2232.
52. *Sacra Virginitas*, *loc cit.*, p. 179. Cf. Address, 12/9/57, AAS 50 (1958), 1, p. 35.
53. Discourse 8/13/41, DR 3, 177. Cf. John XXIII, Hom. in canoniz., AAS 51 (1959) p. 290.

CHAPTER 21

1. 1 Tim. 2, 15.
2. *Serm. 7 de Paradiso Eden.* Works 3, 582.
3. *Adv. Jov.*, lib. 1, n. 27, PL 23, 260.
4. *Serm.* 304, PL 38, 1396–7.
5. *Serm.* 96, c. 8, PL 38, 589. Cf. *De Nupt. et Conc.*, lib. 1, c. 8, PL 44, 419.
6. Haymo of Halberstadt, *In 1 Tim.* 2, PL 117, 791. Cf. Hatto of Vercelli, *In 1 Cor.*, PL 134, 356; Harvey of Bourg-Dieu, *In 1 Tim.* 2, PL 181, 1419.
7. *Sent.*, lib. 7, c. 27, PL 186, 942–3.
8. Book 1, c. 4.
9. *Serm. 6th S. Trin.*, Elliott, p. 457.
10. *De Myst. Theol.*, tr. 2, p. 142.

11. *Laud. Vita Conj.*, a. 30, *Works* 38, 95.
12. *Ibid.*, a. 2, *Works* 38, 60.
13. *In 1 Tim.* 2, 15.
14. *De l'oraison*, p. 2, c. 5, n. 9, *Works* 11, 383.
15. P. 5.
16. P. 6.
17. P. 8.
18. Cf. Lawrence of Brindisi, *3 Quadr.*, fer. 5, Dom. 1, *Works* 6, 160; De la Puente, *op. cit.*, p. 535; Lessius, *De Bono Stat. Cast.*, c. 6, *Opusc.*, pp. 886–7.
19. *Introd. Vie Dév.*, p. 1, c. 3, *Works* 1, 553–4.
20. *Lettre*, 856, *Works* 3, 714.
21. *Lettre* 1767, *Works* 3, 642.
22. *Lettre* 7/16/1608, *Works* 14, 53.
23. *Lettre* 735, *Works* 3, 601.
24. *Lettre* 1774, *Works* 3, 647.
25. *Il Crist. Instr.*, p. 3, r. 25, n. 2, *Works* 2, 843.
26. Cf. Cardinal Bona, *op. cit.*, 24; Bourdaloue, *Pensées diverses*, *Works* 6, 295; Claude de la Columbière, *Refl. Chrét.*, pp. 175–7.
27. Address to Italian Women, 10/14/56, AAS 48 (1956), p. 782.
28. Address, 8/13/41, DR 3, 179.
29. Address to Italian Sodalists, 8/21/58, AAS 50 (1958), p. 534.

I. *Primary Sources* (In Addition to Popes and Councils).

Abelard, Peter, *Opera Omnia*, PL.

Albert the Great, *Opera Omnia*, Paris: Vives, 1894, 38 vol.

Alexander of Hales, *Glossa in 4 Libros Sententiarum*, vol. 4, Florence: Quaracchi, 1957.

———, *Summa Theologica*, Florence: Quaracchi, 1928, Book II.

Alvarez de Paz, Jaime, S.J., *Opera Omnia*, Paris: Vives, 1875, 6 vol.

Ambrose, *Opera Omnia*, PL.

Ambrosiaster, *Comm. in Epistolas Pauli*, PL 17.

Angelomus Luxoviensis, *Opera Omnia*, PL.

Anselm, *Opera Omnia*, PL.

St. Antoninus, *Summa Moralis*, Florence: P. Viviani, 1741, 2 vol.

———, *Summa Sacrae Theologiae*, Venice: Juntas, 1582, 4 vol.

Aquinas, St. Thomas, *Opera Omnia*, Parma: Fiaccadori, 1852–1873, 25 vol.

Ardent, Raoul, *Opera Omnia*, PL.

Athenagoras, *Legatio Pro Christianis*, PG.

Augustine of Hippo, *Opera Omnia*, PL.

Basil the Great, *Opera Omnia*, PG.

Bede the Venerable, *Opera Omnia*, PL.

Bellarmine, Robert, *Opera Omnia*, Naples: J. Giuliano, 1856.

Bernard of Clairvaux, *Opera Omnia*, PL.

Billot, Louis, Cardinal, S.J., *De Ecclesiae Sacramentis*, Rome: P.U.G., 1929, ed. 7a, vol. 2, 477 pp.

Bonacursus, *Libellus contra Catharos*, PL 204.

Bonaventure, *Opera Omnia*, Quaracchi: St. Bonaventure College, 1889.

Borromeo, Charles, *Acta Ecclesiae Mediolanensis*, Paris: J. Jost, 1643, 515 pp.

————, *Homiliae*, Augsburg: I. Vieth, 1758, 750 pp.

————, *Orationes*, Augsburg: I. Vieth, 1758.

Bossuet, Jacques, *Oeuvres Complètes*, Besançon: Outhenin-Chalandre Fils, 1840, 19 vol.

Bourdaloue, Louis, S.J., *Oeuvres*, Paris: Gaume et Cie., 1896, 6 vol.

Bruno of Asti, *Opera Omnia*, PL.

Burchard of Worms, *Liber Decretalium*, PL 140.

Buys, Peter, S.J., *De Statibus Hominum*, Mainz: J. Albinus, 1613.

Cajetan (De Vio Gaetani, Thomas), *Commentarii in Sac. Scripturam*, Lyons: J. & P. Prost, 1639, 5 vol.

Calecas, Manuel, *De Principiis Fidei Catholicae*, PG 152.

Canisius, Peter, S.J., *Epistolae et Actus*, Otto Braunsberger, ed., Friburg: Herder, 1905, 8 vol.

————, *Meditationes*, F. Streicher, S.J., ed. Munich: Officina Salesiana, 1955, 427 pp.

————, *Summa Doctrinae Christianae*, F. Streicher, S.J., ed., Munich: Officina Salesiana, 1933, 398 pp.

Capreolus, John, O.P., *Defensiones Theologicae Divi T. Acquinatis*, Tours: A. Cattier, 1906, 7 vol.

Cassian, *Collationes*, PL 49.

Catechismus ex Decr. Concilii Tridentini ad Parochos, Padua: 1758, 632 pp.

Chromatius, *Opera Omnia*, PL.

Chrysostom, John, *Opera Omnia*, PG.

Clement of Alexandria, *Stromata*, PG.

Climacus, John, *Scala Paradisi*, PG.

Consultationes Zacchaei Christiani, PL.

Contenson, Vincent, O.P., *Theologia Mentis et Cordis*, Turin: J. J. Avondus 1768, 4 vol.

Cydones, Demetrius, *De Condemnenda Morte*, PG 154.

Cyril of Alexandria, *Opera Omnia*, PG.

Cyril of Jerusalem, *Catecheses*, PG.

Damascene (St. John of Damascus), *Opera Omnia*, PG.

Damian, Peter, *Opera Omnia*, PL.

De Granada, Luis, O.P., *Oeuvres*, M. Bareille, tr., Paris: L. Vives, 1868.

De la Columbière, Claude, *Oeuvres Complètes*, Grenoble: Patronage Catholique, 1900, 6 vol.

De la Palu, Pierre, *In 4 Sent.*, Venice: 1493, vol. 4.

De la Puente, Luis, S.J., *De Christiani Hominis Perfectione*, Cologne: 1615, 549 pp.

De Leon, Luis, *La Perfecta Casada*, E. Wallace, ed., Chicago: U. of Chicago Press, 1903, 119 pp.

De Ligouri, Alphonsus, *Opere*, Turin: Marietti, 1846, 9 vol.

De Lille, Alain, *Opera Omnia*, PL.

De Lugo, Juan Cardinal, *Disputationes Scholasticae et Morales*, Paris: L. Vives, 1878, 8 vol.

Denis the Carthusian, *Opera Omnia*, Tournai: Cartusia S.M. de Pratis, 1896, 43 vol.

De Ossuna, *Tercer Abecedario Espiritual*, Escritores Misticos Espanoles, Mir, ed., tom. 1, Madrid: Bailly Bailliere, 1911, 160 pp.

De Sales, Francis, *Oeuvres Complètes*, Paris: Albanel et Martin, 1839, 4 vol.

Dionysius, Exiguus, *Opera Omnia*, PL.

Eck, John, *Homiliae super Evangeliax de Tempore*, vol. 1, 1537.

Eckbert of Schaunang, *Opera Omnia*, PL.

Egbert of York, *Opera Omnia*, PL.

Ephrem the Deacon, *Opera Omnia*, P. Benedict, S.J., ed., Rome: Typographia Vaticana, 1737, 6 vol.

———, *Hymni et Sermones*, T. J. Lamy, ed., Mechlin: H. Dessain 1886, 3 vol.

Epiphanius, *Opera Omnia*, PG.

Ermengaudus, *Opera Omnia*, PL.

Eusebius of Caesarea, *Opera Omnia*, PG.

Fénelon, François, de Salignac de la Mothe, *Oeuvres Complètes*, Toulouse: J. J. Benichet, 1810, 19 vol.

Ferrer, Vincent, *Sermones Aestivales*, Damian Diaz, ed., Antwerp: J. Stelsius, 1572, 935 pp.

Franzelin, J. Baptist Cardinal, S.J., *Tractatus de Sacramentis in Genere*, ed. 4a., Rome: S. C. de Propaganda Fide, 1888, 310 pp.

Fulgentius of Ruspe, *Opera Omnia*, Pl.

Gaudentius of Brescia, *Opera Omnia*, Pl.

Gennadius of Marseilles, *De Ecclesiasticis Dogmatibus*, PL 58.

Gerald of Cambrai, *Acta Synod. Atrebat.*, PL 142.

Gratian, *Decretum*, Venice: 1605, 2 vol.

Gregory the Great, *Opera Omnia*, PL.

Gregory of Nyssa, *Opera Omnia*, PG.

Grou, Jean, S.J., *Le Livre du Jeune Homme*, Paris: V. Palme, 1874, 216 pp.

Halitgar, *Liber Poenitentiarum*, PL 105.

Harvey of Bourg-Dieu, *Opera Omnia*, PL.

Hatto of Vercelli, *Opera Omnia*, PL.

Haymo of Halberstadt, *Opera Omnia*, PL.

Hildebert of Mans, *Opera Omnia*, PL.

Hugh of Amiens, *Contra Haereticos*, PL 192.

Honorius of Autun, *Opera Omnia*, PL.

Hugh of St. Victor, *Opera Omnia*, PL.

Ireneus, *Contra Haereses*, PG.

Isidore of Pelusium, *Opera Omnia*, PG.

Ivo of Chartres, *Panormia*, PL 161.

Jerome, *Opera Omnia*, PL.

John of St. Thomas, *Cursus Theologicus*, Cologne: W. Metternick, 1711, 8 vol.

Jonas of Orleans, *Opera Omnia*, PL.

Justin Martyr, *Apologia*, PG 6.

Lainez, James, S.J., *Monumenta Laini*, Monumenta Historica Societatis Jesu, Madrid: G. Lopez del Horno, 1912, 8 vol.

Lanfranc, *Opera Omnia*, PL.

Lawrence of Brindisi, *Opera Omnia*, Padua: Officina Typ. Seminarii, 1928, 9 vol.

Pierre Le Chantre, *Summa Abelardi*, PL.

Pierre Le Mangeur, *Historia Scholastica*, PL 198.

Lessius, Leonard, *De Justitia et Jure*, ed. 7a, Antwerp: B. Moretus, 1632, 825 pp.

———, *Opuscula*, Antwerp: B. Moretus, 1626, 922 pp.

———, *Praelectiones Theologicae Posthumae*, Louvain: C. Coenestenius, 1645.

Lombard, Peter, *Libri Sententiarum*, PL 192.

Ludolph of Saxony, *Vita Christi Domini*, Venice: V. Bonnello, 1587, 1190 pp.

Lull, Ramon, *Blanquerna*, E. Allison Peers, tr., London: Jarrolds, 1925, 536 pp.

Servatus Lupus, *Opera Omnia*, PL.

St. Martin of Leon, *Opera Omnia*, PL.

Massillon, Jean-Baptiste, *Oeuvres*, Paris: Pourrat Frères, 1842, 2 vol.

Master Bandinus, *Opera Omnia*, PL.

Rabanus Maurus, *Opera Omnia*, PL.

Methodius of Olympus, *Convivium 10 Virginum*, PG.

Gregory Nazianzen, *Opera Omnia*, PG.

Origen, *Opera Omnia*, PG.

Otto of Lucca, *Opera Omnia*, PL.

Ozanam, Frederic, *Oeuvres Complètes*, 2e ed., Paris: Lecoffre, 1862.

Palmieri, Dominic, S.J., *Tractatus de Matrimonio Christiano*, Rome: S.C. de Propaganda Fide, 1880, 427 pp.

Pesch, Christian, S.J., *Praelectiones Dogmaticae*, tom. 7, ed. 2a, Friburg: Herder, 1900, 437 pp.

Peteau, Denis, S.J., *Dogmata Theologica*, Paris: L. Vives, 1867, 8 vol.

Pierre de Poitiers, *Opera Omnia*, PL.

Philastrius of Brescia, *Opera Omnia*, PL.

Philip of Herveng, *Opera Omnia*, PL.

Procopius of Gaza, *Opera Omnia*, PG.

Ps-Gregory the Great, *Epistola ad Augustinum*, PL 77.

Ps-Isidore of Seville, *De Eccl. Dogmatibus*, PL 83.

————, *Papae Evaristi Epist.* 1, PG 5.

Pullen, Robert, *Opera Omnia*, PL.

Paschasius Radbert, *Opera Omnia*, PL.

Ratherius of Verona, *Opera Omnia*, PL.

Reginon, *Opera Omnia*, PL.

Remigius of Auxerre, *Opera Omnia*, PL.

Richard of St. Victor, *Opera Omnia*, PL.

Robert of Melun, *Opera Omnia*, PL.

Rupert of Deutz, *Opera Omnia*, PL.

Salmeron, Alfonso, S.J., *Commentarii in Evangelicam Historiam*, Cologne: A. Hierat and J. Gymni, 1612, 12 vol.

Sanchez, Thomas, S.J., *De Sancto Matrimonii Sacramento*, Venice: B. Milochus, 1672, 3 vol.

Scotus, John Duns, *Opera Omnia*, Lyons: Durand, 1639, 12 vol.

Scheeben, Matthias J., *The Mysteries of Christianity*, C. Vollert, tr., St. Louis: Herder, 1946, 834 pp.

Sedulius Scotus, *Opera Omnia*, PL.

Segneri, Paolo, S.J., *Opere*, Turin: Marietti, 1855, 6 vol.

————, *La Felicità Introdotta nelle Famiglie*, Rome: Pagliarini, 1755, 152 pp.

Segni, Lothair (Innocent III), *De Contemptu Mundi*, PL.

Servatus Lupus, *Opera Omnia*, PL.

Smaragdus, *Opera Omnia*, PL.

Siricius, Pope, *Epistolae*, PL.

Soto, Dominic, *In 4 Sent. Commentarii*, Douai: P. Borremaus, 1613.

Suso, Henry, *Horologium Sapientiae*, C. Richstatter, S.J., ed., Turin, Marietti, 1929, 279 pp.

Tajon of Saragossa, *Opera Omnia*, PL.

Tauler, John, O.P., *Sermons and Conferences*, W. Elliott, tr., Washington, D.C.: Apostolic Mission House, 1910, 786 pp.

Theodore of Studium, *Opera Omnia*, PG.

Theodoret, *Opera Omnia*, PG.

Thomas of Citeaux, *Opera Omnia*, PL.

Thomas of Citeaux, *Opera Omnia*, PL.

Thomas of Strasbourg, *Commentaria in 4 Lib. Sent.*, Geneva: A. Orerius, 1585.

Toledo, Francis Cardinal, S.J., *In Joannis Evang. Commentarii*, Lyons: Officina Junctarum, 1589, 407 pp.

Unknown Author, *Allegoriae in N.T.*, PL 175.

———, *Quaestiones in Ep. Pauli*, PL 175.

Vermeersch, Arthur, S.J., *De Castitate*, ed., 2a, Rome: P.U.G., 1921, 420 pp.

Vincent of Beauvais, *De Eruditione Filiorum Nobilium*, Arpad Steiner, ed., Cambridge, Mass.: The Medieval Academy of America, 1936, 236 pp.

Walter of Mortagne, *Summa Sententiarum*, PL 176.

Werner, *Deflorationes Ss. Pp.*, PL 157.

William of Auvergne, *Opera Omnia*, Paris: P. Auboin, 1674, 2 vol.

William of Auxerre, *Summa Aurea*, Paris: P. Pigouchet.

William of Tournai, *De Instructione Puerorum*, James A. Corbett, ed., South Bend, Ind.: Medieval Institute of U. of Notre Dame, 1955, 50 pp.

Zeno of Verona, *Opera Omnia*, PL.

II. *Studies and Commentaries*

Audet, Jean-Paul, O.P., "Le sens du Cantique des Cantiques," *Revue Biblique*, v. 62, n. 2 (April, 1955), pp. 197–221.

Brown, Raymond E., S.S., "The Johannine Sacramentary Reconsidered," *Theological Studies*, v. 23, n. 2 (June, 1962), pp. 183–206.

De Guibert, Joseph, S.J., *Documenta Ecclesiastica Christianae*

Perfectionis Studium Spectantia, Rome: P.U.G., 1931, 562 pp.

De Vaux, Roland, *Ancient Israel*, New York: McGraw-Hill, 1961, 592 pp.

Fuchs, Josef, *Die Sexualethik des Heiligen Thomas von Aquin*, Cologne: Verlag J. P. Bachem, 1949, 329 pp.

Legrand, L., "The Prophetical Meaning of Celibacy," *Scripture*, 12 (1960), pp. 97–105.

McKenzie, John L., S.J., *The Two-Edged Sword*, Milwaukee: Bruce, 1957, 317 pp.

———, "The Literary Characteristics of Genesis 2–3," *Theological Studies*, vol. 10, n. 4 (December, 1954), pp. 541–572.

Schahl, Claude, O.F.M., *La doctrine des fins du mariage dans la théologie scholastique*, Paris: Editions Franciscaines, 1948, 160 pp.

Stanley, David M., S.J., "The New Testament Doctrine on Baptism," *Theological Studies*, vol. 18, n. 2 (June, 1957), pp. 169–215.

Thomas, John L., S.J., *The American Catholic Family*, Englewood Cliffs, N.J.: Prentice-Hall, 1956, 471 pp.

Wright, John H., S.J., *The Order of the Universe in the Theology of St. Thomas*, Rome: P.U.G., 1957, 223 pp.